EARTHLY
PLENITUDES

EARTHLY PLENITUDES

A Study on Sovereignty and Labor

Bruno Gullì

TEMPLE UNIVERSITY PRESS
PHILADELPHIA

Bruno Gullì teaches philosophy at Long Island University, Brooklyn Campus, and at Kingsborough Community College. He is the author of *Labor of Fire: The Ontology of Labor between Economy and Culture* (Temple).

Temple University Press
1601 North Broad Street
Philadelphia PA 19122
www.temple.edu/tempress

∞ The paper used in this publication meets the requirements of the American National Standard for Information Sciences—Permanence of Paper for Printed Library Materials, ANSI Z39.48-1992

Library of Congress Cataloging-in-Publication Data

Gullì, Bruno, 1959–
   Earthly plenitudes : a study on sovereignty and labor / Bruno Gullì.
      p. cm.
   Includes bibliographical references and index.
   ISBN 978-1-59213-979-8 (cloth : alk. paper)
   1. Labor—Philosophy.   2. Work—Philosophy.   3. Marxian economics.   4. Capitalism.   5. Sovereignty.   I. Title.
   HD4094.G85 2009
   331.01—dc22   2009016341

2 4 6 8 9 7 5 3 1

For Pino, who guides

Que le bonheur soit la lumière
Au fond des yeux au fond du cœur
Et la justice sur la terre

That happiness be the light
In the depths of the eyes, in the depths of the heart
And that justice be on earth

—Paul Eluard, from *Gabriel Péri*

Contents

~~~

Acknowledgements

꧁❦꧂

I want to thank Pedro Canó and André Cechinel for their careful and insightful reading of the entire manuscript. In this sense, my thanks also go to the anonymous Temple reviewers. Sophia Wong read and commented on chapter 5, a section of which I delivered as a paper at the Radical Philosophy conference at San Francisco State University. An earlier version of the material that formed the base for chapters 2 and 3 was published as an article in *Cultural Logic*. A different version of chapter 4 was published in *Workplace: A Journal for Academic Labor* and the section on Schmitt (chapter 2) in *Glossator: Practice and Theory of the Commentary*. The section on Maritain (chapter 2) constituted the material for a paper I delivered at the *Left Forum* conference. The section on Heidegger in chapter 2 was developed as a paper in a graduate seminar taught by Babette Babich at Fordham University. I also want to thank my students at Long Island University, Brooklyn Campus and at Kingsborough Community College / CUNY. The support of Micah Kleit and the staff at Temple University Press was extremely important; so was the encouragement of my friends and family.

Introduction

❧

The history of sovereignties is the history of devastation
—Jean-Luc Nancy, *Being Singular Plural*

Toward the end of Ken Saro-Wiwa's great novel *Sozaboy*, Mene, the main character and narrator (a young lorry driver dragged into a devastating war), says: "I begin to think that the world is not a good place even" (1994: 164). Indeed, it did not seem to be after his town, Dukana, and his private life were destroyed, and sickness and death prevailed, as the war had "uselessed[1] many people, killed many others" (p. 181). Yet, at the outset of the novel, set during an unspecified civil war, which is most likely the Nigerian-Biafran War of the late 1960s, the promise was different. The second paragraph of the novel reads as follows:

> All the nine villages were dancing and we were eating plenty maize with pear and knacking tory [i.e., chatting] under the moon. Because the work on the farm have finished and the yams were growing well well. And because the old, bad government have dead, and the new government of soza [i.e., soldiers] and police have come (p. 1).

At the end of the third paragraph, still on the same page, he says: "Yes, everybody in Dukana was happy. And they were all singing" (ibid.).

However, the novel really starts on a different note. The first paragraph contains only one sentence—a strange sentence, to be sure, which reads as follows: "Although, everybody in Dukana was happy at first" (ibid.). We read almost the same sentence as above, this time introduced by *although* rather than *yes* and concluded with "at first." The novel starts with the word "although" followed by a comma. In its general structural function, "although" is a clause word, introducing an oppositional subordinate clause. At the outset of Saro-Wiwa's novel, it either introduces an *absent* oppositional subordinate clause, or it must be interpreted as a substitute for "yet" or "however," which carries the same oppositional meaning but is a transition word, that is, a transition from another (in this case *absent*) sentence. In either case, we have an absence, the presence of an absence, something which is present and absent at the same time.

The novel starts with, and *as*, a *transition* from a time and place of absence; it is all about this transition, which simultaneously shows and conceals that which remains absent. The transition itself does not point to an empirical time of happiness preceding the war, for that time is now, at the beginning, "at first"—but it is a totalizing moment (and one of misplaced happiness). War itself is total; thus "although" points to a time that is essentially different from the time of now, whose beginning is indicated by "at first," but it is a beginning without end. As Zaza, one of the characters, says toward the end of the novel, "war is war and nobody knows what will happen tomorrow because war is war and *can begin but it cannot end if it have begin*" (p. 147; emphasis added). Thus, "although" really points to a transcendental moment, a time of neutrality when war has yet not begun and cannot begin (for the reason given by Zaza, that is, if it begins, it cannot end). "Although" is a hypothesis and a suspension—the residue of what is now an absence. In what could be read as a reversal of the Hobbesian paradigm (whereby the transition to sovereignty ensures the end of the natural state of war), "although," at the outset of *Sozaboy*, marks the passage *to* a regime of total war. What comes before "although," or in the space (or rather the non-space) between it and the comma, is suspended. This might be a situation of true freedom and happiness, which could be attained by and through a *real* suspension[2] of the regime of sovereignty that brings about war, destroys social life and common wealth, and turns labor into a strictly productive activity. Yet, under this regime, no more singing and chatting under the moon—until the time comes when everybody is killed or *uselessed*, that is, made useless, unproductive, turned into waste.

The above remarks on Saro-Wiwa's novel provide a useful key to the themes of *Earthly Plenitudes*. The main theme, running throughout the book, is the critique of productivity and sovereignty. Other themes, used to highlight and substantiate such critique (and specific to individual chapters), are those of singularity, exception, usefulness, contingent labor, dependency, and disability.

The book introduces the concept of *dignity of individuation* to give the critique of productivity and sovereignty a positive and constructive dimension, a sense of direction. That is, the overcoming of categories such as the sovereign individual can find in the concept of dignity of individuation a new ontological and ethical foundation. I think that this concept, which should not be seen as pertaining only to human reality, but as encompassing all forms of life, all instantiations of being, and which precedes individuality, can be very fruitful as a contribution to the effort of rethinking categories of political ontology. This concept is introduced in Chapter 1, but it is applied in all the other chapters, with particularly interesting results, I believe, in the Chapters 4 and 5.

I prefer dignity of individuation to dignity because the former concept stresses the notion that the dignity of each and any individual being lies in its being individuated as such; in other words, dignity is the irreducible and most essential character of any being (that which, taken away, the being is destroyed). Moreover, dignity of individuation, more explicitly than dignity, relates to a being's constituent moments of singularity, plurality, commonality, and universality. It has singularity as one of its constituent moments because each being is singular in its individuation. Yet, singularity itself is plural, as argued by Jean-Luc Nancy, whose work in this respect I treat in Chapter 1. Thus the dignity of individuation is singular and plural. Yet, it is common, for it belongs to all beings; and it is universal because universality is what makes the singular singular rather than the part of a greater whole, a mere partiality. The singular is the universal. The dignity of individuation is the expression of being in the infinitely small.

The dignity of individuation is one of the main points elaborated in Chapter 1. The focus of the chapter is on Leibniz's ethics and political philosophy, which are very closely related to his metaphysics of individual substances. This constitutes the foundation of the whole book. I particularly deal with Leibniz's common concept of justice, a univocal, neutral structure that, from each individual substance, each singularity, opens to the universal and common. The formulation of this concept of justice is fundamental in Leibniz's early critique or displacement, against Bodin and Hobbes, of sovereignty. Leibniz does not eliminate sovereignty altogether, but he sees it as an attribute of God or as a relative function of the political. This is, however, a great step forward, if one thinks that the concept of sovereignty was usually subscribed to in his times.

In the same chapter, I also deal with the concept of subsidiarity. This concept, a contender of sovereignty, is very important in that it grounds the social, communal, dimension of human life as what in Chapter 5 will appear to be a relation of dependency. Basically, the concept allows for the possibility, in a relation of dependence, of helping others without destroying them—and the only way to do that is to unconditionally recognize the dignity of individuation in everyone.

In Chapter 2, I deal with moments of the defense and critique of sovereignty in the twentieth century. I treat the question of the exception in Carl Schmitt, his logically consistent defense of sovereignty in a world of friend-and-enemy, and his mistrust of solutions that impair the power of decision. Then, I give an account of Jacques Maritain's powerful destruction of sovereignty in the political sphere, the notion that sovereignty is a useless concept. Finally, I speak of Heidegger's political ontology of singularity, which challenges the sovereign decision, and displaces it onto the plane of the uncanny.

I think that Chapter 3 is the most central chapter in the book. In dealing with Bataille's special use of sovereignty (sovereignty as subjectivity, as that which does not serve), the argument finds an exit from the logic of sovereignty—one from which there is no return. Bataille gives sovereignty a revolutionary meaning on the basis of his confusion of the two meanings of "to serve," that is, "to be useful" and "to be servile." As that which does not serve, sovereignty is neither servile nor useful. However, I see this as a problem. I endeavor to distinguish between these two meanings and argue that the category of the useful must still be employed in post-sovereign thought and societies. Bataille's emphasis on consumption and excess is nothing but the logical consequence of mistaking the useful (which is not, of course, the productive in the capitalist sense of the word) with the servile.

With Chapter 4, a new, more "practical" part of the book begins, one that deals with current issues, such as contingent academic labor (Chapter 4) and disability (Chapter 5). At this point, I hope, the validity of the concept of sovereignty has already been undermined, and equal emphasis can be placed on the critique of productivity. Indeed, productivity and sovereignty are part of the same logic, bent to ruthless domination, a logic of raw power and violence, oblivious to (or, in its utter stubbornness and stupidity, even unable to see and recognize) the traits of the human face, let alone the dignity of individuation. Chapter 4 very specifically deals with contingent academic labor, but the argument can be applied to other instances of a similar contingency. The fact that contingency in the workplace is so generally accepted is an insult to what is dearest to the human condition (made of anxiety and hope), the certainty of having a home, the clarity of a return, the recognition of one's achievements. Contingency means being able not to be. Although this is a general existential truth (for anyone can die at any moment), the fact that it is cynically enforced in situations of everyday life, in one's performance of daily, useful activities, only shows the sovereign terror bent to cripple and destroy singularities. In concrete terms, it is the terror of capital crippling and destroying living labor, living labors. In academia, in the institutionally designed space for the production of knowledge, this terror takes on the form of a disfigurement of the process of teaching and learning, a miserable disabling of vital and rich potentialities.

Following Kittay's dependency critique of equality and concept of dependency work, as well as Elizabeth Diemut Bubeck's concept of care as a substitute for productivity, the final chapter sees in the labor of care an exit from the sovereign regime of capital geared toward profit and exploitation. Stressing the fact that disability is a social construct (made on the basis of actual physical and/or mental impairment), it studies its place within our society from the viewpoint of the critique of the logic of inclusion and exclusion typical of the paradigm of productivity and sovereignty. In the first section of the chapter, attention is also given to the question of gender, the fact that care is usually construed as "women's work." The point, it is argued, is to explode the category and make of care an anti-sovereign and anti-productivist, general and common, modality of human relations and creative praxis. Moreover, given that, as Kittay says, dependency is the inescapable condition of human life, disability, the most serious form of dependency, must become the measure of humanity. In this sense, disability ceases being the exception against the norm. The fact that someone has a physical and/or mental impairment ceases being a disqualifying condition at the political, social, and existential levels. On the basis of the dignity of individuation, human agency can flourish in a manner adequate to each being's being.

I think of *Earthly Plenitudes* as of a sequel to *Labor of Fire* (2005). In the latter, I sought to disambiguate the concept of productive labor, often used both in the sense of the labor that produces and increases capital and in the sense of creative labor. In *Labor of Fire*, I argued that a distinction between these two forms is necessary if we want to exit the logic of productivity and profit, domination and sovereignty, typical of many modes of production, but certainly, and specifically, of the capitalist mode. I called attention to the fact that in Marx living labor is not always the same as productive labor, that the latter is a historically determined instance of the former, but one which constantly loses its creative character. Strictly speaking, productive labor is the labor productively employed by capital. The labor of care, for instance, is by definition *unproductive*. To give the labor of care pre-eminence over other, "productive," forms of labor means to recognize the social usefulness of being unproductive (in the capitalist sense of the word), and thus to challenge productivist logic as such. Indeed, nothing could be more useful to societies than our desire and ability to deactivate and smash the machinery of capital before we are all *uselessed* by it.

PART I

Critique of Sovereignty

CHAPTER ONE

Singularity or the Dignity
of Individuation

֍

*The singularity of a thing is no impediment to the abstraction
of a common concept.*

—John Duns Scotus, *Philosophical Writings*

In the *Communist Manifesto*, Marx and Engels's famous description of the communal society to come is built on the absence of sovereignty—an absence that is the presence of a new essential difference. They say:

> In place of the old bourgeois society, with its classes and class antagonisms, we shall have an association, in which the free development of each is the condition of the free development of all. (1994: 176)

The free development of each individual, the free development of all, their dialogical and dialectical relationship, can only be understood outside of the logic of domination, the logic of sovereignty, underlying all history (with some possible exceptions), and certainly (and specifically) the history of capitalist societies. Here the sovereignty of capital over labor becomes the omnipresent form of violence and domination, but it also engenders a political struggle, the class struggle at every point of everyday life. The free development of each is not an end in itself, as it would be in a theory of individualism, nor is it simply a means used in the construction of an abstract concept of society—a means whereby the individual would ultimately be crushed. At the same time, the free development of all is not a generality and an abstraction. These "all" to freely develop do so on the basis of the free development of "each," not the other way around—also because, as Aristotle says, " 'all' is ambiguous" (1998: 1261b19–20), and its reality and disambiguation lie in the "each." Moreover, the other way around would entail the structure of a closed society, a "totalitarianism," which is completely foreign to Marxian thought, although often ascribed to it because of the century of failed attempts at revolutionizing human society. The relationship between "each" and "all" is not the relationship between individuality and generality, but rather that between singularity and universality.[1] It is then important to understand the philosophical nature of this "each," that is, not simply what it is to be an individual, but rather the ontology of individuation, the constitution of the singular, which, because of its deep structure of commonality, universality, and plurality, makes an association possible. To guide our analysis will not be the concept of the exception, which must rather be refused by a political ontology of individuation intending to be a critique of all forms of sovereignty. To guide our analysis will be, instead, the *thisness* of everyday life, the constant and various individuation of the most common, its constant movement, its plurality, its difference and identity—identity with itself and with the most common, difference from the most common and from any other; identity with any other and profound difference from itself. The most important aspect is the absence of any hierarchical structure of domination, the notion of sovereignty. I call this *singularity*, or the *dignity of individuation*.

On the one hand, one could take singularity, as it relates to the concept of "person," in the characteristically medieval sense of the word, shared by both Thomas Aquinas and John Duns Scotus (despite their difference as to the role of the will), as the *ability to master one's own acts*.[2] This would replace the concept of sovereignty, perhaps displacing it into that of subjectivity, as it happens in Bataille (see Chapter 3).[3] However, the concept of "person," or "individual," can serve only as an introduction to the real and more fundamental meaning of the *dignity of individuation*, for the dignity of the individual, its singularity, as Jean-Luc Nancy (2000) shows, is the translation into "one" ("me" or "you," etc.) of more original and originary singularities (in this sense, see the remark on Jean-Luc Nancy, below). And even the ability to master one's own acts is what *comes to* "one" from what is *not one*, but *any this*, *many thises*. But the notion runs into difficulties when it faces the reality of *dis-ability* (I return to this in Chapter 5). Thus, to replace sovereignty will not be subjectivity, the sovereign individual, but something other than this.

On the other hand, singularity as the *dignity of individuation* can be understood as the translation into political ontology of the metaphysical principle of individuation.[4] With its long history from Greek philosophy (for instance, Aristotle's *tode ti*, "this") to Duns Scotus's *haecceitas*, "thisness," to Leibniz's individual substance and simple individual substance or monad and beyond, the principle of individuation is still one of the richest and most problematic concepts not only of metaphysics, but also, particularly today, of ethics, of psychology, and even of political ontology. This is shown, for instance, by Giorgo Agamben's use of it, in the form of *any this*, or to use Agamben's own expression, *whatever*, in *The Coming Community* (pp. 17–20). The translation I am proposing intends to add to it a stronger ethical and political connotation and to make it particularly useful in the context of a critique of the concept of sovereignty from the viewpoint of a radical ontology of labor. This is, fundamentally, the notion of a labor liberated from all forms of domination. It names the certitude of its ontological, social, and historical importance, the notion that each and all of its instantiations, of its expenditures, contribute to the free development of a genuinely and commonly wealthier world—an idea of justice, if there is one—of political and social justice. This is what in *Labor of Fire* (2005) I called the *solitude* of labor, that is, the return of labor to itself, to its immediacy. But what must be said now is that speaking of labor entails no *reductio ad unum*. It is, to use the metaphor with which Deleuze (1994: 35) illustrates Duns Scotus's concept of univocity, a *clamor* raised in our case not by a *single voice*, but by many voices, the many labors, the many activities, the singularities of all doing(s). "Solitude," which I use in *Labor of Fire*, means autonomy from the form and content of capital, but it does not name the condition of being one, alone, independent.[5]

Remark: Nancy on Being-With

In *Being Singular Plural*, Jean-Luc Nancy says that the human being "is nothing other than the idea of a 'value in itself' or a 'dignity'" (p. 74). Arguing for the concept of being-with as constitutive of Being, Nancy points out the necessary simultaneity of the singular and the plural in the human condition. He says:

> If "humanity" must be worth of something, or if Being in general must "be worth of something" under the heading "humanity," this can only be by "being valuable" *singularly* and, simultaneously, in "being valuable" by and for and with the *plural* that such singularity implies, just as it implies the fact of "value" in itself. (Ibid.)

Singularity is here understood not as individuality, but as "the punctuality of a 'with'" (p. 85). It is the effect of the spacing, the dis-position, a "between" (pp. 19, 27), which seems to constitute the only ontological ground (if an ontology is still needed), for Being as such is dismissed (pp. 76–77).

The individual itself is "an intersection of singularities" (p. 85). Thus, "dignity" is not to be found, first and foremost, in the individual, but in the distance, the distinction, the ipseity, or the punctuality of any *this*. It is that "Self" that Nancy sees as more originary than, as well as the condition of, "me" and "you," and "we" and "they." It must be understood as the "as" of Being (for Being is always being-as), equal to "what ex-ists as such" (p. 95). There is here an essential rethinking of the categories of individual, person, and subject. Nancy stays away from both subjectivity *and* intersubjectivity, and thus he arrives at something that constitutes the condition of both: the "plurality of origins." However, speaking of origins for Nancy does not entail any notion of "anteriority": "co-originarity is the most general structure of all con-sistency, all con-stitution, and all con-sciousness" (p. 40). I think that this is essential to what I try to conceptualize with the expression of *dignity of individuation*. This dignity is not in "one," for the simple fact that "one" *is not* one; "one" becomes one, and it is in this becoming, the individuating process, that the dignity resides. This means that dignity is not a feature to be recognized at the point of arrival, at the end of a process, and as the result of that process (this may be the case only with the dubious dignity of dignitaries), but rather at the points of departure. It is not after the constitution that dignity appears, but in the constituting moments. Nancy says this very well when, speaking of the "plurality of origins," he says that "each being belongs to the (authentic) origin, each is originary . . . and each is original" (p. 83). The only problem I have with Nancy's discussion, and I say more about this below, is his repudiation of commonality and universality.

Justice and the Dignity of Individuation

I am aware that in speaking here of justice I gloss over many important questions.[6] Nancy, for instance, sees a possible focus on justice as a type of resignation to "a weak, instrumental, and slavishly humanist thinking" (p. 133). This is certainly the case when justice is understood as a strictly juridical concept, that is, when it is reduced to a system of laws and to the necessity of obeying the law. However, when justice is understood as an ethical and politico-ontological concept, when, for instance, it "decides what is just" (Aristotle1998: 1253a38), not what the law determines of it, then the situation is different. In this case, justice is a common and univocal concept, as Leibniz shows (see below). Even beyond the ethical and political definitions of it, even "beyond justice," to use Agnes Heller's expression and book title, one finds justice—for what is goodness, the good life, if not justice itself? In her teleological account, Heller says that the good life is "the goal of justice" and is, consequently, "*beyond justice*" (p. 326; Heller's emphasis). Here the instrumental nature of justice is evident. I do not wish to deny the moment of instrumentality necessarily (but only to a degree) attached to justice, but I would argue that, in the case of justice, the means equals the end. This is to say that true justice, both ontologically and ethically speaking, is the same as the good life.

The focus of this chapter is on the *dignity of individuation*. But one of the functions of this concept is precisely to recast the concept of justice, to reappropriate it in ways that might be more useful today. The conceptual reality addressed by the dignity of individuation is not new. "Dignity" is a central concept in practical philosophy (notably, Kant) and in political praxis (for instance, with the Zapatista movement), in the North and the South of the world. And "individuation" is one of the essential concepts of ontology. What I am proposing is not the crude combination of two concepts into one. Rather, what I am wording as "dignity of individuation" is the common fact of existence, the fact of singularity, the time and space of each occurrence. It is common (and plural, in Nancy's sense) because it knows no exception, no extraordinary event. The concept of dignity, that of *value*, cannot be applied only to humanity (because of the obvious danger that this would entail— e.g., that if a group of people is construed as "less than human," typically, "the enemy," then dignity is not applicable). It might be that, as Sartre says, "man has a greater dignity than a stone or a table" (1985: 16). However, value and dignity must be generalized, applied, for instance, to Brother Fire and Sister Earth, as Francis of Assisi sang. It is this "posthumanist" thinking that the concept of *dignity of individuation* tries to formulate, with evident implications for questions of ecology, which are among the most pressing questions that ontology, ethics, and politics face. Thus justice is not simply an instrument whereby a world in which all things are regarded as having intrinsic dignity and value, that is, a better world, can be brought about. Justice is that world's very configuration. In fact, how can social justice be merely instrumental? A means to what end? The good life? But how can the good life be different from one in which social justice "reigns"? Certainly, to say this substantively, one has to avoid the easy and dangerous answers of liberalism, which is what Nancy also wants to avoid. This means that one has to avoid reducing everything to the individual, its autonomy and liberty. As the editors of a very recent volume on critical disability theory say, "Liberalism tends to put great emphasis on the individual, assuming that the self is both sovereign and a foundational unit for analysis" (Pothier and Devlin

2006: 16). In reality, they add, the question as to who is the self, the question of its authenticity, remains very much open.[7] We can recall Nancy's suggestion of the "plurality of origins," and we can also call attention to a certain similarity between Nancy and Heidegger in this respect. In Heidegger, "the selfhood of humanity" (2000: 153) is understood, *poetically* (p. 154), in terms of the twofold manifestation of *deinón* (the uncanny, the singular and frightening) as the overwhelming power (*dikē*) that gives order and structure and as violence-doing (*technē*). *Dikē* is the Greek word usually translated as "justice," but for Heidegger it should be translated as "fittingness," that is, arrangement and enjoining structure (p. 171). Heidegger says: "Being as *dikē* is the key to beings in their structure" (p. 177). The twofold meaning of *deinón* as *dikē* and *technē* is at work in the very definition of the selfhood of humanity. According to Heidegger:

> The selfhood of humanity means this: it has to transform the Being that opens itself up to it into history, and thus bring itself to a stand (p. 153).

The Being that opens itself up is the overwhelming (*dikē*), which must be transformed into history by means of *technē*. However, in contrast to Nancy, he continues:

> Selfhood does not mean that humanity is primarily an "I" and an individual. Humanity is not this any more than it is a We and a community. (Ibid.)

The idea is then to welcome Heidegger's suggestion only in part, that is, instead of discarding "justice" altogether, it might be fruitful to understand it as what is "fitting" and "proper" (*Ereignis*; another important concept of Heidegger's). Thus understood, the concept of justice also acquires ontological substance. It is no longer simply a juridical category, nor is it ethical in the sense in which ethics regulates and determines behavior, the sense of the *ought*; rather, it is ethical in the sense of the plurality of possibilities inscribed in the *could* modality: it is ethical *and* ontological at the same time. Similarly, speaking of the way in which the proper only returns (i.e., a returning "with"), an idea that I discuss below, Nancy refers to an ontology that "must be both an *ethos* and a *praxis*, identically" (2000: 65).

Commonality and Universality

In political ontology, the concept of justice can be attained by means of a logic of neither/nor, a negative method that intends to unveil the ontological ground, the ontological structure of the concept. The point is not to retreat to a realm of eternal truths—despite my relying on Leibniz at this point—but rather to reach into the plane of universality and commonality. However, the relation of the common and universal to the individual and singular should not be understood as an unbridgeable metaphysical gap between the unchanging forms and the merely empirical, but rather as an "incessant emergence" and a constant passing over of the ones into the others (Agamben 1993).[8] Indeed, even when the singular is explicitly understood—as it should be—as the singularly plural (see the remark on Nancy, above), the question of its relation to the universal and common remains important. If the plane of the universal and common is forgone, justice remains an empirical concept, enmeshed in the ambiguity of the empirically given. As an empirical concept, justice (right) is often simply equated with the law, and its ground is obscured. Unveiling its ontological structure, or rather its ontological movement, is fundamental in the attempt to establish a clear link between labor and sovereignty, showing the uselessness of the latter concept and presenting the former, once freed from the yoke of sovereignty, in its universality and commonality as the concept of justice itself, embodying the dignity of individuation, the solidity and plurality of the singular. The link between the universal and common to individuation, and thus to the particular and empirical, makes it possible for us to understand the idea of justice as the effect of human doing, of labor, the many labors. In fact, the notion of justice as a system superimposed on the many labors, the subjects of history, is one of the most problematic aspects of political and ethical theory. What must be recognized is that true justice flows with and from labor's praxis—a doing freed from the regards of external law, following its own laws, and being in touch with the ontological ground, the source of its power. In this sense, the aberrant mode of practices such as the anti-strike laws (the Taylor law in the state of New York, for instance), the law that makes it illegal for sectors of the workforce to say no to the violence and exploitation of capital, becomes apparent. When looked at from this point of view—namely, the view that there is no justice but that which flows from labor, for labor is the power constituting the social world—then the question can no longer be one of whose interests are hurt more in a strike against blind and exploitative productivity, as was the case with the debates around the MTA strike in New York City in December 2005. In substance, it is no longer a legal dispute; it cannot be left to legal arbitration, for the law shows itself to be lacking in universality. It is, instead, a matter of political ontology, that is, the theory and practice of the production of common life, the good life. Political ontology, particularly the theory of labor's subtraction from all forms of sovereignty, gives full legitimacy and justification to an action such as an "illegal" strike, for it finds in labor's dignity of individuation (that is, in being what it is, in the immediacy with itself) the only possible justice.

Universal Justice

Traditionally, the idea of justice associated with labor is distributive justice, the principle of equity, to give to each her due. The theory of natural right, Leibniz says, distinguishes among commutative, distributive, and universal justice. It is in distributive justice that

> the political laws of a state belong, which assure the happiness of its subjects and make it possible that those who had a merely moral claim acquire a legal claim; that is, that they become able to demand what it is equitable for others to perform. (Leibniz 1972: 172)

However, this works only in the context of a theory of the state; otherwise, distributive justice presents its problems. Marx's later slogan "from each according to his ability, to each according to his needs" qualifies the principle of distributive justice in ways that have yet to be considered, let alone implemented.[9] It seems to me that the kind of justice embodied in the doing of labor is not only distributive justice, but also and primarily universal justice, not in the sense of living honestly or piously (as Leibniz also says), but in the more fundamental sense of allowing labor to return to itself, to its immediacy and dignity, and thereby build a new world devoid of the separateness always inscribed in the logic of exploitation, domination, and sovereignty—a kingdom of ends without *price* (see the remark on Kant, below).

The Antinomy of Sovereignty

Leibniz's language is Christian and, notwithstanding his preference for Plato, Aristotelian. Obviously, it has nothing explicit to do with Marxian theory; yet, his discourse, based on the critique of traditional sovereignty and on the common concept of justice, is very useful to a renewal of radical political theory. When Leibniz goes back to speaking of commutative justice (strict right) and of distributive justice (equity or charity), he says:

Simple or strict right is born of the principle of the conservation of peace; equity or charity strives for something higher—[namely] that while each benefits others as much as he can, he may increase his own happiness in that of the other. And, to say in a word, strict right avoids misery, while the higher right tends toward happiness, but only such as is possible in this life. (p. 173)

Obviously, as a believer, Leibniz does not stop here; he goes beyond into the realm of theology. What is important for us is that, even from the point of view of a philosophy of transcendence, he illuminates the realm of imma-nence, the earthly plenitudes, with a discourse that is certainly profoundly moral but has, at the same time, a distinctive political resonance: no sover-eignty in the realm of immanence; this is, of course, not Leibniz's explicit teaching, but undeniably it is the direction toward which his teaching points. As it becomes clear when he deals with questions of international law, sover-eignty loses its absolute status and becomes a relative concept. But this is a clear challenge to the concept of sovereignty as such, for, as Alan James notes in traditionally Bodinian and Hobbesian fashion, sovereignty is an "abso-lute . . . condition" (1986: 25). Thus Leibniz's early critique of sovereignty really points to the necessity of its elimination—and indeed, in the past fifty years, sovereignty as the power of a state to make its own decision has decid-edly weakened. As Philippe Sands writes, "Notions of sovereignty have changed with growing interdependence. To claim that states are as sovereign today as they were fifty years ago is to ignore reality" (2005: xvii). This is the result of the growing importance of international law, as well as, according to Sands, of the process of globalization made possible by it. Indeed, as Sands says, "international law underpins globalization" (p. 16), and there "would be no globalization without international law" (p. 15). The doctrine of sover-eignty, in its "internal" and "external" aspects, is then in crisis.[10] However, this does not mean that we live under a regime of international law and uni-versal justice. In fact, the opposite is the case, and we often find ourselves in a "lawless world" (Sands 2005). This is due particularly to the double stan-dard, the exceptionalism, which the United States, as the only imperial superpower, has adopted vis-à-vis international law, supporting it when it favors and enhances U.S. economic and strategic interests and ignoring it when it might limit and harm them. Thus, more than to a regime regulated by international laws, the shrinking of state sovereignty is giving rise to an imperial sovereignty under U.S. hegemony (see Hardt and Negri 2000). In-ternational law often becomes instrumental to imperial (and imperialist) policies, at the service of the globalizing hegemonic forces: the United States above all, but also the former imperialist nation-states, today the empire's "vassals," as Ignacio Ramonet (2002) has dubbed them. Although international law should in theory reduce the sovereignty of all states, control their power, in reality the situation is very uneven. Sovereignty becomes a "game" between the absolute form defining the old established and most powerful states and the *quasi-states*, the ex-colonial states, which, according to Robert H. Jackson (1990), enjoy a negative sovereignty in that they are formally independent—an independence guaranteed and supported by the postcolonial international order—but lack the empirical, institutional, and thus positive sovereignty enjoyed by the former. For Jackson, the quasi-states are the creation of the new balance of power in international relations that comes with the process of decolonization. This amounts to what he calls "sovereignty plus" (p. 40), which guarantees the very existence of "otherwise weak and vulnerable Third World governments" (ibid.), at the expense, however, of other peoples' claims for independence and self-determination, including some peoples nominally represented by those very governments. According to Jackson:

> Numerous peoples which were not colonies could not claim this new right of self-determination and have accordingly been barred from entering the international community. (p. 41)

Jackson actually says that self-determination "has become a conservative right of quasi-states" (p. 42). Those *nations without states* that are the object of Montserrat Guibernau's study (1999)—nations that would qualify as sovereign entities according to Bodin's classic theory of what makes a *république*, that is, a commonwealth (Bodin 1993)—are deprived of self-determination and autonomy, of sovereignty. For Guibernau, the question of the nations without states can be solved by the adequate implementation of the principle of subsidiarity, that is, the political and juridical principle based upon the decentralization of power (pp. 184–186).[11] In his optimistic vision, the negative condition of some nations deprived of sovereignty and statehood could become a positive and universalized feature of the new global political actors:

> In my view, the recognition of nations without states as global political actors does not necessarily involve them becoming independent. My argument is that while some nations without states may secede [he gives the example of Quebec] most of them are likely to achieve greater political autonomy within the political institutions which are currently

being developed. For instance, there are strong chances that further European integration will favour a greater presence of nations without states such as Catalonia, Scotland, the Basque Country or Flanders in the international political arena. (pp. 27–28)

This remark on a contemporary question of international relations shows the importance and fruitfulness of Leibniz's early critique. When coupled with the universalizing doctrine of individual substances, sovereignty, a "legal condition" (cf. James 1986: 25), shows the limits and dangers inherent in the concept of the law as command, the constitution of unitary political entities at the expense of other realities and experiences, which are silenced and neutralized by being included and excluded at the same time. Yet the doctrine of individual substance posits in singularity and the dignity of individuation the measure for a genuine theory of justice, one that (to use a different language) gives human rights and dignity priority over sovereign rights and that is able to challenge, and perhaps reverse, the status quo in international law whereby, as Jackson says, the "cosmopolitan society of humankind is legally—not to mention politically—inferior to the international society of sovereign states" (1990: 46). In his discussion, Jackson also employs the contradiction between human rights and sovereign rights (or at least the limited scope of the doctrine of sovereignty and self-determination) inherent in the 1960 Declaration on the Granting of Independence to Colonial Countries and Peoples (UN Resolution 1514). For, if on the one hand it proclaimed that "all peoples have the right to self-determination," on the other it condemned "any attempt aimed at the partial or total disruption of the national unity and the territorial integrity of a country" (pp. 77–78). "Consequently," Jackson remarks,

ethnonational self-determination is now illegitimate and the prospect of independence for the numerous ethnonationalities of the Third World [and of the world in general, we might add] are bleak. (p. 78)

And again:

Decolonization clearly was an extension of self-determination and sovereign rights to numerous governments which previously had not been independent. But it was not always an extension of human rights to the populations under their jurisdiction. (p. 159)

The antinomy of sovereignty is here clearly shown: by legitimizing some forms of power, it makes other forms (perhaps, this time, forms of life) illegitimate. In Leibniz, as we shall see, the distinction is between right and law.[12] But it must be said now that the concept of dignity of individuation is more far-reaching and less ambiguous than that of right.

Universal Love

In "Codex Iuris Gentium," Leibniz says that justice is virtue, and virtue should be taken, I believe, in the etymological sense of power. He says that justice as virtue "regulates that affection which the Greeks call . . . [philanthropy]" (1972: 171), that is, love of humanity, universal love. He defines it as "the charity of the wise man, that is, charity which follows the dictates of wisdom" (ibid.). Leibniz is here speaking of important concepts in the tradition of philosophy: wisdom, happiness—concepts that he rereads in the light of the Christian tradition, but that remain important even for secular ways of thinking. So let us see what he means by charity, and how it relates to happiness, that is, to the good life. He says that charity is "a universal benevolence, and benevolence [is] the habit of loving or willing the good" (ibid.). From the language of Christianity we are back, conceptually, to Aristotle and post-Aristotelian philosophy. On the one hand, we have universal love; on the other, the idea that the good life is the result of our choices, of habit. But how do love and happiness relate to each other? According to Leibniz :

> Love . . . signifies rejoicing in the happiness of another, or, what is the same thing, converting the happiness of another into one's own. (Ibid.)

In the short piece called "Felicity," Leibniz says: "To love is to find pleasure in the perfection of another" (p. 83). But what is this perfection? From his metaphysics of individual substances, we know that there are many kinds of perfections, that everything is perfect in its kind, that there is no exception, no extraordinary event, no miracle.[13] Everything is perfect in its individuation. Perfection is the dignity of individuation. Obviously, this goodness or perfection implies the capacity to recognize the perfection of another, to be in the place of the other: "The place of others is the true point of perspective in politics, as well as in morality" (p. 81). In fact, what is justice, the universal law, if not a sense of the dignity of the other? It is here that the concept of the singularly plural, the plural origins of the singular, shows its full force and importance. However, it must also be admitted that the place of the other is the capacity to recognize the universal, to *be* the universal.[14] Indeed, these concepts cannot be mutually exclusive; we simply cannot choose to repudiate the universal on the basis of singularity and its plural constitution—not of course the plural as a collection of empirical phenomena, but as the original indeterminacy of what could be. In truth, the plural is precisely what mediates between the singular and the universal.[15] A way out of the problem would of course be offered by Sartre's concept of the "singular universal." In his study of Flaubert, Sartre says that to understand what a human being is, one should consider, not the category of the individual, but that of the singular universal, that is, the totalizing and universalizing process whereby one becomes what one is (1981: ix). For Sartre, one is universalized by one's time, which is in turn universalized in the production of one's singularity. The problem of losing the essential and originary moment of plurality thematized by Nancy seems neutralized by the fact that the universal is not a point of departure, but rather the effect of the totalization and universalization process. Perhaps the only problem is that, in Sartre, who writes in this respect in the tradition of Kierkegaard, the singular universal necessarily sets itself apart from the whole, reconstituting the whole in its singularity. Thus, it might be good to make the universalizing moment explicit and stronger and stay at the level of the process, rather than close it with a finished product having the air of absoluteness. In this sense, I would propose Robert McRuer's immensely fruitful concept of "temporary or contingent universalization," which would replace what he calls "a banal, humanistic universalization" (2006: 157). I refer again to McRuer's work on disability and queerness more extensively in Chapter 5, but this concept can be extracted at this point and used in a perhaps wider sense than McRuer himself might intend. With this concept in mind, charity based on wisdom is not, then, a patronizing, "humanistic" way to deal with the other. It is instead an active conversion of "the happiness of another into one's own," that is, the wisdom, the capacity to see the universal in the particular, and to understand that the self—as Randy Martin has also recently observed—"is made out of something other than itself" (2002a: 98). Moreover, anticipating Kant, Leibniz holds this universal love to be disinterested, for "the happiness of those whose happiness pleases us turns into our own happiness, since things which please us are desired for their own sake" (1972: 171). Wisdom, then, the highest moment in philosophy as well as in life, "is nothing but the science of happiness itself" (ibid.). But the reference to Kant, who is in this respect very close to Leibniz, should also make us understand that the universality implied in the notion of the place of the other rules out the empirical gesture of switching places with the other, which is ultimately an impossible thing to do and can be done only at the level of feelings and the imagination. Instead, the task is here *transcendental*, and it has to do with the pronounced parallax that Kojin Karatani explains and elaborates upon in his superb reading of Kant (a part of his book on Kant and Marx). This transcendental task or position is the view emerging from a logic of neither/nor and neutrality—a view that is, for instance, neither subjective nor objective.[16] Accordingly, "the place of the other" opens the realm of universality because it is not the empirical, but the transcendental other, that is at stake here. In Karatani's words,

> this other is not one who can be identified with the self in any sense of intersubjectivity or common sense. . . . Nor is this other a one who introduces relativism into our thinking, but rather the one who makes us face the problem of universality. (2003: 52–53)

Yet, by not being empirical, the other, the place of the other, is not removed from experience, as if it lay in a *transcendent* realm:

> The transcendental other—as distinct from the transcendent other, the sacred other (God)—is a quintessentially secular other who is everywhere and everytime in front of us. (p. 70)

The relation between the transcendental and the empirical is also explained by Slavoj Žižek's notion of universality, in particular with respect to Hegel's "concrete universality":

> Universality is not the neutral container of a particular formation, their common measure, the passive (back)ground on which the particulars fight their battles, but this battle itself, the struggle leading from one particular formation to another. (2006: 30)

Žižek also says:

> Concrete universality is not merely the universal core that animates a series of its particular forms of appearance; it persists in the very irreducible tension, noncoincidence, between these different levels. (p. 31)

However, it must be noted that neutrality and commonality are not canceled by universality, both because, at the most general level, the latter is determined by the former two concepts and because, more specifically, "neutral" also refers to the parallactic neither/nor and "common" to the very tension whereby the particular reaches into the universal. This is also acknowledged by Žižek when, speaking of Spinoza, he describes the passage from the "One *qua* the neutral medium/container of its modes" to "the One's inherent gap" as "the very passage from Substance to Subject" (p. 42).[17]

Right and Law: Three Illustrations

In "Caesarinus Fürstenerius" (his main work on sovereignty), Leibniz attacks Hobbes's concept of sovereignty. He says: "In explaining the concept of sovereignty, I confess that I must enter into . . . a field which is thorny and little-cultivated" (1972: 113). The truth is that the concept of sovereignty, starting with Bodin and Hobbes, always referred to a supreme, absolute, and unitary power.[18] For Leibniz, and this is where he says that in dealing with this subject one "lacks the aid of great writers" (p. 114), this allegedly supreme and unitary power is in actual reality divided. For him, there remains a universal power, such as the Holy Roman Empire, which has *majestas*, a medieval concept that Bodin still equates with sovereignty, rather than sovereignty itself. But for Leibniz, sovereignty itself can only be understood as a relative term. As Patrick Riley says in the introduction to the Cambridge selection of Leibniz's political writings, later incorporated in his monographic study (Riley 1996), Leibniz "removed the character of absolute supremacy from the concept of sovereignty, making it only a comparative rather than a superlative standard" (Riley 1972: 27). Of course, once this is done, it is no longer of the traditional concept of sovereignty that one is speaking. Riley points out that Leibniz's concept of sovereignty was "descriptive and non-legal" (ibid.). For Riley, Leibniz's "reasons for wanting to undermine the idea of sovereignty" were not only "practical," but also "purely philosophical" (ibid.). One of these philosophical reasons was his aversion to "the Hobbesian doctrine of law as command" (p. 28). For Leibniz, in fact, "Right cannot be unjust, it is a contradiction; but law can be" (Leibniz 1972: 50).[19] The point, of course, is to understand what the distinction between law and right really implies. I have already said how justice (or right) follows from labor, and I believe that it is only in this sense that the force of law loses meaning. In Leibniz, as Riley points out, what we have is a "radical distinction between positive and natural law," the latter referred to by Leibniz as "universal jurisprudence" (Riley 1972: 28). Today we cannot simply say that beyond positive law there is natural law, for the critique of essentialism in the realm of ethics complicates a distinction that might be too neatly made, and rightly so; or, to put it another way, this would be doing metaphysics in the most traditional sense. Hence the universality of a hypothetical natural law, a higher law that stands behind the system of positive law, a right that is always just behind the law, which can be just or unjust, becomes highly problematic. Yet, we cannot renounce the idea that there is a measure of justice not necessarily encountered by the law, the positive law, for this is what history and everyday life show. The suggestion is that justice is the dignity of individuation, that is, the capacity to recognize the dignity of the other—a claim already made above. Thus, to make a concrete historical example, John Brown's actions would not make sense without what is for him an appeal to a higher, divine, law, and what we might reinterpret as the justice unfolding from labor, from human doing in touch with universality and plurality, not determined by the particularity of one group's interests. Thus, John Brown, after his capture and before his execution, typically says:

> I think I feel happy as Paul did when he lay in prison. He knew if they killed him, it would greatly advance the cause of Christ; that was the reason he rejoiced so. On that same ground "I do rejoice, yea, and will rejoice." Let them hang me; I forgive them, and may God forgive them, for they know not what they do. I have no regret for the transaction for which I am condemned. I went against the laws of men, it is true, but "whether it be right to obey God or men, judge ye." (Du Bois 1987: 278)

Of course, John Brown could not have fought against slavery, "the sum of all villanies" (p. 74), by following the positive law. Notwithstanding his religious rhetoric, it was action—and violent action at that—it was *labor* that gave him the measure of right and wrong. For, and this must be stressed here, what is meant by labor is not strictly the working activity, such as in the factory, but all doing constituting, producing the social. This universal labor is what we see at work in the John Brown example. Another illustration of how the confrontation between labor and sovereignty (the law) gives rise to an adequate idea of justice is the classical figure of Antigone, who challenges Creon's prohibition and gives proper burial to her brother Polyneices. When Creon says to Antigone: "And yet you dared to violate these laws?" Antigone answers:

> *What laws? I never heard it was Zeus*
> *Who made the announcement.*
> *And it wasn't justice, either. The gods below*

Didn't lay down this law for human use.
And I never thought your announcements
Could give you—a mere human being—
Power to trample the gods' unfailing,
Unwritten laws.
(Sophocles 2001: lines 450–457)

These "unwritten laws" are established by the doing of labor, by praxis, notwithstanding here again the religious language. To her sister Ismene, who first deserted her but later wants to share responsibility for her action, Antigone says: "I have witnesses: the gods below saw who did the work" (line 542). The work was done in accordance with the requirements of justice; it is just work, capable of upsetting the whole establishment of society, of destroying and reconstituting society. It was done at the margins of the political, for Antigone says: "I have no place with human beings, / Living or dead. No city is home to me" (lines 851–852). There is no sovereign power in it. It is rather the potency of the immediacy of labor, its subjectivity, the immediacy of doing and praxis, in touch with the ontological ground, which here appears as "the gods below." There is no sovereignty in the act that subverts the law, but the act itself, the work done, subverts the law and eliminates all elements of sovereignty by virtue of its intimacy with the common concept of justice: "It wasn't Zeus who made the announcement, and it wasn't justice, either." But before continuing with a discussion of Leibniz's common concept of justice, it might be good to give another example of the problematics linking sovereignty, labor, and justice. This time I use a movie, *La promesse* (1996), by Jean-Pierre and Luc Dardenne, casting the exceptionally good Jérémie Rénier (as Igor, the son), Olivier Gourmet (as Roger, the father), and Assita Ouedraogo (as Assita, Amidu's wife). When Amidu (Rasmane Ouedraogo), an undocumented immigrant from Burkina Faso, who works for Roger in Liège (Belgium), falls from a scaffold during a labor inspector's visit and soon dies for lack of medical care, the almost perfect, idyllic relationship between Roger and Igor is ruined. Igor, who promises Amidu to take care of his wife, Assita, and their small son, recently arrived in Belgium from Burkina Faso, is forced to break with Roger, who wants to hide the fatal accident at all costs. Roger's whole business relies on the exploitation of undocumented immigrants, whom he provides with the bare necessities of life when they get to Belgium. Reporting the accident to the authority would entail the end of his business and serious criminal charges against him. Yet, to keep his promise to Amidu, Igor does not give in to Roger's threats and implorations; he sides absolutely with Assita, helps her and her son in all possible ways.

Igor's break with Roger is not easy. They are not only father and son, but also boss and apprentice, as well as friends (before Amidu's accident and death, Igor is learning from his father, whom he calls Roger, not only the skills of carpentry but also those necessary to manage the enterprise and be a boss). However, when I say that Roger and Igor are *also* friends, I need to explain, for even friendship can be tainted by dynamics of domination, and then cease being sincere or true friendship. Some scenes in the movie make this evident. For instance, when Roger finds out that Igor is helping Assita by asking one of his associates to give her money, he beats him up. This is, after Amidu's death, the main turning point in the relationship between father and son. Although Roger soon tries to restore the old relationship, it will not last long. Right after beating him up and announcing "no more cheating between us," Roger tries to cheer Igor up, by cuddling and tickling him (and Igor unconvincingly reacts and laughs), by finishing the tattoo he is drawing on his son's arm. Then Roger asks Igor if he has ever been with a woman, if he would like to try, adding that he should. In the next scenes, Roger and his girlfriend and Igor and a date are in a pub. In a movie without soundtrack, Roger and Igor sing on the mike, and then the four of them sing and laugh at the table. This scene has the nostalgia of fireworks, which will not last; it is a tribute to what might have been. In fact, the situation soon deteriorates. Back to their routine and everyday life, Igor and Roger will not be able to relate to one another as they used to. When Igor lights a cigarette for Roger, which he normally does before lighting his own, Roger refuses it, implying that a modality of their relationship is over. And when Igor asks Roger, who tricks Assita into believing that Amidu is waiting for her in Germany, what he will do when she finds out the truth, he answers, "That's my problem."

It is at this point—when he realizes that in taking Assita to Germany, Roger intends to sell her as a whore—that Igor rebels against his father. The first, spontaneous movement of rebellion, or noncompliance, was when, at the time of Amidu's death, Igor refused to empty the wheelbarrow filled with cement on Amidu's body, which Roger was burying. But that was an act of resistance due more to the incapacity to act—he was petrified—than to anything else. When he now jumps into Roger's car and drives away with Assita and her child, the rebellion becomes a conscious one. At this point, what is important for Igor is not only to take care of Assita and the baby but also to tell Assita the truth. However, he cannot bring himself to do that until the moment when, at the end of the movie, Assita is about to take the train to Italy, where she has a relative. At this point, Igor tells her that Amidu is dead and buried in cement, that he wanted to take him to the hospital after the accident, but that, "to avoid problems," he "obeyed" his father.

What moves Igor is neither John Brown's God nor Antigone's gods below. Yet, it is the same concept of justice, secularized this time, which hits and shatters the same sovereign power—and here, too, its vehicle is labor, in the wide sense of praxis, doing.

Throughout the movie we see the many labors Igor engages in, which oscillate between the legal and the illegal, the ethical and the unethical: he is an apprentice mechanic but also (if the occasion arises) a thief, someone who turns in illegal migrant workers to the police but also Assita's friend and self-appointed carer. But the real oscillation is between accepting sovereign power (whether it comes from his master mechanic or from Roger) and living the freedom and dignity of his individuation (which he experiences when he builds a go-kart with his friends in his free time or when he renounces everything for the sake of the promise he made to the dying Amidu).

When we consider these three examples, we see that Leibniz's comparative concept of sovereignty makes a lot of sense, for sovereignty is everywhere, perhaps permutated from state power, or perhaps eminently attributed to it. Thus, the sovereignty of the United States vis-à-vis the slaves, the fugitive slaves, and the abolitionists, is not, in its substance, different from the more ambiguous (because at one and the same time official and personal) sovereignty of Creon, nor is it different from that which Roger has over Igor. This sovereignty, which is everywhere, has the only purpose of crushing labor, not simply the employed labor force, but all labor, all doing that does not accept a Hobbesian command, a superimposed order, an external law bent to ruthless domination (although for the purpose of mutual assistance). But we have seen that it is labor itself, in its return to itself (a return that is apparent in all of the three examples I gave), which subverts the law, destroys sovereignty, and renews justice. This justice is nothing but the dignity of individuation, which is a task of the return to illuminate. John Brown, Antigone, and Igor accomplish the return. In the solitude and the immediacy of their being, yet in deep involvement with the other, they regain the dignity of individuation, which has no tolerance for any form of sovereignty. But they do so by becoming, in their singularity, universal subjects, that is, contingent universalizations.

In the section on co-appearance, Nancy says that "one should not say the 'with'; one should only say 'with'" (p. 62). This "with" is not "the essence of a common Being" (pp. 64–65) that must be reappropriated, "but rather a *with* of reappropriation (where the proper does not return, or returns only *with*)" (p. 65). The space and time of "with," this co-ontology, the event of reappropriation, can be seen as universal and common not in the sense of pointing to an essence lying beyond, for all remains within the plane of immanence, as Nancy's discussion shows. Yet, contrary to Nancy, one can still speak of universality and commonality insofar as this is the structure of the "with of reappropriation," of the "proper returning only with." The three illustrations given above exemplify this structure. In fact, plurality constitutes the mediation between the singular and the universal. It is not John Brown, Antigone, or Igor as a mere individual that grounds the event of justice and gives translucence to the dignity of individuation. It is rather the "with" of slavery and the resistance to it. It is the "with" of Creon's positive law and the being-with of Antigone and Polyneices, of life and death, for, before dying, Antigone, who had no home, says: "I'm coming home forever, to be held in / With my own people, most of them dead now" (Sophocles 2001: lines 892–893). To Polyneices, she says, "Look: this is my reward / For taking care of you" (lines 903–904). And referring to the law she has followed, she says, "There is no ground to grow a brother for me now" (line 912). And again, the dignity of individuation is in the "with" of migrant labor abuse in Belgium and Igor's struggle against identifying with a "we" of authority and command, docility and obedience, based solely on a logic of inclusion and exclusion: Assita, Amidu, are "the other," with whom one must not identify, in whose place one must not enter. And this is illustrated, in the movie, by Roger's prohibition to Igor to visit Assita in her room. But the course of action chosen in all these cases is universal in character, perhaps in the Kantian sense, that is, answering solely to the moral law. But in Kant, too, if the law is universal, objective, and necessary, following it is a subjective endeavor, contingent, and *tending toward* the universal—and it is in this *tension* that the pronounced parallax studied by Karatani is revealed. In fact, from the point of view of each of the individuals in question, it is a way of reaching into the universal, a contingent universalization of their singularity. Yet, it is so because it is not done in isolation, and it could not be done in isolation. It is done out of what is really and already "one's own" (to refer to Antigone again) returning as "with": speaking of Creon, Antigone had said, "He has no right to keep me from my own" (line 48). Thus a new community emerges, beyond the law: the community that repudiates slavery, the king's unjust law, the boss, the father, and the system of exploitation of migrant labor. It is the community that repudiates sovereignty.

Rejecting Sovereignty

Obviously, Leibniz does not give us a theory of revolution or even of resistance to any form of sovereignty, his main political interest being the "reunification of 'Christendom'" (Riley 1972: 1), modeled after the "universal monarchy" under God (Leibniz 1972: 105). In one of his political letters, he said:

> As for the question, whether subjects can resist the sovereign power, and in what cases, I am strongly of the opinion of Grotius, and I believe that as a rule resistance is forbidden to them. For ordinarily the evil of rebellion is greater than that which one claims to remedy. (p. 187)

Leibniz does not at all challenge the idea of God as "sovereign wisdom" and "sovereign power"—an idea that serves as a metaphysical *and* moral principle:

> As for me, I put forward the great principle of metaphysics as well as of morality, that the world is governed by the most perfect intelligence which is possible, which means that one must consider it as a universal monarchy whose head is all-powerful and sovereignly wise, and whose subjects are all minds [*esprits*], that is, substances capable of relations or society with God. (p. 105)

Nor does he challenge the notion that a prince has supreme power within a given territory. Thus, his political theory is certainly not democratic and, despite his emphasis on universal justice, it is rather conservative.[20] Yet, his critique of the traditional concept of sovereignty—particularly of Hobbes's notion of the indivisibility of sovereign power—opens important spaces for the elaboration of a radical theory capable of displacing sovereignty altogether. Indeed, as Hinsley says in his classic history of the concept of sovereignty, after Hobbes, who "exalted" it (Hinsley 1966:144), sovereignty was generally accepted. According to Hinsley:

> Among later thinkers of any stature perhaps Leibniz alone . . . attacked sovereignty as being merely an academic formulation, on the ground that all human authority is necessarily relative and conditioned. (Ibid.)

Hinsley explains that, generally speaking, even those who opposed Hobbes did not reject sovereignty as such, but spoke of the people as sovereign, not advancing in this from the positions of Althusius and Milton (p. 146). Moreover,

Leibniz's metaphysics of individual substance, as the only indivisible, becomes fruitful when applied to the essentially revolutionary concept of dignity. Of course, in the course of a revolutionary struggle, there are moments when resorting to the concept of sovereignty is very important, as is the case today with the Bolivarian Revolution in Venezuela (cf. Lebowitz 2006; Harnecker 2005). Thus, in 1993 Hugo Chávez said: "The sovereign people must transform itself into the object *and the subject* of power" (quoted in Lebowitz 2006: 116). And in the long interview with Chávez by Marta Harnecker, there is a whole section on the question of building a sovereign nation, with particular regard to Venezuela's international policy. But the theme of sovereignty recurs throughout the book. However, this does not cancel the truth that, ultimately, it is the dissolution of sovereignty as such and the upholding of a philosophy of dignity, the constitution of a society based on justice and dignity that gives meaning to revolutionary struggles. In relation to the Venezuelan Revolution in particular, there is a clear example of the process toward the elimination of power as command in the story told by Chavez to Harnecker of the president of a Community Development Council who, to his question as to whether she was in charge, answered that no one was in charge there because they had a horizontal organization with no managers but only a coordinator (Harnecker 2005: 171). And at the end of his book on the new socialism, Lebowitz remarks that "the goal is the full development of human potential" (pp. 116–117). After a balanced and critical assessment of the Revolution's achievements, shortcomings, and dangers, Lebowitz looks at it as a re-embodiment of the Marxism of Che Guevara, of his idea of the new human being, and he says that, of course, the Bolivarian Revolution is not Venezuelan in character. Instead, on the basis of his reading of the new constitution, he calls attention to the fact that the Revolution's task is the struggle for human development and radical needs, "the understanding that people are transformed as they struggle for justice and dignity" (p. 118). The emphasis on dignity is, of course, also a feature of the philosophy of the Zapatista revolt, in which, because of the Zapatista opposition to the idea of taking power, sovereignty does not figure at all. As John Holloway says, with a reference to Subcomandante Marcos:

> The fight for dignity cannot be restricted to national frontiers: "dignity," in the wonderful expression used by Marcos in the invitation to the Intercontinental Gathering held in the Lacandon Jungle in July 1996, "is that homeland without nationality, that rainbow that is also a bridge, that murmur of the heart no matter what blood lives

in it, that rebel irreverence that mocks frontiers, customs officials and wars." (1998: 168)

In *Change the World without Taking Power*, Holloway equates dignity with "anti-power" (2000:159), and that means, of course, anti-sovereignty.

The Common Concept of Justice

To return to Leibniz, one of the most important aspects of his thought is the emphasis on universality, and this is true whether he deals with logic and language or ethics and justice. For Leibniz, the concept of justice "must be common to God and to man" (1972: 48). This is what he says in the "Meditation on the Common Concept of Justice"—which makes one think, as Patrick Riley also notes (1996: 205), of John Duns Scotus's doctrine of univocity, that is, the neutrality of being with respect to any qualifying determinations. Analogously, in Leibniz's concept of justice, we find the neither/nor of the law, its neutrality, but also its commonality and universality. At the outset of his essay, Leibniz implicitly refers to Plato's famous formulation of the problem of justice in the *Euthyphro*: "Is the pious being loved by the gods because it is pious, or is it pious because it is being loved by the gods?" (Plato 2002: 10a). Leibniz's own essay starts by saying:

> It is agreed that whatever God wills is good and just. But there remains the question whether it is good and just because God wills it or whether God wills it because it is good and just: in other words whether justice and goodness are arbitrary or whether they belong to the necessary and eternal truths about the nature of things, as do numbers and proportions. (1972: 45)

Of course, Leibniz's answer, just like Socrates' and Plato's, is that there is universality and necessity in goodness and justice. Metaphysically, and theologically, the question is also answered in *The Monadology*, where Leibniz distinguishes between God's will and understanding, as well as between contingency and necessity, and in *Discourse on Metaphysics*. In *The Monadology*, he says that

> we should not imagine, as some do, that since the eternal truths depend on God, they are arbitrary and depend on his will, as Descartes appears to have held. . . . This is true of contingent truths. . . . But necessary truths depend solely on his understanding . (Leibniz 1989b: 218–219)

In *Discourse on Metaphysics*, we read:

> Thus, in saying that things are not good by virtue of any rule of
> goodness but solely by virtue of the will of God, it seems to me that
> we unknowingly destroy all of God's love and all of his glory. For
> why praise him for what he has done if he would be equally praise-
> worthy in doing the exact contrary? Where will his justice and wis-
> dom reside if there remains only a certain despotic power, if will
> holds the place of reason, and if, according to the definition of tyrants,
> justice consists in whatever pleases the most powerful? (1989a: 36)

Here we are again at the center of the problem of sovereignty. With the primacy of God's understanding over his will, Leibniz is again confronting
Hobbes, particularly his *decisionism*, namely the idea of the law as arbitrary
command. According to Ernst Bloch, "Hobbes secularizes the doctrine of
the primacy of the will of God over the reason of God" (1987: 47), and he
continues by saying that this was the doctrine that "Duns Scotus had established in the preabsolutist period" (ibid.). Bloch explains that for Scotus,

> the good is not good because God willed and commanded it, be-
> cause God could just as well have ordained murder, thievery, and
> adultery in the commandments and then not murdering, not steal-
> ing, and not committing adultery would be sins. (Ibid.)

Bloch continues: "In short, the good would not have been able to be a preor-
dained idea in accordance with God's unlimited power of issuing decrees"
(ibid.). This is a difficult point, to which I return when I deal with sovereignty as decisionism in Carl Schmitt. Fundamentally, Duns Scotus's theory,
reported by Bloch, says that the good is good in itself. Thus he agrees with
Plato before him and with Leibniz after him. Even in his philosophy of the
primacy of the will, it is not possible to hold that what is just could also be
unjust. In this sense, despite Bloch's attempt at establishing a direct link between Duns Scotus and Hobbes, there is an important difference between
them. If for Hobbes, as Bloch also points out, "autoritas, non veritas facit
legem"—a principle fully accepted by Carl Schmitt—for Scotus the making
of the law is not the primary concern of the theory of the primacy of the will,
nor is the will itself identified with the principle of authority. Instead, the
principle of charity, which we shall find in Leibniz too, sets an important
limit to the possibly capricious authority of the law. In Scotus's philosophy of
contingency and freedom, it is not the *nature* of things that is chosen, but

their event, or eventualization. This is so also because in Duns Scotus we have the formation of the will as such (Loiret 2003: 21), not simply its employment at the empirical level. God, in Scotus's and Leibniz's theologies, or human beings, in ethics and in secular thinking, have the will to say yes or no to a just or an unjust world, thereby *contingently causing* the one or the other, but they cannot bring about a situation in which the just is unjust and the unjust just. In Scotus, in particular, the will is a rational will. Or rather, as François Loiret says, the will *as* will implies "a new determination of rationality itself;" it *is* rationality itself (p. 51). *Autoritas*, the sovereign, can choose a policy of murder and genocide, but it cannot choose it as just and good. It can choose to outlaw charity, care, and human solidarity, to make them crimes, but it cannot change their essential nature. The doctrine of sovereignty from Hobbes to Schmitt, the doctrine of decisionism and of the exception, remains deprived of ontological and ethical grounding. It is important for the theory of the law and for that *threshold*, or *zone of indifference*, which for Agamben is "neither external nor internal to the juridical order" (2005: 23), which suspends the law and yet reiterates it. But it does not reach into the ontological ground of the neither/nor of the law. It remains the task of a political ontology to see beyond the law, not simply what makes the law possible, any law possible, but the universal and common concept of justice shining in the dignity of each individual being. It is upon such an *intuition* (for this is how individuation is experienced and grasped, as intuition) and, within that intuition, in the most common that one finds the measure of a better world.

Rationality and the Will

I have established a link between Leibniz and Duns Scotus, but there is at least one important difference that must also be addressed. It has to do with the concept of the will, central in the philosophy of Duns Scotus, but subordinated to reason in Leibniz. Thus, in "The Common Concept of Justice," Leibniz says: "And to say *stat pro ratione voluntas*, my will takes the place of reason, is properly the motto of a tyrant" (1972: 46). However, this important difference is ultimately only formal. In fact, the rational will in Duns Scotus shows the limits of the law as command, and thus of sovereignty, just as much as Leibniz's primacy of reason does. In both cases, the most important concept is that of contingency and of its relation to the ontological constitution of its specific character. Contingency does not mean that everything is always equally possible and that the reality we know might henceforth be underestimated because a different modality of the real would always be possible. Rather, what it means is that when something occurred, the opposite could also have occurred. In other words, contingency does not deny necessity; *it only denies natural necessity*—this is at least Duns Scotus's teaching (see Loiret 2003: 55). In Leibniz, contingency denies necessity, but it does not deny certainty, which can be seen as a special kind of contingency itself, as shown in *Discourse on Metaphysics* (1989a: 12). With respect to justice, it does not mean that the will is free to make an action just or unjust. Rather, it means that it is free to choose between doing and not doing a just action, as well as doing and not doing an unjust action. As Leibniz says, "It is one thing to be just and another to pass for it, and to take the place of justice" (1972: 47). For Leibniz, the problem does not reside within the will, but within the understanding, for the confusion as to what makes an action just or unjust has to do with the "failure to distinguish between right and fact" (ibid.). Thus,

> to say that "just" is whatever pleases the most powerful is nothing else than saying that there is no certain and determined justice which keeps one from doing whatever he wants to do and can do with impunity, however evil it may be. (Ibid.)

However, Leibniz's attack is not on the will as will, the rational will of Duns Scotus for instance, but on the will as crude power, that is, the will that is merely appetite, and not love.[21] What Leibniz calls "formal reason of justice" (1972: 48) also implies a redefinition of rationality, just as Duns Scotus's concept of the rational will does. For Leibniz, the formal reason is the concept of justice itself, "common to God and to man" (ibid.). Although Leibniz makes no mention of the will here, it is evident that what he has in mind is not simply the understanding that understands, but a "legislating" concept, a universal ontology of which the seemingly easily graspable empirical is but a result. For Leibniz, this ontology includes what he calls "the necessary and demonstrative sciences" (p. 50), from logic and metaphysics to geometry and ethics, which, he says, "are not founded on experiences and facts, and serve rather to give reasons for facts and to control them in advance" (ibid.). And he shows the limits of the law by adding that this same regulating and legislating process "would [also] happen with respect to right, if there were no law in the world" (ibid.). Although this falls short of stating the uselessness of the law as command and of sovereignty, it certainly shows the way toward it. Leibniz continues: "The error of those who have made justice dependent on power comes in part from confounding right and law" (ibid.). And then, there is the already quoted: "Right cannot be unjust, it is a contradiction; but law can be" (ibid.). Leibniz does not argue against Hobbes's tautology that *autoritas facit legem*. For him, this is not the most important point. Rather, the important question is whether the law is just or unjust. Indeed, it goes without saying that power gives and maintains the law (this is why I speak of a tautology), and at the level of the empirical, the understanding understands as much. However, "if this power lacks wisdom or good will, it can give and maintain quite evil laws" (ibid.)—a notion fully accepted by Kant.[22] Riley says: "Without a certain kind of will, then, wise charity cannot serve as the heart of a justice which is more than sovereign-ordained law" (1996: 61). It must, however, be said that wisdom or good will is not necessarily the same as will, and this, as Riley notes, "is of course the central moral problem in [Leibniz's] theory of substance" (ibid.). The implication is that the dissolution of power and the law is not the dissolution of justice, but rather, perhaps, the coming to the fore of its common concept. It is obvious that this implies a new form of rationality, one which must be willed—a new form of justice.

The Reality of Justice

As Patrick Riley remarks, for Leibniz "it was merely an empiricist prejudice to see justice as "unreal" if it did not consist of tangible commands backed by power and threats" (p. 16). This "new" form of justice, then, is already there from the beginning: it is real in the most eminent sense—and it is what Leibniz calls a *formal reason*, probably not always readily apparent, certainly hindered by the empirical, yet already present. For Leibniz, it is an eternal truth. And, as Riley says,

> Leibniz used the notion of objectively certain "eternal verities" politically and morally to attack the idea of justice as base superior power; the "formal notion" [or reason] of justice, he observed in a commentary on Hobbes, has nothing to do with the more "sovereign" command of authorities. (Ibid.)

Instead, and here Riley quotes Leibniz, it depends on "the eternal rules of wisdom and goodness, in men as well as in God" (ibid.).

Here we find again the meeting of understanding and will, the rational will, for, as Leibniz says, "wisdom is in the understanding and goodness in the will" (1972: 50). And in the next sentence he says: "And justice, as a consequence, is in both" (ibid.). He is here still speaking about the formal reason of justice:

Justice is nothing else than that which conforms to wisdom and goodness joined together. (Ibid.)

Power, Leibniz says,

is a different matter, but if it is used it makes right become fact, and makes what ought to be really exist, in so far as the nature of things permits. (Ibid.)

Power, which is "naturally a good, . . . does not become a certain good until it is joined with wisdom and goodness" (ibid.), and that means, with charity and love.

The practical importance of grasping the common concept of justice has to do, for Leibniz, with the need to go beyond the ambiguity and the confusion that reigns at the empirical level, the level of opinions in Plato's sense, the need to build a universal jurisprudence, a universal grammar of the ethical, to unveil the ontological ground of the practice of right and power. Leibniz says:

Most of the questions of right, but particularly that of sovereign and of peoples, are confused, because everyone does not agree on a common concept of justice, with the result that everyone does not understand the same thing by the same name, and this is the cause of endless dispute. (p. 53)

For Leibniz, justice is not given by simply refraining from harming others; it requires an active involvement of the will toward benevolence, and this is what he calls the *charity of the wise*, "that is to say goodness toward others which is conformed to wisdom." He adds, "And wisdom, in my sense, is nothing else than the science of felicity" (p. 54). For Leibniz, good and evil are negatively related to one another; the negation of the one lies in a continuum in which the positing of the other becomes probable or even certain:

Whether one does evil or refuses to do good is a matter of degree, but that does not change the species and the nature of the thing. One can also say that the absence of good is an evil and that the absence of evil is a general good. (p. 55)

This active disposition toward benevolence is what Leibniz also calls the principle of equity, "which orders that we give each his due: *suum cuique tribuere*" (p. 56), and we know what is due by putting ourselves in "the place of the other" (ibid.). At first sight, this might seem to hold only within the framework of individualism, but in truth it can be universalized, and Leibniz himself proposes that. In a short work called "Notes on Social Life," he says: "The place of others is the true point of perspective in politics as well as in morality" (p. 81). Hence, "the wise" does not have to be one restricted group of people, ultimately dominating over all others. Leibniz notes that

> nothing can contribute more to the happiness or the misery of man than men. If they were all wise, and knew how to treat each other, they would all be happy, so far as happiness can be attained by human reason. (p. 57)

The importance of Leibniz's philosophy within the context of a discourse on labor and sovereignty, moving from positions that are certainly different from Leibniz's, lies in the awareness that radical social change requires that fundamental categories we live by be rethought and some of them, such as sovereignty, eliminated. Leibniz is one of the philosophers showing the way. He calls into question the accepted notion of the law as command—widespread in his day, as well as in ours. He does not get rid of the political concept of sovereignty, but limits it to situations of internal, territorial control. However, as Riley points out, Leibniz's "efforts to recast sovereignty led to a broad attack on Hobbes and Pufendorf and, ultimately, to a more general critique of legal positivism" (1972: 2). This critique is, of course, the most important result of the critique of sovereignty itself—a result that is very important for us today if we want to think differently about power and the law. What we need in order to do that is a political ontology (i.e., a science of the constitution of the social world) that disregards the law as command, disregards sovereignty, and upholds social justice. A simple reversal of the law, of who commands and who obeys, will not do—but commanding and obeying are modalities that must be overcome. In "Opinion on the Principles of Pufendorf," Leibniz says:

> Whoever, indeed, does good out of love for God or for his neighbor, takes pleasure in the action itself (such being the nature of love) and does not need any other incitement, or the command of a superior. (1972: 72)

Leibniz is here criticizing Pufendorf, according to whom, "Obligation is properly introduced into the mind of a man by a superior" (quoted in Leibniz: 74).

To conclude, the lesson we can draw from Leibniz's doctrine of the charity of the wise, his universal jurisprudence, is that singularities, individual substances, individual women and men, find their dignity beyond the empirical law, and become thus capable of bringing about a new form of the empirical, through the praxis of a labor geared toward the production of common and social wealth, not just in the economic sense, of course—perhaps what Leibniz calls charity, benevolence, and love. In Chapter 5 of this book, this new praxis will appear as the labor of care.

Remark: Kant on Price and Dignity

In *Grounding for the Metaphysics of Morals*, Kant says that in

> the kingdom of ends everything has either a price or a dignity. Whatever has a price can be replaced by something else as its equivalent; on the other hand, whatever is above all price, and therefore admits of no equivalent, has a dignity. (1981: 40)

Kant's "kingdom" has no king, but every rational being, as a legislator, "belongs to it as sovereign" (ibid.). To be a legislator means that one subjectively brings oneself to stand under the objective and universal moral law. Generalized and disseminated, sovereignty remains: everybody is sovereign, which really entails—as we shall also see with Bataille—that nobody needs to be one. In Kant, the real sovereign is the moral law. But it is probably because of this remainder that dignity is not the only option, the only modality of being, in the kingdom of ends, as one would expect, but it has to share its space with price. On the one hand, this simply seems to be restating the logic of means and end contained in the very definition of the kingdom of ends, according to which

> all rational beings stand under the law that each of them should treat himself and all others never merely as means but always at the same time as an end. (p. 39)

On the other hand, if the co-presence of means and end is understandable—for realistically the absence of the former would compromise any concept of the useful, and we have to be able to *use* each other, see each other, as well as ourselves, as means and not only as an end—the co-presence of price and dignity presents more problems. In fact, here we do not simply have the category of the useful, which cannot be dispensed with at the level of practice, but we have a category of the market economy: price. One could at first sight be tempted to draw a parallel between price and dignity in Kant and the Marxian categories of exchange value and use value, productive labor and living labor. Price in fact also characterizes "[s]kills and diligence in work" (p. 41). However, why have price (and the type of skills and diligence in work that goes with price) in the kingdom of ends? Answering that this is so because Kant belongs in the bourgeois phase of Western thought cannot be fully acceptable. Karatani, for instance, unequivocally denies that. He says: "Kant was not in the least a bourgeois philosopher" (2003: vii), and he sees the kingdom of ends as a description of communism (pp. viii, 128–129). Thus, the utopian element contained in the concept of kingdom of ends points to something capable of transcending price and the market economy. Kant looks at the moral law and the autonomy of the will, and this compels him to stay away from the empirical content. Thus, he cannot ground the law in the actual practice of labor, the form of living labor, that is, the fact that something must be done and will be done, although the direction of this doing can be determined and defined in many different ways: It can be done because of the price attached to it, or it can be done out of the dignity of individuation. In the former case, the determining factor is the law of the market; in the latter, the law that Kant calls of morality and humanity. But this does not have to apply only in typically moral situations, such as "fidelity to promises and benevolence" (p. 41). The concept of dignity should be broadened, in a Leibnizian sense, to relate to and define each and every individual substance, each and any singularity, even the monads, the "true atoms of nature," "the elements of things" (Leibniz 1989b: 213). In the last instance, the determining factor should not be the subjective representation of a universal but abstract *ought*, for this risks becoming a mere formality again. Instead, the determining factor should be a practical engagement in the tension of *what-could-be*, not in the sense of simply following one's inclinations (to keep close to Kant); rather, the *could*, which replaces the *ought*, should be determined by the principle of need, the principle of usefulness, and the principle of common wealth. For it is obvious that many things could be. However, the choice must be made on the basis of what is called into being with greater and most common urgency, the singularity that most certainly and adequately meets the requirements of the common. This is not a utilitarian claim, nor is it communitarian. The determining factor should not be the greatest number, the vast majorities, or the closed community. Rather, it should be what in its simplicity most closely approaches nothing. The most important point is to realize that this cannot happen within the realm of necessity and the *ought*, but rather within that of contingency and the *could*.

The seemingly necessary character of the law might be explained by Leibniz's concept of certainty, which remains within the contingent. By certainty Leibniz means the highest degree of probability, the happening of something when all the conditions for it have been fulfilled. Thus, in working toward the constitution of a better world, a world that—now everybody recognizes—is possible, there might come a time when its certainty and adequacy will also be absolutely evident. However, this does not imply any notion of necessity, although one might have the impression that such a notion is involved. This should also say something about the Marxian notion of the transition from one mode of production to another, too often understood in mechanical, deterministic terms, as if a genuinely communist society would necessarily come by itself. Instead, it is clear that the very fact that a better world is possible and probable can bring about the certainty of its reality—but this is always a matter of contingency, never of necessity. It is because of this contingency, the potentiality allowing change based on reason rather than only on the will, that Leibniz calls this world the best possible world. It is not the best on account of its empirical, factual, historical configuration; it is the best in virtue of its contingency; for whatever we call the real, the universe, includes the potential, and each singularity is a mirror of it. In other words, the best possible world, a notion often ridiculed as too silly and idealistic (notably, in Voltaire's *Candide*), is a world whose contingency makes it better than others. It is a world in which, as Patrick Riley notes at the end of his study, what Leibniz calls "universal jurisprudence"—that is, true justice—is a clear possibility.

Remark: The Principle of Subsidiarity

Although there is a vast literature on subsidiarity, for the purpose of this remark I rely exclusively on Paolo Carrozza's essay "Subsidiarity as a Structural Principle of International Human Rights Law" (Carrozza 2003). This allows me to make the relationship between subsidiarity and dignity immediately evident. At the same time, I cannot hope to render here the richness and complexity of Carrozza's essay.

The history of the concept of subsidiarity can be certainly traced back to Johannes Althusius (1557–1638) and perhaps, according to some scholars mentioned by Carrozza, even as far back as ancient Greek thought (Carrozza 2003: 40–41). It was then formally established in Catholic social thinking by Leo XIII's encyclical *Rerum Novarum* of 1891 as a middle ground between liberalism and capitalism on the one hand, and communism on the other. However, "its principal purpose was to justify and encourage the protection of workers from the effects of unrestrained capitalism" (p. 41). From social philosophy it was transposed into law in the constitution of the German Federal Republic, and later it was given special relevance in European Union Law at the 1991 Maastricht Treaty (p. 50).

But what is subsidiarity? In a footnote, Carrozza gives a provisional and "very simplified working definition," which reads as follows:

> Subsidiarity is the principle that each social and political group should help smaller or more local ones accomplish their respective ends *without, however, arrogating those tasks to itself.* (p. 38; emphasis added)

The phrase that I have emphasized is very important, the idea often reiterated: subsidiarity must provide "a help that does not destroy" (p. 44); "any form of totalitarian impulse that seeks to subsume every individual or every social group into the whole is incompatible with the basic presumptions of subsidiarity" (pp. 44–45); as for the international community, the principle of subsidiarity "would generate a responsibility for that order to intervene and assist, but would prohibit it from taking over what more local communities can accomplish by themselves" (p. 57); the goal of subsidiarity is "to assist but not to usurp" (p. 66). In one word, subsidiarity is care.

Carrozza is interested in the application of the principle of subsidiarity to international law and, particularly, to the question of human rights. What is important is that

> in international law subsidiarity can be understood to be a conceptual alternative to the comparatively empty and unhelpful idea of state sovereignty. (p. 40)

Even more important is subsidiarity's intimate connection to the ideas of dignity and freedom:

> That is, its first foundation is a conviction that each human individual is endowed with an inherent and inalienable worth, or dignity, and thus that the value of the individual human person is ontologically and morally prior to the state or other social groupings. Because of this value, all other forms of society, from the family to the state and the international order, ought ultimately to be at the service of the human person. Their end must be the flourishing of the individual. (p. 42)

Yet, for all that, subsidiarity does not engender a theory of individualism, for the individual is always understood as "naturally social" (ibid.), in a way that perhaps, adds Carrozza in a footnote, "turn[s] on its head Aristotle's conclusion that the *polis* exists prior to the individual" (ibid.).

Subsidiarity shares its "first foundation" with the idea of human rights, which is also to be seen as social and relational (p. 46). One might say that Carrozza's analysis seems to be pointing to a "kingdom of ends" in which there is dignity, but there is no price. It is

> a recognition that each individual is unique and unrepeatable, thus incapable of being absorbed by any collectivity without doing violence to his inalienable dignity. (p. 45)

Thus, the principle of subsidiarity must be applied to all situations and spheres of life, "the sum total of the conditions necessary for individual human flourishing" (p. 46)—for instance, even in the family or in a friendship. And it is here that the close relationship of subsidiarity and care becomes evident (cf. Chapter 5).

One of Carrozza's main concerns is to stress, along with other scholars on whose work he also relies (scholars such as Gráinne de Búrca and Ken Endo), the status of the principle of subsidiarity as one of mediation between the particular and the universal (p. 54)—a relationship that he calls an "anxious dialectic," which sovereignty is unable to address, let alone resolve (p. 64). This is subsidiarity's paradoxical status, its internal tension (p. 68). The particular and the universal, pluralism and the common good can be brought together by the implementation of the principle of subsidiarity. But for this to happen, sovereignty must be discarded: "The idea of subsidiarity leaves no room for sovereignty as such" (p. 69). Sovereignty and subsidiarity oppose one another. What is this to say if not that domination (including price) and dignity oppose one another? However, subsidiarity and dignity are not the same, for, although subsidiarity is "a general principle, not a clear rule" (p. 79), still it is a regulative principle, and indeed the dignity of individuation may be understood as subsidiarity ontological ground. But how, in practice, can pluralism and the universal/fundamental common good coexist? Carrozza's answer is that

> the freedom and human dignity sought to be achieved through the adequate protection of human rights will be most fully realized where the decision over the reasonable balancing of aspects of the

common good is taken at the closest level to the affected person as is effectively possible. (p. 73)

This is perhaps a different way of formulating the notion of justice as "the place of the other"—a notion we have discussed above. After all, subsidiarity is characterized by "unity-in-diversity" (p. 75), a tension that needs no resolution but must be lived as a tension. Yet, who makes the decision? The danger here is that of reintroducing the figure of the sovereign. Perhaps, "the affected person," evidently "the other," should be able to determine what she needs, and whatever this is, it should not really be understood as a *subsidium*, but rather as what the dignity of individuation demands, as that without which this dignity is taken away.

In conclusion, Carrozza says that subsidiarity

values the freedom and integrity of local culture without reducing particularism to pure devolution and decentralization of authority; it affirms internationalism and intervention without the temptation for a superstate or other centralized global authority. (p. 78)

It would seem that, from the individual to local culture, subsidiarity becomes a safeguard against domination and oppression. And sovereignty is neutralized. For this to really be the case, however, one would need a form of global governance based on human rights. This would still fall within the logic of law, and ultimately of sovereign power. Who, for instance, has the right to intervene? This presents as many problems as the notion that the dignity of individuation must become, in Leibniz's sense, common, in Benjamin's, divine. But this latter option truly does away with all instances of sovereignty. As an epigraph to his essay, Carrozza chooses Rudolf von Jhering's sentence, "Every individual should say the phrase of Louis XIV: 'I am the state'" (p. 38). Perhaps not.

CHAPTER TWO

Exception and Critique

~❖~

Sovereignty is NOTHING

—Georges Bataille, *The Accursed Share*

In Leibniz sovereignty becomes a relative concept when applied to the political sphere, and full sovereignty only obtains in the sphere of theology. But there, too, it does not have (to use Schmitt's expression) a *decisionist* character; rather, it has a rational one. In other words, it is not based on the will, but on reason. Or God would also operate in accordance with the logic of tyrants (see Chapter 1).

For Carl Schmitt, who follows Hobbes, the concept of sovereignty, as used in political philosophy and in juridical theory, is the secularization of a theological concept—but of a decisionist rather than rational theology. Sovereignty is decision and domination. It is not simply a technical concept in state theory (which could be understood according to its internal and external aspects)[1] but rather the personal privilege of the ruler: "Sovereign is he who decides on the exception"; this is how *Political Theology* famously starts (2005: 5). But what is it, precisely, to decide on the exception? In a sense, the answer is contained in the paradoxical figure of the sovereign, in sovereignty as a "borderline concept," "one pertaining to the outermost sphere" (ibid.). Schmitt says that although the sovereign "stands outside the normally valid legal system, he nevertheless belongs to it" (p. 7). He belongs to it precisely in virtue of his capacity to decide on the exception. As Tracy B. Strong notes in his foreword to *Political Theology*, for Schmitt "it is the essence of sovereignty *both* to decide what is an exception *and* to make the decisions appropriate to that exception" (p. xii). Here one sees the complexity of this apparently simple and straightforward truth. The question is: What enables the sovereign to decide on the exception and thus be sovereign? The answer is found not in Schmitt, but in Walter Benjamin: violence, and the violence always "implicated in the problematic nature of the law itself" (1978: 287). But let us pursue this more slowly. The question I just posed can also be rephrased as follows: What gives the sovereign that special capacity to see that there is an exception, a state of emergency, and consequently decide on it? Does the sovereign become sovereign because he can decide on the exception, or is it rather the case that he can decide on it because he is already sovereign? Depending on the answer, the hyperbolic truth enunciated by Schmitt acquires a different meaning: In the first case, any person with special powers (or even simply a special sensibility) should be recognized as sovereign. This would be an honorary status conferred on him. The implication here would be that there actually is, objectively speaking, an exception and the sovereign is he who can recognize and handle it. But of course Schmitt does not speak of any sense of recognition, understanding, and judgment, but only of decision—although one would think that a decision can only come after a judgment is made on rational grounds. It is perhaps the concept of "genuine decision," of which Schmitt speaks in the preface to the second edition of *Political Theology* (p. 3), which comes close to this first sense of the statement. A genuine decision is not necessarily that which is made by those who have the legal, constitutional power to decide. In fact, they can be, and most of the time are, completely mistaken in their decisions. A genuine decision requires some inherent and special powers. In this case, the decision itself would decide of the sovereign. In making the decision, X would rise to the status of sovereign.

In the second case, the sovereign is he who has the power (in the strictly political, institutional sense—a power always grounded in violence) to decide on the exception. This is, for instance, the case of G. W. Bush rebuking the United Nations before attacking Iraq: "We don't need permission," or his decision to open the detention camp at Guantanamo. As I write (June 12, 2008), a divided U.S. Supreme Court has ruled that the Guantanamo "enemy combatants" have the right to challenge their detention. The Associated Press reports that Justice Anthony Kennedy, writing for the court, said, "The laws and constitution are designed to survive, and remain in force, in *extraordinary* times" (emphasis added). This is a blow to Bush's sovereignty and a challenge to the Schmittian notion of sovereignty. To be sure, it would challenge only the second of the two meanings of Schmitt's truth given by Strong, that is, the sovereign may very well decide on what constitutes an exception, but he has to listen to other institutional voices and sites of power before deciding on the appropriate measures—he can disagree, but he has to abide.

Thus, the sovereign is sovereign only to an extent. Probably, Schmitt would blame this state of affairs on constitutional liberalism and the rule of democracy. In any case, it would be difficult to prove here that (and if) the decision made by the sovereign is a genuine one. In fact, the exception itself can be a mere fabrication of the sovereign, which acquires dubious legitimacy on the basis neither of ethics nor of the violence travestied as the force of law, but of mere and raw violence. In this case, it is not the exception, the state of emergency, which calls forth the sovereign decision, but the other way around: the sovereign decision creates the exception, or state of emergency. Then, the state of emergency is not, in Benjamin's sense, a *real* one. In Strong's important explication of Schmitt's truth, it is the first meaning of "decide," which is also the least apparent, which lends Schmitt's theory of sovereignty an ontological, rather than simply technical (i.e., juridical), dimension. However, contrary to Strong, I doubt that Schmitt's decisionism can be weakened on that account.

We have seen that in Leibniz's philosophy of individuality there is no exception, and this is so because every individual being is complete, unique, and thus exceptional. But when the exception can be so generalized, it also loses its meaning and reason to be. In Schmitt, on the contrary, the concept of the exception makes sense because it is contained in the concept of the sovereign; it *is* the sovereign. Using Leibniz's language, one could say that the exception is the predicate of the sovereign subject. Thus, it is not the case that the sovereign realizes that there is an objective state of need and thereupon he acts decisively. Instead, the sovereign chooses which state is to be raised to the level of the exception, or simply fabricates it. An illustration would be the war on terror, and particularly the war against Iraq. One would think that there are many other more urgent situations in the world that require attention and perhaps intervention, for instance, poverty, child labor, inadequate education. Yet, none of these are raised to the status of the exception, and the reason for this neglect must be sought precisely in the fact that they are not contained in the concept of the person of the sovereign, as a predicate in a subject. They are other than the sovereign; in fact, they are instances of bare life.

It is easy to see that, despite its brilliance[2] and internal logical coherence, Schmitt's doctrine is also deeply flawed. It says that the decision on the exception is a privilege of the sovereign, that the sovereign is a sovereign precisely by virtue of his capacity to decide; yet, it does not say how he receives this capacity nor why this capacity is not generalized to become a privilege of each individual, the dignity of individuation, which is probably the only *real* exception. Ultimately, the justification for Schmitt's theory is the fear determined by the supposedly evil character of human nature. In the last chapter of *Political Theology*, he says:

> Every political idea in one way or another takes a position on the "nature" of man and presupposes that he is either "by nature good" or "by nature evil." (p. 56)

However, this is not correct, and not only today when the question of human nature has ceased to have the importance it did have in the seventeenth, eighteenth, and nineteenth centuries. Long before, even Aristotle's political science was built on the idea that the human being is by nature endowed with the twofold capacity of being just or unjust, and that this capacity changed into a state depending on the decision one made and on the habit built thereafter. But by nature, one is neither just nor unjust, neither good nor evil, as this would eliminate the possibility for change, because what is by nature in one condition cannot be brought into another condition:

> A stone, for instance, by nature moves downwards, and habituation could not make it move upwards, not even if you threw it up ten thousand times to habituate it. (Aristotle 1999: 1103a21–23)

It is true that Schmitt intends to meet this objection when he adds: "The issue [of human nature] can only be clouded by pedagogic and economic explanations, but not evaded" (2005: 56).

Yet, I think that the objection still stands. In the case of Aristotle, for instance, the importance of education does not simply explain away the issue of human nature; more fundamentally, it provides a structure for the practice of human freedom, which Schmitt of course intends to dispense with.

We have already seen Schmitt's concept of "genuine decision" (p. 3). This is to be found in the context of the notion that "the political is the total" (p. 2) and of the description of the three types of legal thinking: normativist, institutional, and decisionist. The first emphasizes impersonal rules and leads to the bureaucratization of society; the second "leads to the pluralism characteristic of a feudal-corporate growth that is devoid of sovereignty" (p. 3); the third, which relies on personal decision and which Schmitt opts for, needs to be able to determine what a *genuine* decision is. For Schmitt, "genuine" does not have anything to do with an ethical or politico-ontological situation, or with existential authenticity. It is political in the Schmittian sense of the distinction of friend and enemy. However, despite Schmitt's assertion to the contrary, this is not the only possible sense of the political. I do not disagree with Schmitt's critique of liberalism. Yet, "political" should not be seen as an either/or between Schmitt's totalistic conception (which in principle is not incorrect) and liberalism. In fact, besides this either/or (and one could say: at the level of neither/nor, i.e., of potentiality), "political" also addresses the capacity for social transformation. This can be utopian, anarchist, yet it is the modality of the political that has no use of sovereignty. It is not that which calls forth a normativist or institutional legal theory, both of which risk trampling the individual, nor is it individualistic; rather, it highlights the tension between what-is and what-could-be, the moment of non-law, that is, a world devoid of any law that is not the one of the dignity of individuation. Of course, Schmitt would find the idea of a radical transformation of the social completely unrealistic. Yet, his defense of sovereignty is, realistically, unable to bring about security for all—given that this is its main aim. Thus, in *The Concept of the Political*, starting from the premise of an irreducible antagonism between friend and enemy, Schmitt very logically shows the impossibility of perpetual peace (although he is not addressing Kant's concept here). The fact is that for Schmitt the permanent regime of war, which seems to be a natural foundation of the social and the political, could only be ended by "a war against war" (1996: 36)—in other words, a paradox. That would be a war of the pacifists against the nonpacifists, but still a war, and, as such, a political position and a political act. Interestingly, the end of war is also the end of the political, and the situation becomes really paradoxical: "the last absolute war of humanity." Schmitt continues:

> Such a war is necessarily unusually intense and inhuman because, by transcending the limits of the political framework, it simultaneously degrades the enemy into moral and other categories and is forced to make him a monster that must not only be defeated but also utterly destroyed. (Ibid.)

Thus, there is no exit from war. A regime of war, understood as the antagonism of friend and enemy, is preferable to the end of war with the utter destruction of the enemy. Schmitt does not see any alternative for humanity to emerge from the logic of violence and domination that is apparently connatural to it. As a consequence, he chooses to give a theoretical justification for this fact. To an extent, this might be understandable, as Schmitt was writing *The Concept of the Political* and *Political Theology* in the aftermath of World War I. However, with World War II the notion of the utter destruction of the enemy became tragically concrete,[3] both with the Nazi final solution and with the American (sovereign) decision to use the atomic bomb against

Japan.[4] What Schmitt had articulated as the paradox of pacifism became the utmost degree of the total war. This makes Schmitt's partisan philosophy of the political prophetic and realistic on the one hand, yet also difficult to accept on the other. The state of the exception, from Auschwitz and Hiroshima to Guantanamo and Abu Ghraib, proves to be outside of the political, in the realm that belongs to violence, cruelty, gangsterism, and criminal justice.

There is no alternative for humanity because, as Schmitt says, "Humanity is not a political concept" (p. 55). Humanity "has no enemy" (p. 54). But what if humanity's enemy is precisely something like this logic of sovereignty that seems to be unassailable and necessary? From Schmitt's position, it follows logically (again) that humanity "as such cannot wage a war" and this "because the enemy does not cease to be a human being" (ibid.). But what if humanity's war is not simply political in the Schmittian sense, but politico-philosophical, that is, ontological, in the sense of aiming at reconstituting the essence of humanity itself? In other words, what if the enemy is not a group of particular, concrete human beings, but the conditions of possibility of violence, domination, and the very antagonism of friend and enemy? Indeed, physically eliminating human beings perceived and conceived as enemies is what gangsters and the various mafias do very well. One does not need a theory of the political for that. Certainly, there is more than this in what Schmitt says. He says that the word "humanity" is confiscated, invoked, and monopolized by one state or an alliance of states to wage war against an enemy who is denied "the quality of being human" (p. 54). He is correct in saying:

> When a state fights its political enemy in the name of humanity, it is not a war for the sake of humanity, but a war wherein a particular state seeks to usurp a universal concept against its military opponent. (Ibid.)

It is in this context that he refers to the extermination of the Native Americans—and it is evident how relevant this type of rhetoric is today with the notion of humanitarian war. But again, against Schmitt's extreme realism, or cynicism, one can hold on to the idea, advanced by many, that, with an incredible amount of work and commitment, there is hope for humanity to exit the logic of war, of politics in the Schmittian sense, of violence and domination. For this to happen, however, the concept of sovereignty must be discarded, or even utterly destroyed.

If politics is antagonism and war, or the ever-present possibility of war, if this antagonism cannot be eradicated, and if "justice does not belong to the concept of war" (p. 49), then the possibility of a world of social justice is ruled out *a priori*. As I have said, I agree with the critique of liberalism, but not necessarily for the reasons given by Schmitt—or perhaps I would not characterize liberalism in exactly the same way. What I am saying is that liberalism is not characterized by an open (and never-ending) dialogue, but by the emphasis on individual rights, including property rights, which are established only by means of a logic of inclusion and exclusion. Thus, I agree with the critique of liberalism insofar as it presents a clear exposition of the limits and flaws of individualism. Yet, individualism should not be confused with the theory of individuality, grounded in singularity and the dignity of individuation, which makes possible the full development of the individual. Under liberalism, for Schmitt, the "state turns into society" (p. 72) and politics (the politics of antagonism) is abandoned. Yet, precisely, he says, "State and politics cannot be exterminated" (p. 78). True, Schmitt points out the hypocrisy of liberal rhetoric, and of pacifism in particular:

> War is condemned but executions, sanctions, punitive expeditions, pacifications, protection of treaties, international police, and measures to assure peace remain. (p. 79)

This is indeed an accurate description of the new world order of the last two decades. Schmitt continues:

> The adversary is thus no longer called an enemy but a disturber of peace and is thereby designated to be an outlaw of humanity. (Ibid.)

The consequence is the notion of the last war of humanity, which I have discussed above. In sum, there is no exit from the friend/enemy distinction, and an

> allegedly non-political and apparently even antipolitical system serves existing or newly emerging friend-and-enemy groupings and cannot escape the logic of the political. (p. 79)

Schmitt is criticizing in particular the attempt at dissolving the political into the ethical on the one hand and the economic on the other. For him, this would be an impossible task. But let us consider what might be the most fundamental friend-and-enemy relation, that between labor and capital. First of all, it must be noted that there is here no reduction of the political to the economic, as is often understood and Schmitt himself seems to understand. The antagonism of labor and capital is in fact fully political, even in the narrow sense given to the word by Schmitt. Capital tries to assert its sovereignty over labor, and labor, in its most radical expression, tries to free itself from the yoke of capital. But labor has two enemies: capital and the productive form of labor, that is, the form of labor that produces capital. For Marx, the struggle of the proletariat is the struggle for the dissolution of all classes, including the dissolution of itself as a class. From the point of view of labor, the enemy is certainly not a group of people that must be physically eliminated, but rather practical categories and structures of domination equal to the very form of the political antagonism. This should say clearly that the aim of the political struggle is the overcoming of the political, or perhaps its redefinition along lines that are neither those of the friend-and-enemy split, nor those of the split between economic competition on the one hand and the (legal) construction of ethical and cultural patterns of discourse on the other. Rather, the aim of the political struggle is to open up the potential by enduring the tension between what-is and what-could-be. The real enemy is this what-is, which Schmitt sees as unavoidable and necessary, the apparently unsurpassable structure of the empirically given. But Schmitt does not consider the moment of contingency.

At the end of his critique of the state of exception, Giorgio Agamben addresses the question of contingency, which is very important in all of his work, when, with a reference to Benjamin, he speaks of "the urgency of the state of exception 'in which we live'" (2005: 86).[5] This is also to be understood as the restricted sense of the real imposed on life as "an empty space, in which a human action with no relation to law stands before a norm with no relation to life" (ibid.). It is the paradox of a state of exception become permanent. The exit for Agamben is a redefinition, or recuperation, of politics, that is, a *space for human action* without regard to the law. He says:

> Politics has suffered a lasting eclipse because it has been contaminated by law, seeing itself, at best, as constituent power (that is, violence that makes the law), when it is not reduced to merely the power to negotiate with the law. The only truly political action, however, is that which severs the nexus between violence and law. (p. 88)

In his eighth thesis on the philosophy of history, Walter Benjamin says:

> The tradition of the oppressed teaches us that the "state of emergency" in which we live is not the exception but the rule. We must

attain to a conception of history that is in keeping with this insight. Then we shall clearly realize that it is our task to bring about *a real state of emergency*. (1968: 257; emphasis added)

Both Agamben and Benjamin challenge the logic of sovereignty that Schmitt defends. Benjamin's *real* emergency, which conceptually also pertains to Agamben, is the exit from the exception that has become a rule. This real emergency is not what suspends the law, but what destroys it, what opens a space for existence other than the law. For Benjamin, what destroys the law is divine violence, or (still) sovereign violence (Benjamin 1978: 300). As William Rasch says in his concise and clear exposition of the main distinction in the work of Schmitt, Benjamin, and Agamben:

Whereas Schmitt locates himself firmly within the political as defined by the sovereign exception, both Benjamin and Agamben imagine the possibility of a politics that exceeds the political. (2007: 99)

Rasch continues saying that, however, neither Benjamin nor Agamben can say what this post-sovereign politics really is, and it is with this type of more practical question that I deal with in Part II of this book. They only say, according to Rasch, that "if and when it comes, it will come with an all consuming but bloodless violence that, in Benjamin's terms, will be divine, . . . neither law-making nor law-preserving" (ibid.), but precisely law-destroying (Benjamin 1978: 297).

The paradoxical regime of a permanent state of exception, more evident in our own time, is a general feature of the logic of sovereignty and domination, of the antagonism that for Schmitt characterizes the political. As Machiavelli says, the fundamental antagonism is between those who want to dominate and those who do not want to be dominated.[6] The aim of the latter group, which is called *more honest* by Machiavelli, evidently points toward the end of domination as such, that is, of a world in which the law is not necessary because "good habit" (*buona consuetudine*) suffices.[7] But this would amount to *deciding against the decision*, which at the end of *Political Theology* Schmitt derides Bakunin for doing:

the odd paradox whereby Bakunin, the greatest anarchist of the nineteenth century, had to become in theory the theologian of the antitheological and in practice the dictator of an antidictatorship. (2005: 66)

However, leaving Bakunin aside, there is no real paradox in deciding against the decision, provided that the person who decides is not the sovereign but anyone choosing freedom and dignity over domination. I return to this in the next chapter when dealing with Bataille's concept of renunciation, and we shall see there that Bataille's own problem is his claim that the renunciation must happen in a sovereign manner.

Critique of Sovereignty

We have seen that for Schmitt, sovereignty, like all other political concepts, is the secularization of a theological concept. For him, this suffices to grant it, particularly in political philosophy and state theory, full validity; it seems that its theological provenance is a good enough proof, as against the critique of the concept often coming from jurisprudence, of its soundness. However, Jacques Maritain, while also recognizing the link between theology and political philosophy with respect to the concept of sovereignty, thinks very differently about this. To be sure, like Schmitt, Maritain sees the limits of a juridical critique of the concept, but he brings this insight to a completely different end. In fact, while Schmitt offers a defense of the concept of sovereignty, Maritain holds that a correct philosophical analysis points to the necessity of its elimination.

In his analysis of sovereignty—a chapter of *Man and the State* (1998) first published in 1951 and also included in W. J. Stankiewics, *In Defense of Sovereignty* (1969)—Jacques Maritain holds that sovereignty is another name for absolutism and that, as such, it must be discarded from the discourse on the political sphere—discarded, as we shall soon see, not because it is obsolete, but because it is wrong. In the conclusion of the essay he says that "we have to discard the concept of Sovereignty, which is but one with the concept of Absolutism" (p. 49). Writing from the point of view of a Catholic philosopher, Maritain thinks that the concept of sovereignty (more precisely, "genuine Sovereignty") makes sense in the spiritual sphere, that is, the sphere of theology: "In the spiritual sphere there is a valid concept of Sovereignty" (ibid.). This is so because in that sphere we have the concept of *separation*, which is necessarily included in that of sovereignty: "God, the separate Whole, is Sovereign over the created world" (ibid.). For Maritain, "with Sovereignty separation is required as an *essential* quality" (p. 35). However, this is not the case in the political sphere, where the separation and transcendence posited by the theorists of sovereignty—Jean Bodin being the first among them—to justify the concept of sovereignty itself is in reality the result of a philosophical (logical and metaphysical) error. To be sure, Maritain says that for Bodin, "the father of the modern theory of Sovereignty" (p. 30),

> the king did not possess supra-mundane Sovereignty, which has absolutely nothing above itself. God was above the king, and the supreme power of the king over his subjects was itself submitted to "the law of God and nature,"[8] to the requirements of the moral order. But the king was Sovereign, the king was possessed of human Sovereignty. (pp. 30–31)

For Maritain, the error lies in grasping the position of the (human) sovereign as *above the peak* rather than *at the peak* (p. 36)—that is, inside and outside at the same time—and in overlooking the medieval notion of *vicariousness*, according to which the prince is the "vicar of the multitude" and not truly divided from it. Thus the right that the prince exercises is the right of the people (ibid.), regardless of the fact that the people have divested themselves of it. As Maritain says, Bodin's position—of which he offers a close textual reading—is "perfectly clear" (p. 34). And I need here to quote at length this extremely important and clear passage:

> Since the people have absolutely deprived and divested themselves of their total power in order to transfer it to the Sovereign, and invest him with it, then the Sovereign is no longer a part of the people and the body politic: he is "divided from the people," he has been made into a whole, a *separate* and transcendent whole, which is his sovereign living Person, and by which the other whole, the immanent whole or the body politic, is ruled from above. When Jean Bodin says that the sovereign Prince is the image of God, this phrase must be understood in its full force, and means that the Sovereign—submitted to God, but accountable only to him—transcends the political whole just as God transcends the cosmos. Either Sovereignty means nothing, or it means supreme power *separate* and *transcendent* . . . and ruling the entire body politic *from above*. That is why this power is absolute (ab-solute, that is non-bound, separate), and consequently unlimited, in its extension as well as in its duration, and not accountable to anything on earth. (Ibid.; Maritain's emphasis)

But this is not truly the case even with the absolute monarch of the modern age. Indeed, in the next section, on Hobbes, Maritain says that the concept of sovereignty, absent in the Middle Ages—where "St. Thomas treated of the

Prince, not of the Sovereign" (p. 36)—relates to *absolute monarchy* (ibid.).[9] Thus, if it is true that with modernity "an essence other than common humanity was to be ascribed to the person itself of the Sovereign" (p. 35), it is not as true that this ascription is justified by anything other than an error of evaluation of the ontological nature of that concept. What Maritain really holds and demonstrates is that the absoluteness of absolute power is untenable from an ontological point of view. The "absolute" monarch, with his *divine right* typical of Louis XIV (p. 37), does *not* have absolute power, if words are to have a meaning. And since absolutism and sovereignty belong together, having "been forged together on the same anvil" (p. 53), it follows that the human sovereign is not sovereign. For Maritain—he concludes thus his analysis—the two concepts of sovereignty and absolutism "must [also] be scrapped together" (ibid.).

To get a better understanding of Maritain's radical move and conclusion, we need to consider the presuppositions of his argument, based as they are on an endeavor of semantic and conceptual rectification. However, as I have already suggested, at stake here is really a question of ontology—the ontology of the concept, which includes, and is included in, the ontology of being. And since we are here speaking of political ontology and of history, it is historical being, history itself, which must hereby be "rectified." The categories handed down from past history still shape our present and future, our mental habits as well as our everyday practices. It is then not simply a question of precision and clarity that we are here examining. Maritain's effort and endeavor reach into the region of historical being with a force capable of erasing the preconditions of the repetition of an error that becomes historical truth and of replacing them with a new structure and a new vision—structure and vision of immanence, of earthly and secular plenitude, notwithstanding his distinction between the spiritual and political spheres before which we have to part from him. But history does not have less truth only because it is based on an error. The point is then not that of changing the contingent in it, as one would do in rewriting history, but of changing—to use Duns Scotus's notion—the *contingently caused*, namely, the source of historical necessity.

It is in this sense, precisely, that Maritain starts his essay—after briefly reviewing some important studies of the concept of sovereignty from the point of view of juridical theory—by calling attention to the need of a philosophical investigation of the concept itself (pp. 28–29). Thus he immediately argues that

> political philosophy must get rid of the word, as well as of the concept, of Sovereignty—not because it is an antiquated concept, or by

virtue of a sociological-juridical theory of "objective law"; and not because the concept of Sovereignty creates insuperable difficulties and theoretical entanglements in the field of international law; but because, considered in its genuine meaning, and in the perspective of the proper scientific realm to which it belongs—political philosophy—this concept is intrinsically wrong and bound to mislead us. (p. 29)

Interestingly, in the above passage Maritain has a footnote that refers to Hugo Preuss, who drafted the constitution of the Weimar Republic and to whom Carl Schmitt also refers in his *Political Theology*. For Maritain, Preuss only rejects the concept of sovereignty because it is antiquated, not because of its inherent philosophical and political inadequacy. Yet, Maritain and Preuss agree as to the end of their critique, that is, the abolition of the concept of sovereignty. Schmitt, who is critical of Preuss and is interested in defending the concept of sovereignty, says:

Preuss rejected the concept of sovereignty as a residue of the authoritarian state and discovered the community, based on associations and constituted from below, as an organization that did not need a monopoly on power and could thus also manage without sovereignty. (2005: 25)

But for Schmitt, Preuss's organic theory of the state, with its rejection of sovereignty, is precisely what must be avoided. Sovereignty for Schmitt is the decision that establishes the exception. The exception is to politics and law what the miracle is to theology: "The idea of the modern constitutional state triumphed together with deism, a theology and metaphysics that banished the miracle from the world" (p. 36).

For Schmitt, "Sovereign is he who decides on the exception" (p. 5). However, we have seen that this formula, which sounds definitive and profound, is highly problematic and ultimately void. Following Maritain, we can say that in the field of politics, the equation of sovereignty and decision, of decision and exception, or rather, the equation of sovereignty and exception by means of decision, is untenable, or it makes no sense. What kind of decision does Schmitt have in mind? Answer: The genuine decision. But who has the competence to determine the genuineness of the genuine decision? It is like a vicious circle. In truth, the decision is equal to the *separation* that for Maritain is necessarily included in the concept of sovereignty. To be sure, "decision" always means "separation," for it literally points to a "cutting *off*," a "cutting *away from*," which, precisely, separates. Thus all decisions we make in practical life separate us from whatever remains undecided, the immense potential that we might have considered in the process of deliberation. Yet, notwithstanding the fact that each and any decision we make is, by virtue of its singularity and uniqueness, exceptional, none may be sovereign, unless we extend the latter concept to include any singularity. In that case, we would all be sovereign, and, again, the concept would become irrelevant. In truth, the separation that characterizes sovereignty is only a theological concept, and Maritain is right in pointing out that its political use is based on a mistake. This is particularly clear when, at the end of his *Political Theology*, Schmitt speaks of de Maistre and Donoso Cortés. For de Maistre, sovereignty is the same as *infallibility*, and for him "making a decision is more important than how a decision is made" (pp. 55–56). For Donoso Cortés, decisionism is dictatorship, and dictatorship is the only solution to the endless talks that, for him as well as for Schmitt, characterize liberalism. But the pretense to infallibility, defended with army and police, does not make infallibility a valid concept; nor does dictatorship ever separate itself enough from those upon whom it imposes itself to avoid a multitude of other decisions, of counter-decisions, capable of making it collapse. What de Maistre and Donoso Cortés mean by decision is brute force, violence, which is not an acceptable political concept—or perhaps it is in Schmitt's understanding of the political. It is also very problematic to say that what counts is making the decision, regardless of its modality and nature. One could say, with Walter Benjamin, that the decision that brings about a state of exception must be weighed as to its universality or lack thereof, and that it is only thus that it can be granted ontological validity or not. In Benjamin, this is the difference between mythical violence and divine violence, and of course it is only the latter that has ontological validity:

> If mythical violence is lawmaking, divine violence is law-destroying; if the former sets boundaries, the latter boundlessly destroys them; if mythical violence brings at once guilt and retribution, divine power only expiates; if the former threatens, the latter strikes; if the former is bloody, the latter is lethal without spilling blood. (1978: 297)

After a careful examination of Jean Bodin's theory, Maritain asks the question of the meaning of sovereignty and says that it means two things:

> First, a right to supreme independence and supreme power which is a *natural* and *inalienable* right. Second, a right to an independence

and a power which in their proper sphere are supreme *absolutely* or *transcendently*, not *comparatively* or as *topmost part* in the whole. (1998: 38)

On the basis of this twofold definition, he goes on to show that neither the body politic nor the state is sovereign; nor are the people. He holds that the body politic has a right to *full autonomy*, which is what sovereignty should give way to in the political sphere; and he insists that this autonomy must be both internal and external (pp. 40–43).

"The right of the body politic to such full autonomy derives from its nature as a perfect or self-sufficient society" (p. 41); whereas one can speak of "limited autonomy" when a body politic enters a federal political society. This right of the body politic to full autonomy is, Maritain says, a *natural* and *inalienable* right (ibid.), and in this sense it "implies the *first* element inherent in genuine Sovereignty" (p. 42). Yet, if this part of the concept of sovereignty, its first meaning, corresponds to that of full autonomy, full autonomy itself is a more precise and certainly correct expression. What is important, however, is that the second element of the meaning of sovereignty not be implied in it. The reason for this is central in Maritain's argument, and it is repeated twice:

> For it is clear that the body politic does not govern itself *separately from itself* and *from above itself*. (Ibid.)

This means that "its supreme independence and power are only comparatively and relatively supreme" (ibid.), not *absolutely* or *transcendently* supreme, as required by the genuine concept of sovereignty.

In reality, from the point of view of a thoroughly immanent philosophy, the concept of a *supreme* power in its absolute and transcendent character is evidently untenable; and so is, from the point of view of a radical ontology of labor (which I deal with shortly) even the comparative and relative character of a supreme power. In this sense, although Maritain's critical analysis of the concept of sovereignty goes a long way to show how untenable this concept is in the political sphere, more is needed to truly *radicalize* political theory and practice. Certainly, Maritain's argument shows great force in that it denies the state any sort of genuine sovereignty; and to the state neither the first nor the second meaning of sovereignty belongs, the state itself being an "instrumental agency" of the body politic (p. 43). But he places a lot of importance on the functions of the state and still retains the notion of the state's supreme authority, which should "in no way be called sovereignty" (p. 24); he thus misses the more radical view, present in Hinsley's analysis for instance, that the notion of "a final and absolute political authority in the community" (1966: 17), which accompanies the emergence of the state, constitutes the germ of the concept of sovereignty. I am saying that Maritain's analysis, fundamental for his critique of sovereignty in the political sphere, finds its limit in the displacement of the concept onto the sphere of transcendence and in his insistence on the necessity of nonsovereign, yet supreme state power.[10] Unlike the state, the people, just like the body politic, lack the second meaning of sovereignty, and in their case, too, it is of full autonomy that one can speak. It is here that Maritain repeats the reason for the inapplicability of the concept of sovereignty to a self-sufficient entity, and, in the last analysis, of its non-interchangeability with the concept of full autonomy. He says that

> it would be simply nonsensical to conceive of the people as governing *themselves separately from themselves and from above themselves.* (1998: 44)

He attributes this nonsensicality to Rousseau and his concept (Maritain says "myth") of *Volonté Générale.* He says:

> The myth of the *Volonté Générale* . . . was only a means of having the separate and transcendent power of the absolute king transferred to the people while remaining separate and transcendent, in such a way that by the mystical operation of the General Will the people, becoming one single Sovereign, would possess a separate, absolute, and transcendental power from above over themselves as a multitude of individuals. (pp. 44–45)

For Maritain, this shows that Rousseau was against democracy and actually "pointed toward the totalitarian state" (p. 45). He adds: "Rousseau's State was but the Hobbesian Leviathan, crowned with the General Will" (p. 46).

The philosophy of Maritain is genuinely concerned with democracy, although certainly not with radical or direct democracy. He presents a clear concept of representative democracy, whereby the power of the state is an instrumental function of the power of the people and the body politic, which directly emanates from the people themselves. For Maritain, the state is necessary to ensure a system of social justice. But the people are "above

the State, the people are not for the State, the State is for the people"
(p. 26). The concept of the people, "the highest and noblest" of the basic
concepts he analyzes—Maritain says in chapter 1 of *Man and the State*—
"means the members organically united who compose the body politic";
whereas the body politic "means the whole unit composed of the people"
(ibid.). For Maritain,

> the people are the multitude of human persons who, united under
> just laws, by mutual friendship, and for the common good of their
> human existence, constitute a political society or a body politic.
> (Ibid.)

There is an idealistic element in this definition because very often, if not always, the situation in which the people find themselves, and thus the formation of a body politic, is strongly determined by the institutional powers of
the state and its economic structures. Maritain is aware of this, and he calls
for a renewed form of the state, one which brings the state "back to its true
nature" (p. 27), whereby its only function becomes that of the exercise of
justice and of facilitating the free development of the body politic. For this
to become a reality, the state must be "freed from the notion of its so-called
sovereignty" (ibid.), for, as we have seen, for Maritain the state has no real
sovereignty. The state, as Maritain says in the last chapter of his book, must
be freed of its Hegelian or pseudo-Hegelian characteristic of being considered as a person or a suprahuman person and be only understood as the
highest part of the body politic (p. 195). Indeed, for Maritain the fact remains that the people "have a special need of the State" (p. 26); however, it
is political society (and, in the last analysis, the people themselves) that must
exercise a control over the state itself precisely in order to impede the formation of the state's spurious sense of sovereignty. In this sense,

> it is necessary that many functions now exercised by the State should
> be distributed among the various autonomous organs of a pluralisti-
> cally structured body politic. (p. 27)

The idealistic moment I have underlined above is also one in which a greater
radicality is reached. Yet some problems also arise, and I would say that the
main problem that Maritain faces here, in addition to his defense of the state,
is that of the justification of the law—the just laws under which the people
are united, for this "under" risks to reinscribe within his discourse the notion of sovereignty he wants to discard.

It is evident that with Maritain the critique of sovereignty is not at all a question of terminology, although some questions arise as to his ability to effectively overcome the concept. For us, the critical approach represents a way of revealing, beyond its juridical use, the philosophical grounding of the concept of sovereignty and of disposing of it within the context of a radical ontology of labor, for it is by labor that the social texture that precedes and sustains the various institutional entities (among which the state and its pretence to supreme authority and sovereignty) is formed. Our endeavor is that of producing such ontology—a philosophy of labor capable of overcoming all theoretical positions in which the concept of labor, if philosophically employed at all, always occupies a marginal space. In this endeavor, we start from the Marxian approach, as well as from the anarchist theoretical and practical experience, to find ways of radicalizing and reproposing such positions based on labor in the new world economy and culture. The effort to radicalize presupposes clarity, and radicalizing the philosophy of labor means, first and foremost, dispensing with the concept of sovereignty, grasping, in an initial moment, the force of the alternative concepts of independence and full autonomy, self-sufficiency, and self-determination; however, these concepts must also soon be called into question on the basis of the reality of dependency.[11] They give way to the concepts of the solitude of labor and of labor's return to itself, to its dignity and freedom. Maritain's contribution is important in that it provides guidance in exiting the logic of sovereignty, although it will not go past the notions of independence and autonomy. In emphasizing the notions of *separation* and *transcendence* always included in the concept of sovereignty—an inclusion whereby all spurious usages of the word sovereignty always involve its *genuine* concept—Maritain's analysis brings to the fore a major problem of political philosophy, and certainly one to be reckoned with by all attempts at producing a true philosophy and practice of the common,[12] a theory and practice of radical social change. For a philosophy of immanence, which a radical ontology of labor ought to be, the implications of Maritain's analysis, in itself not concerned with establishing a philosophy of immanence, are clear: any use of the concept of sovereignty inscribes political thought in the order of the transcendent.

As Maritain says:

No doubt it is permissible to use the term Sovereignty in an improper sense, meaning simply either the natural right of the body politic to full autonomy, or the right which the state receives from the body politic to topmost independence and topmost power. . . .

Yet in doing so one runs the risk of becoming involved in the worst confusion, since the word Sovereignty always connotes obscurely its genuine, original meaning. (p. 43)

He also explicitly says:

The question is not a question of words only. Of course we are free to say "Sovereignty" while we are thinking full autonomy. (p. 49)

The point is that thinking the concept of full autonomy, of separation in solitude, yet within a context of social and historical relations, a sort of monadic separation, is not the same as thinking an absolute that, as such, remains beyond the sphere of historical and social, temporal, and human relations. As I have noted, for Maritain, this is the sphere of the spiritual, so much so that "in the last analysis, no earthly power is the image of God and deputy of God" (p. 50). For us, however—given the fact that we place ourselves on the plane of immanence, of earthly plenitude, of the "absolute secularization and earthliness of thought" (to use Gramsci's explanatory expression for "historicism"), of the "humanism of history" (Gramsci 1971: 465)—thinking, not full autonomy, but human solitude, that is, human finitude, without sovereignty is the essential requirement for a true philosophy of labor. The same can be said of the essential requirement for a philosophy of the common, which is really one with the philosophy of labor, and which also cannot be adequately thought unless the concept of sovereignty is overcome and discarded.

The idea of this section was to examine Maritain's view of sovereignty in order to show the inadequacy of the concept in the sphere of radical political ontology and of the ontology of labor in particular. I have chosen Maritain because through his analysis, based on a philosophy of transcendence, and perhaps precisely because of this, the irrelevance of the concept of sovereignty in political thought is made absolutely evident. Maritain does not renounce all forms of sovereignty. He says that sovereignty belongs only to the sphere of the spiritual, of theology, of transcendence. For him sovereignty means absolute separation and a standing outside of the order upon which it is imposed. However, the supreme political authority, which for Maritain belongs to the state, is at the peak of that order, but it essentially belongs to it, and it derives its nature from it. I fully accept Maritain's elimination of sovereignty from the political sphere and, only provisionally, his emphasis on full autonomy and self-sufficiency. But I disagree with him as to the necessity of the state institution endowed with supreme authority. It can be argued that this authority is still another name for sovereignty, and that, therefore, Maritain undoes what he has accomplished.

The Political Ontology of Singularity

The poetic spirit of the river makes arable in an essential sense; it prepares the ground for the hearth of the house of history.
—Martin Heidegger, *Hölderlin's Hymn "The Ister"*

It is not through man that the world can be what it is and how it is—but also not without man.
—Martin Heidegger, *Only a God Can Save Us: The* Spiegel *Interview*

The critique of sovereignty can be enriched by a critical look at Heidegger's political ontology of singularity. In this sense, I then try to highlight the essential dimension of Heidegger's relation to the political; in particular, I try to understand why Heidegger's political ontology remains important for progressive, left thinking, despite his evidently wrong choices at the level of the empirical. These are his commitment to the Nazi party (which he shares with Carl Schmitt), the acceptance of the rectorship, his praise for "the inner truth and greatness" of the movement (2000: 213), and, otherwise, his silence. These choices have their importance at the empirical, biographical, and ideological levels, but their analysis will not give access to political ontology. To attack Heidegger for his allegedly Nazi philosophy can only be based on an ideological motif. In fact, I do not think that Heidegger's philosophy can be described as National Socialist in character. And I am in agreement with Samuel IJsseling, who says that, in any case, we would need to "ask what, exactly, is National Socialism" (1992: 5). And when one considers some of its most important aspects, such as "propaganda, racism, biologism, the glorification of youth, and enthusiasm," one realizes that "these are precisely characteristics that never could be seen as applying to Heidegger's thinking" (p. 6). Yet, Emmanuel Faye, for instance, argues that "Heidegger's Nazism is . . . not limited to a few speeches of the moment," and that "Heidegger taught his philosophy students the very doctrine of Hitlerism" (2006: 55). But anyone who reads Heidegger seriously realizes immediately how mistaken these charges are. Certainly, there is in Heidegger a special attention toward the *völkisch*, which is what Faye stresses and which is in Heidegger the closest to any concept of National Socialist ideology. However, this is a concept that belongs to all populist ideologies, right and left, and to National Socialism and fascism insofar as they are precisely populist in character. Thus, it is more than an exaggeration to say that "Heidegger, through the *völkisch* and racist principle which is explicitly his starting point, destroys man in his very being" (p. 65). And it is a total absurdity to state that Heidegger's work "is not, in its foundations, a philosophy, but rather an attempt to destroy philosophy" (p. 66). In any case, whoever reads Heidegger without a preconceived mind will realize that it is not the destruction, but rather the problematic aspect, of philosophy and human reality that is at stake in his thought. After saying that "[a]t the foundation of Heidegger's work, one . . . finds not a philosophical idea, but rather a *völkisch* belief in the ontological superiority of a people and a race," Faye himself has to admit:

> Of course, no true philosophy can align itself with the project of the extermination of human beings, a project to which the Nazi movement was committed. Therefore, I do not wish to say that Heidegger produced a National Socialist philosophy, but rather that he did not hesitate to utilize philosophical expressions such as "truth of Being" or "essence of man" to express something else entirely. (p. 58)

In addition to this, it is also important to consider Heidegger's criticism of National Socialism. As Babette Babich says:

> Heidegger reproves or challenges the then-current regime, that is to say, National Socialism, as he explicitly names it in the *Beiträge*, as representing the *same* dynamic politicizing, the *same* technologizing order and ordering momentum as other (and otherwise different) imperial cultures. (2007: 46)

If the question of the empirical can be set aside, what I would like to do, in keeping with Heidegger's own method of essential questioning, as well as with the method of immanent reading, is engage in a "confrontation" with Heidegger's thinking, seeking to unveil *the political* as a fundamental concept of poetic ontology, with an emphasis on the concept of singularity, that is, on the essential way in which something comes to be individuated and realized as the something that it is. By poetic ontology I mean the science of the constitution of human societies, an expression that is informed by Vico's concept of poetic metaphysics (Vico 1948), as well as by Marx's notion of living labor (Marx 1973).[13] My claim is that Heidegger's thought can be seen as a constant attempt to leave traditional metaphysics behind and accomplish a passage into poetic ontology. However, this passage is complicated by the fact that Heidegger, more strongly than Vico or Marx, emphasizes the non-human-made as the ground of poetic ontology—and it is this ground that constitutes the focus of his thinking. Because of this, he weakens his chances to succeed in the passage to poetic ontology, yet he also opens up a space and time for reflection, as is the case, for instance, when he speaks of the danger of technology as a danger that lies at the level of the *essence* of technology, not at the empirical level. What I intend to do in this "confrontation" is look at the question of the political from this *essential* (not essentialist) point of view.

Poiēsis

I deal particularly with *Introduction to Metaphysics* and *Hölderlin's Hymn "The Ister,"* but I also refer in important ways to *The Question Concerning Technology* and *The Will to Power as Art*, the first volume of Heidegger's lectures on Nietzsche. The conceptual key to my reading will be provided by Heidegger's identification of *physis* and *pélein* in *Hölderlin's Hymn "The Ister"* (from now on referred to as "*The Ister*"), and *physis* and *poiēsis* in *The Question Concerning Technology*. A study of these concepts will reveal the political as what is *granted* and thus *endures*; in other words, it will reveal the prepolitical ground of the political itself. In "*The Ister*," reading *Antigone's* lines from Sophocles: "Manifold is the uncanny, yet nothing more uncanny looms or stirs beyond the human being," Heidegger describes *pélein* as "stirring and looming, abiding in itself amid change, emerging forth from out of itself, yet as this coming and going, remaining nevertheless within itself." He continues: "This is what the Greeks otherwise call [*physis*], and this is the word for being" (1996b: 108). The "stirring and looming" of *deinón* (i.e., that which is not at home, the unfamiliar, the uncanny, hence the danger) finds its "pole" (p. 86) in the poetic activity of the human being, and it is this activity that grounds the *polis*, the political, history, as a *singular* event. It *is* the event itself (*Ereignis*), without which there is no grounding. However, this poetic activity is prepolitical in its first grounding because the "stirring and looming" (*pélein*) of the danger (*deinón*) is the same as that which arises of its own accord (*physis*), and this arising itself is poetic, a form of *poiēsis*, its highest form. As Heidegger says in *The Question Concerning Technology*:

> Not only handcraft manufacture, not only artistic and poetical bringing into appearance and concrete imagery, is a bringing-forth,

poiēsis. Physis also, the arising of something from out of itself, is a bringing-forth, *poiēsis. Physis* is indeed *poiēsis* in the highest sense. (1977: 10)

Accordingly, poetic and political ontology, that is, the constitution, in the open, of a world, a culture, a state, a "people," will not be for Heidegger the effect of a decision [*Entscheidung*], in the Schmittian sense of the word, namely the act of the sovereign. For, as Schmitt says in the famous opening of his *Political Theology*, "Sovereign is he who decides [*entscheidet*] on the exception" (2005: 5). Instead, poetic ontology, insofar as it is the condition of the political, really precedes the possibility of the logic of sovereignty, for the decision in this case is not of the sovereign, but it is first granted as such. Whether this yields a conservative or progressive political direction at the empirical level must remain, as far as I am concerned here, an open question. Indeed, it would be an empirically political question, not the *essential* way of questioning the political as such. Yet, this is an important point, for one thing I wish to understand and highlight here is the reason for the relevance of Heidegger's thought to left political theory. The reason for this cannot be attributed to the fact that some left theorists are led astray by postmodernism, Heideggerianism, and Nietzscheanism, as some critics maintain.[14] Instead, the reason may provisionally be indicated in the importance of what in the political is not immediately political, the ontological ground, which is neither right nor left, neither progressive nor conservative—in the present case, in the structure of *neutrality* (in the ontological sense) of Heidegger's concepts. In other words, although there is no doubt that Heidegger was politically conservative, a reactionary at the "ontic" level (if I may put it this way), the fact remains that his treatment of concepts greatly appeals to ontologies of liberation. It might be that Heidegger was essentially misguided, by his own judgment, in his political choices, and that his positions are closer to a philosophy of genuine communism than one might at first suspect—that is, when "communism" is properly understood as outside of any dogmatic orthodoxy and as pointing to the ontology of the common, "the singularity of the common," as Stefano Harney says in a different context (2002: 81). After all, in the dialectical treatment of the homely and the unhomely, which I deal with more later, it is the loss of the common that comes to the fore as the homelessness which, as Heidegger says in *Letter on Humanism*, "is coming to be the destiny of the world" (1998: 158). Here Heidegger makes a rare reference to Marx, and to his concept of alienation. He says:

What Marx recognized in an essential and significant sense, though derived from Hegel, as the estrangement of the human being has its roots in the homelessness of modern human being. (p. 158)

This homelessness is not, of course, the loss of one's abode in the sense of one's private property, but rather the disappearance of the singularity of the common. Addressing what he understands as Sartre's shortcoming in this respect, and actually anticipating Sartre's famous statement as to the unsurpassable character of Marxism as a philosophy, Heidegger says:

Because Marx by experiencing estrangement attains an essential dimension of history, the Marxist view of history is superior to that of other historical accounts. (p. 259)

Heidegger complains about the lack of the conditions for a dialogue between Marxism on the one hand and phenomenology and existentialism on the other, and in a paragraph on labor and materialism he astonishingly comes very close to positions that today, from within the Marxist perspective, emphasize the importance of the subjectivity of living labor. Heidegger says:

For such dialogue it is certainly also necessary to free oneself from naïve notions about materialism, as well as from the cheap refutations that are supposed to counter it. The essence of materialism does not consist in the assertion that everything is simply matter but rather in a metaphysical determination according to which every being appears as the material of labor. The modern metaphysical essence of labor is anticipated in Hegel's *Phenomenology of Spirit* as the self-establishing process of unconditioned production, which is the objectification of the actual through the human being, experienced as subjectivity. The essence of materialism is concealed in the essence of technology, about which much has been written but little has been thought. Technology is in its essence a destiny within the history of being and of the truth of being, a truth that lies in oblivion. (Ibid.)

In *The Question Concerning Technology*, *technē* is understood in terms of *poiēsis*, the common bringing-forth of the true, the singularity of the event, and a destining. The event itself is that of *destining* [*Geschick*], out of which "the essence of all history [*Geschichte*] is determined" (1977: 24). This destining is that within which the essence of technology, Enframing [*Ge-stell*], also belongs (p. 25), and this essence is the danger, the supreme danger. What is said of technology can also be said of the political. The danger also lies in the prepolitical ground, the essence of the political. It is, as Giacomo Leopardi says in his last poem *The Broom, or the Flower of the Desert*, "the terror that first forged / for human beings the social bond / Against the savagery of nature" (1997: 81; lines 145–147). For Heidegger, "the coming to presence of technology gives man entry into That which, of himself, he can neither invent nor in any way make" (1977: 31). Again, the same can be said of the political, which is also part of *technē*, just as art is. It would be tempting to translate all this, perhaps simplistically, by saying that what makes the world and human societies, what makes humanity, is not simply human praxis and labor, but more fundamentally the fact that there is a world that arises, the earth itself that produces something in the sense of bringing-forth, a first movement of *poiēsis*, a "stirring and looming" and a danger, and that at the same time humans are given those capacities whereby they can face the danger in a special way, dwell, create and build, or destroy and be destroyed. In other words, this means that the fact that there is labor and a world to be made is not a human decision, but it is rather the singularity of the event whereby humans are first de-cided, that is, separated from the rest in a special, singular, way. In other words, again, the world is certainly human-made, but the conditions whereby a human-made world and humanity itself become possible are not themselves human-made. This is not in itself a great discovery, yet I think that it is around this that much of Heidegger's thinking turns. Not a great discovery, yet it becomes important from an ontological, as well as political and ethical point of view, because it calls attention to the danger upon which all is founded, the earth as the ground of the world (and it is in this sense that Heidegger also becomes important to questions of ecology), the concealed as the ground of the open. If Heidegger spoke theologically or according to the language of traditional metaphysics, he would simply be retracing the path of transcendence, but because he does not, it must be recognized that he is attempting something different and new, or perhaps ancient, close by his own admission to the pre-Socratic tradition, for instance to what Heraclitus says, namely, that the world is common, made neither by the gods nor by humans. In fact, he speaks of the earth and the river, of the unity of *physis* and *poiēsis*, and of *pélein*, that is, being there, presencing, in the manner of "stirring and looming."

It seems then safe to say that Heidegger's political ontology of singularity, or, which is the same, poetic ontology, has nothing inherently conservative and that, again, it is instead of great aid to the endeavor of rethinking the most fundamental categories of the political with a view to an ontology of liberation. But we have to bracket the question of the empirical. For Heidegger, the essential question of the political is the question of singularity as individuation and selfhood, as the "who" of humanity beyond humanism. In *Introduction to Metaphysics*, he says:

> The selfhood of humanity means this: it has to transform the Being that opens itself up to it into history, and thus bring it to a stand. (2000: 153)

This is very similar to the abovementioned discussion of the founding of the *polis* as the "pole." As explained at the end of this section, the pole is precisely the site where things are brought to a stand. Heidegger continues:

> Who is humanity—we . . . only [learn] when humanity steps into the confrontation with beings by attempting to bring them into their Being—that is, sets beings into limits and form, projects something new (not yet present), originally poetizes, *grounds poetically*. (pp. 153–154; emphasis added)

Indeed, to say that the decision that grounds history is first granted in its singularity means to challenge the traditional concept of sovereignty and to look, beyond sovereignty, at alternative ways of thinking the historical and the political. It is evident that the danger at this point is that of a mystic turn, that is, the notion that there is an original event (*Ereignis*) preceding human *poiēsis* and *praxis*. This danger is always present in Heidegger's thought, and this fact must be continually borne in mind. Yet, is not forgetting that not everything is human-made even more dangerous? This constant reminder is perhaps one of Heidegger's most important contributions to philosophy in general and to political theory in particular. Thus, without taking a mystic path, we can gain a lot from Heidegger's articulation of the structure of singularity, the singularity of the event that grounds history and the political. The relation of *pélein* (being there in the mode of "stirring and looming"), *physis* (arising out of itself), and *poiēsis* (bringing-forth) described above not only indicates that, in its essential constitution, in its essential dis-position and dis-placement, the political is not political—and this in the same way in which the technological is essentially not technological—but it possibly also offers elements that can be useful to a materialist ontology. It is in this sense that Heidegger can be placed alongside Marx and that one can speak of left-Heideggerianism, as Stuart Elden among others does (Elden 2004: 101). In his article, which is mainly on Lefebvre, Elden also emphasizes Heidegger's concept of "poetic dwelling" (p. 92), which comes to Heidegger from Hölderlin and which is linked to Lefebvre's "politics of space." For Elden, Heidegger makes it possible to understand that "there is a politics of space because politics is spatial" (p. 99). Using the distinction between "politics" and "the political" (p. 89), he also says, "The political, as the ontological foundation of politics, is where politics *takes place*" (ibid.). This is indeed what an analysis of the *polis* as the "pole" and of the concept of *pélein* also shows.

Decision

Heidegger's philosophy is built on the centrality of questioning, with a special emphasis on the essential character of the question, on "the question of all true questions," as he says in *Introduction to Metaphysics* (2000: 7). This is the question of being, that is, the grounding question of philosophy. The grounding question, the question of being as such, is opposed to the guiding question, that is, the question of the being of beings, which is typical of traditional metaphysics. Asking the grounding question is, according to Heidegger, what metaphysics precisely cannot do. Heidegger's endeavor is to initiate a thinking that is other than the metaphysical, less than the philosophical, and able to ask the grounding question, of being as such. This is a very important point, repeated by Heidegger in many of his works. In particular, in the first volume of his Nietzsche lectures, *The Will to Power as Art*, there is a most central section on this topic—a section called "The Grounding Question and the Guiding Question of Philosophy" (1979: 67–68). Here Heidegger explains that the guiding question of philosophy, which all metaphysics asks, is only the *penultimate* question. The *ultimate* question, which asks about the ungrounded ground, is the grounding question, and that is, "what is Being itself?" (p. 67). For Heidegger, not even Nietzsche, who brings metaphysics to completion but does not overcome it, is able to ask the grounding question: "The grounding question remains as foreign to Nietzsche as it does to the history of thought prior to him" (ibid.).[15] If the grounding question is not asked, "Being remains forgotten" (2000: 20). This is from *Introduction to Metaphysics*, but it is also the opening of *Being and Time*: "This question has today been forgotten" (1996a: 1). This forgetfulness constitutes, for Heidegger, the history of metaphysics proper, as well as the history of nihilism, which is equal to it. For the question of being to be asked, it is necessary to face a decision, and the decision implies a willing. This willing, as Heidegger says in *The Will to Power as Art*, is

the submission of ourselves to our own command, and the resolute-
ness of such self-command, which already implies our carrying out
the command. (1979: 40)

The decision to be faced with respect to "an originary way" (2000: 100) of
asking the question of being has to do with the distinctions of being discussed in *Introduction to Metaphysics*, that is, being's relation to becoming,
seeming, thinking, and the Ought. All these distinctions (*Unterscheidungen*)
are modes of the decision (*Entscheidung*) that grounds history: "With decision, history as such begins" (p. 116). Here, de-cision [*Ent-scheidung*]

does not mean the judgment and choice of human beings, but rather
a division (*Scheidung*) in the . . . togetherness of Being, unconcealment, seeming and not-Being. (Ibid.)

It is evident that this is not the decision of the sovereign, but that which is
granted in the first place, which opens up space. This creates a problem because it says that wanting to ask the question of being is not a sufficient
condition for actually and successfully doing it. On the one hand, this points
to the limitations of human thinking and doing; yet, on the other, it also
says that asking that question, with all the consequences that it implies
(a different thinking, a different doing and dwelling), requires more than a
mere choice at the empirical level. Perhaps, to use Heidegger's own language,
it also requires that one bring oneself into the open region where being
and truth belong together—and it is only in this sense that human reality, *Dasein*, opens up to the possibility of unconcealment. This may, on the
one hand, sound mystical; yet, on the other, it redirects human praxis toward a new relation with the materiality *and* spirituality of that which is and
can be. In fact, asking this question, rather than bringing about a sort of
quietism, may unveil the truth that there is much to be done; in terms of
production, for instance, not, of course, in the strictly economic sense, but in
the poetic sense—self-production perhaps, that is, a bringing-forth of the
selfhood of humanity into the open region of singularity and individuation,
namely, the region where history and politics can begin again, in the sense of
being displaced into a different mode: a path to utopia. I do not think that,
even in Marxian terms, one could name the revolution without addressing
essential questions of this kind, unless one limited the concept of revolution
to a mere change at the economic level, as has often been the case. What
Heidegger also allows us to think is the possibility of an essential change as

the effecting of a separation, a division, a decision, which, again, is not that of the sovereign, but is rather the result of the singularity of the eventful co-belonging of being and truth, which is often unheeded, forgotten, but always already there.

The link between the *question* and the *decision* is found at the outset of *Introduction to Metaphysics*. There, Heidegger says that "the question seeks a decision with respect to the ground that grounds the fact that what is, is in being *as* the being that it is" (2000: 3). What-is, the merely empirical, is linked to the *as-structure*, discussed by Heidegger in *Being and Time*, where the *as* constitutes interpretation (1996a: 140). Interpretation requires language, but this is the language constitutive of what-is, not that of the statement; it is the poetic language that makes something *as* something, not the language that simply speaks *about* something; again, it is the language that is immediately an ontological and poetic power, not the instrumental language used to exchange information and to chat.[16] For Heidegger, it is the language arising from the region where being and truth belong together—and it is this co-belonging, this *there*, which is named in the *as-structure*—a structure of neutrality, to be sure, and of ontological depths. It is at that level that the *de-cision* is made. Indeed, Heidegger equates decision with apprehension, "the taking up that takes in" (2000: 178). Apprehension (*noein*, usually translated as "thinking" in Parmenides' fragment in which he equates it with "being") is

> a happening (*Geschehen*) in which humanity itself happens, and in which humanity itself thus first enters history (*Geschichte*) as a being, first appears—that is, [in the literal sense] itself comes to Being. (p. 150; brackets in the text)

And again: "apprehension is the happening that has the human being" (ibid.). This means that originally at least the human being does not decide, but rather *is* de-cided. And it is in this, perhaps forceful, de-cision that the danger also lies. And it is because of this danger that the human being is called upon its poetic task—a task that is also political and historical.

Singularity

In *Introduction to Metaphysics*, the decision that is apprehension is seen in terms of violence: "such essential deciding . . . has to use violence" (2000: 179). This is the violence that grounds history, "the violence that humanity has to surmount in order to be itself first of all—that is, to be historical in doing violence in the midst of being" (p. 167). We will see that this violence, no longer thematized as such, is related to the danger, the uncanny, of which Heidegger speaks in "*The Ister.*" In *Introduction to Metaphysics*, Heidegger also says:

> This act of violence, this de-cided setting-out upon the way to the Being of beings, moves humanity out of the homeliness of what is most directly nearby and what is usual. (p. 179)

This passage into the unusual, unhomely, and extraordinary—after all, "Philosophizing is questioning into the extra-ordinary" (p. 13)—is the condition for the return into the familiar, the home, the hearth, of which Heidegger says a lot in "*The Ister.*" This is also an important theme in *The Will to Power as Art*, where the emphasis is on willing, power, and art as legislation and command. Indeed, there we read, "In willing we come toward ourselves, as the ones we properly are" (1979: 52). This is the same idea of "self-assertion" (p. 61) present in the rectoral address of 1933, "The Self-Assertion of the German University." In his lectures on Nietzsche, Heidegger says that in self-assertion there is something creative, the will to power itself is creative, and this "often seems to suggest that in and through will to power something is to be produced." However, Heidegger adds:

> What is decisive is not production in the sense of manufacturing but taking up and transforming, making something other than . . . *other in an essential way.* (p. 61; emphasis added)

It is not of productive labor that Heidegger is speaking, but of *living labor, creative labor.* This is the *singularity* whereby something *essentially different* can ultimately come to the fore. The passage points out the consistency of singularity, the thisness of production in terms that, as Heidegger stresses, are not economic and calculative, but poetic. What is other in an essential way is the potential included in a nonpositivistic conception of the real, what-could-be at the horizon, or at the center, of what-is, that which is usually simply taken as nothingness. It is "the essential difference" problematized by Marx in the *Grundrisse* (1973: 85),[17] the difference of living labor, which gives singularity its proper *mode*, its characteristic—a mode of production which, as Marx says, is not simply an economic dimension, but a "general illumination" of societies (p. 107). It is, at the same time, the singularity that alters the "apprehension" of the common, the decision on the common, or the common as decision, the return from the exception and the extraordinary, which, to be sure, are highly problematic concepts, to the freedom of what is proper. It is precisely because it is *of* the common that it accomplishes the return from the uncanny into the proper. And this is also Heidegger's concept of *Ereignis*; this is the event, the singularity of the event as the singularity of the common.

It is this concept of singularity that becomes thematic in "*The Ister,*" that is, the idea of the journey into the foreign, the other, and the uncanny, and hence the return into the homely and proper. Speaking of the river, Heidegger says, "Becoming homely demands a going into the foreign" (1996b: 142). The return is for him already inscribed in the originary journey:

> This venturing is no mere leaving something behind but is already the first and therefore decisive act of return to the home. (p. 133)

The already of the return is the already of the there, the space and place of the open, the tumultuous relation to the unity of the homely and the unhomely, of what one is and is not. In a sense, one never leaves. One never leaves the open, never leaves being, because "Being is the hearth" (p. 112), and also because place and journey, "space and time," belong together (p. 39). History, Heidegger says, "is nothing other than such return to the hearth" (p. 125). One never leaves, but is "turned round," such as in bidding farewell, in such a way that he "always retain[s] the attitude of someone who's departing," as Rilke suggests at the end of his eighth Duino elegy (1939: 71). Indeed, one never leaves and remains within "the sphere of being" because being "sets no limits to the one who ventures forth in all directions" (Heidegger 1996b: 108). Here we find again that element of a materialist ontology I mentioned above. Heidegger says that even the unhomely (the uncanny and foreign) "remains within the sphere of being" (ibid.) and thus ultimately of the homely itself, in much the same manner in which for Aristotle the very fact that we say that nonbeing *is* nonbeing belongs to the many senses in which being itself can be said (1979: 1003b11). For Aristotle, being is manifold and one only "by reference" (Owens 1951: 437). That the unhomely remains within the homely Heidegger says when, speaking of Antigone, he stresses the "unhomely being homely of human beings upon the earth" (1996b: 120), and he calls this state "poetic." And then again he speaks of the human being's "being unhomely-homely in the midst of being" (p. 121). But also when, in the difficult analysis of Hölderlin's lines: "namely at home is spirit / not at the commencement, not at the source. The home consumes it" (p. 129), Heidegger says that the spirit at the commencement is not homely at the source precisely because the home consumes it; he says the same thing:

there is no exit from the unhomely-homely tumult that must unfold as a venturing and a return, there is no exit from being, from being there in the open, from being essentially unhomely at home, at the source and at the beginning. Being consumed is the same as being forced to leave, leave the hearth, "the hearth as being," yet unable to leave being altogether. It is here, in the section on "the hearth as being," that Heidegger identifies *physis* with *pélein*, the stirring and looming that yet abides in itself, the venturing and the return, the other and the same. And it is this same movement that, Heidegger says in *The Question Concerning Technology*, constitutes the highest expression of bringing-forth, of *poiēsis* (1977: 10–11).

This bringing-forth, which is prepolitical, grounds the *polis*. Bringing-forth, *poiēsis*, which is the movement of *pélein*, of the stirring and looming that yet abides in itself, as well as of *physis*, that is, "the arising of something from out of itself" (p. 10), is the unity of the venturing into the open and of the return to the home. This bringing-forth is the labor of the poets, the labor of the rivers:

> Yet the rivers are the poets who found [*stiften*] the poetic, upon whose ground human beings dwell. The poetic spirit of the river makes arable in an essential sense; it prepares the ground for the hearth of the house of history. The poet opens that time-space within which a belonging to the hearth and a being homely is possible in general. (1996b: 147)

The historical and the political would not be possible without such grounding. But the grounding itself remains foreign to the political, for the essence of the political is not itself political (p. 83). The *polis* itself "is not a 'political' concept" (p. 80). The *polis* is "the pole . . . in which and around which everything turns" (p. 81). *Polis* means "state"—not in the political, historical, and sociological sense—but in the sense of a place of permanence in the midst of becoming. It is "the site [*die Stätte*] of the abode of human history that belongs in the midst of beings" (p. 82). But the place *of* such place is not a state, but rather the "singular," the "supreme level of the uncanny" (p. 68), which in Sophocles' *Antigone* describes human reality. When the *polis* becomes a political concept, when it is institutionalized, it also becomes the measure of inclusion and exclusion. Thus, Creon, the sovereign, can say: "A city belongs to its master. Isn't that the rule?" But Antigone says: "No city is home to me." The effort is to keep the uncanny, the danger, out of the city, for it is what is and must remain foreign to it. Yet this uncanny, Heidegger explains, the "unity of the fearful, the powerful, the inhabitual" (p. 64), is precisely "that which is not at home—not homely in that which is homely" (p. 71). And Heidegger adds that human beings are not homely "in a singular sense" (ibid.). Singular means essential—"What is essential to all essence is always singular" (p. 64), but it also means de-cided, that is, separated, or perhaps, with a different terminology, still Heideggerian, *thrown*. Yet, thrown in a singular way, poetically projected into the open of doing, building, dwelling— the open of labor. One of Heidegger's most important contributions to philosophy is, I repeat, this calling attention to the truth that, notwithstanding the human poetic essence, not everything is human-made, and this essence itself, its singularity, is not either. This is certainly what all religious thinking already knows. But Heidegger's discourse is not religious. It is instead akin to those of the poets; of Hölderlin, who follows the rivers; of Leopardi, who praises the broom, the flower of the desert, for being wiser and less unstable than humans. By not making any recourse to the transcendent, by being completely earthly, Heidegger's political ontology of singularity provides important elements to a thinking intending to challenge the concept of sovereignty—a concept that cannot be thought without the transcendent.

CHAPTER THREE

Bataille's Special Use of the Concept of Sovereignty

꒰꒱

What if each people . . . each singular intersection . . . substituted a
wholly other logic for the logic of the sovereign (and always sacrificial)
model . . . a logic where singularity was absolute and without an
example at the same time?

—Jean-Luc Nancy, *Being Singular Plural*

In his Nietzsche-inspired philosophy *against servility*, in the space of turbulence it opens up, Georges Bataille also deals with the concept of sovereignty in important ways. Indeed, volume 3 of *The Accursed Share*, *Sovereignty*, offers an interesting, although unusual, analysis and employment of the concept. In the first part of the volume, which bears the title of "What I Understand by Sovereignty" and the subtitle of "Theoretical Introduction," Bataille says:

> The sovereignty I speak of has little to do with the sovereignty of States, as international law defines it. I speak in general of an aspect that is opposed to the servile and the subordinate. (1993: 197)

However, as we shall see, Bataille's use of the concept of sovereignty is ultimately mistaken, not because it is used in a way other than usual, but because in his case too the concept of full autonomy or, as he himself holds, of *subjectivity*, or solitude, would be sufficient, and indeed more adequate, to describe the conceptual and practical reality to which he attaches the name of sovereignty. In Bataille, the mistake has to do not only with the critique of the concept of sovereignty that we have already seen in reading Maritain, but also with an equivocation on the concept of *the useful*, and in particular of useful labor. It seems to me that Bataille understands the words "useful" and "servile" as synonyms, but it is evident that they are not. Thus, when he says that sovereignty indicates the condition of "that which does not serve"—a definition that is formally correct and punctual—two equally important points of criticism must be made. One has to do with the fact that Bataille does not distinguish between the two senses of "to serve," which means "to be a servant" but also "to be of use." From the point of view of a radical ontology of labor, which is the direction toward which Bataille moves, the critique of that concept makes sense only insofar as servility is under attack; however, to extend the critique, as Bataille does, to the concept of the useful is a dangerous move because it raises the question of the status of labor, or of all doing for that matter.[1] The other point of criticism, which follows directly from the first, involves the concept of living labor. Here, it is clear that Bataille did not consider the fundamental difference between ontology and political economy, that is, between productive labor as a category of capital and its more essential, living, and creative aspect that makes capital itself want it.[2]

Bataille's mistake occurs precisely because he subsumes the notions of freedom, autonomy, and subjectivity under the concept of sovereignty. Although his use of sovereignty is unorthodox, it still has a regard for its formal definition: the one first given by Jean Bodin, crystallized in the Westphalian form of the modern state, and hence in international law. We have seen Maritain's critique of this. We can also add at this point that, although there are times when a struggle for sovereignty might appear to be progressive, for instance in wars of liberation and for self-determination, the fact remains that the concept of sovereignty always carries with it something of a reactionary nature. Once subsumed under the concept of sovereignty, liberation, autonomy, independence, and self-determination are institutionalized and lose their fundamentally progressive and revolutionary character. They do not belong to the *schema* of sovereignty, as Bataille thinks. These are immanent and concrete forms of the general concept of freedom; whereas sovereignty always implies a structure of domination. Thus, it is difficult to simply accept Bataille's statement in "Method of Meditation": "Sovereignty is revolt, it is not the exercise of power. Authentic sovereignty refuses" (2001: 96). Indeed, one of the requirements of radical political ontology is the elimination of the concept of sovereignty. As Michel Foucault says: "In political thought and analysis, we still have not cut off the head of the king" (1990: 88–89).[3] Bataille's influence on Foucault is well known, and this statement is conceptually very close to Bataille's figure of the acephalous. So what I am saying is not that Bataille argues for a philosophy of domination, but rather that he does not realize that sovereignty must be totally destroyed. Bataille tries to transform sovereignty into a revolutionary category, and he equates it with subjectivity. But this cannot be done. The source of Bataille's confusion lies in the fact that in the concept of sovereignty the two senses of "to serve" are actually suspended or eliminated: the sovereign is truly he who does not serve in the twofold sense of not being servile and of not being of any use. The sovereign, in fact, is completely useless, a mere parasite. Distinguishing between a traditional concept of sovereignty and a different, revolutionary one—as Bataille does—does not help. As we have seen with Maritain, to be useless is what most essentially pertains to the concept of sovereignty itself—a concept that must be discarded. It would be meaningless and wrongheaded to recuperate and apply it to situations in which it would be repugnant. If sovereignty points to the condition of that which does not serve in an absolute sense, it cannot be applied to revolutionary subjectivity, which, in radical rupture with the paradigm of servility, does not forfeit *use* and *usefulness*, but valorizes them for itself, the other, and the world. But we should substantiate our argument with a close reading of passages from *The Accursed Share*.

In volume 1 of *The Accursed Share, Consumption*, the concept of sovereignty is presented within the definition of a general economy in which, precisely, "the 'expenditure' (the 'consumption') of wealth, rather than production, [is] the primary object" (Bataille 1991: 9). Sovereignty, which will be given as "primordial" and irreducible in the third volume of the work (Bataille 1993: 284), is here described as "man's return to himself" (1991: 140). However, it seems to me that sovereignty is neither primordial/irreducible, nor is it a return. What is primordial and irreducible is a being-there, an open and perhaps disquieting sense of finitude, the solitude that more than with sovereignty can be equated with subjectivity, the many solitudes that posit the conditions for the coming of language culture and a world, the common obscure intuition of a project and a *telos*, dictated by need and desire, to which labor will give content and form. Similarly, the return cannot be to sovereignty or be sovereignty itself; it must instead reach into something more essential than sovereignty (which is, as we have seen, a useless concept)—perhaps a return to a labor without sovereignty, a life without sovereignty: a return that for now we can only term aesthetic-ethical. But it is the nature of such a return that we need to understand and describe.

Bataille's inversion of the primacy of the terms of political economy on the one hand and of ethics and political philosophy on the other, that is, his emphasis on consumption rather than production and on that which does not serve (the sovereign) rather than the useful, has the unwanted consequence of obscuring the importance of his discovery of a radical subjectivity, arising with the "effervescence of life" (p. 10), arising *as* that effervescence, pure movement, dynamism, and (excess of) energy. This *radix* that Bataille is nonetheless able to point out requires that—if it is to be fully grasped and experienced—the ontological structure of its constitution also be shown. This structure cannot be other than a *neither/nor* that neutralizes all thought of a primacy and that, in particular, discards the concept of sovereignty as well as the idea of a relationship of opposition between production and consumption (for, as Marx shows in the *Grundrisse*, they cannot be understood in that relationship but as moments of the same process, and one cannot be without the other). Only thus will this radical subjectivity, which is the real object, as well as the subject, of Bataille's work, acquire full stature and luminosity.

To be sure, Bataille takes important steps in that direction, but it does not seem to me that he actually gets there. Thus, when, still in the preface, he introduces the notions of "productive expenditure" and "nonproductive expenditure," he does not theorize the neutrality of consumption and/or production. And yet he is on the way toward it, that is, toward the logic of neither/nor, as the following passage clearly shows:

> But real life, composed of all sorts of expenditures, knows nothing of purely productive expenditure; in actuality, it knows nothing of purely nonproductive expenditure either. (p. 12)

But Bataille does not realize that he is using "productive" and "nonproductive" in a sense dictated solely by the logic of capital, and that only by following the route of their double negation could an exit from that logic be found.

The ambiguity between political economy and other aspects of life is all contained in Bataille's central notion of *surplus*. Indeed, when surplus is used as excess of energy in the general sense of life activity, it has a different value than when it is used as a strictly economic category. In fact, not all economies are based on the existence (the production and consumption) of a surplus. As Marshall Sahlins says in *Stone Age Economics*, "The DMP [Domestic Mode of Production] is intrinsically an anti-surplus system" (1972: 82). To this we must add that the notion of excess of energy is always problematic. In fact, how can energy be excessive? Or perhaps a better question would be: In what sense can one speak of excess? The answer to this question is that one can speak of excess only in a relative sense. Absolutely, there is no excess, as there is no surplus. The problem, rather, is finding the proper channels of use for what is otherwise understood and expended as excessive. Life needs all of life's energy. The world could use the excessive, as it could use the extraordinary. In fact, neither one nor the other has to be construed as such, but both of them could be liberated into practical and poetic use in the construction of a different everydayness, one in which, above all, there is no longer poverty. The anti-surplus system proper to the domestic mode of production of which Sahlins speaks is not one in which there is scarcity, but rather one in which an adequate balance between production and consumption is attained. In such a system, energy is not wasted, but it is put to a different use, and that is, the construction of *the good life*. Certainly, it is not the capitalist system that can serve as a model for the equilibrium proper to the concept of the good life. With its unevenness between production and consumption, its pathologies within the sphere of circulation and in distribution, its crises due to overproduction, its constant drive for profit and its intrinsic need of a system of exploitation, capitalism is bound to create a logic of surplus and excess, which is then often accepted in the light not of its contingency, but of a metaphysical necessity—as if life itself were excessive. But life is what it is, and even in its effervescence and explosions moves from the neutrality of its potency, as Spinoza notably shows. This potency knows nothing of excess or surplus. It then falls upon men and women in the world to choose between a way of immanence, a materialist thought, or that which points to a beyond—to which excess and surplus also belong—typical of traditional metaphysics; to choose, that is, between this earthly plenitude, the many earthly plenitudes of our finitude and contingency, or the path that leads into nothing, already forbidden by Parmenides himself.

Perhaps we can say that Bataille's emphasis on consumption is too strong. Certainly, as Marx (1973) shows, consumption is part of production, and there is *expenditure* in both. But consumption cannot be hypostatized; it cannot be understood outside of the process of production. The point is, obviously, that of distinguishing between ways in which production takes place, that is, modes of production. Thus, even the gift economy described by Marcel Mauss (1990), which has consumption as its central moment in the form of the potlatch, is understood as a system of production and reproduction—not of inert commodities, of course, but of living social and spiritual relations, which the things exchanged precisely produce. This shows that consumption does not happen for its own sake, but, as Marx says, it is itself productive—although not necessarily in a capitalist sense. Bataille is not mistaken when he describes the *profitless* way in which consumption as freedom and as destruction takes place. Indeed, he points out that "[f]rom the standpoint of profit the pyramid is a monumental mistake" (1991: 119). Yet, "profitless" is not the same as "useless." And once the latter category is redefined and broadened, the act of consuming in freedom and destruction may have a higher value, from a social and spiritual point of view, than the mere and proper use of what has been produced—when "proper" is taken in its most empirical, instrumental, and commonsensical way. In fact, the truly proper use of something is that which engenders the trajectory of a return, which is the only route to a renewed subjectivity: the return to itself of energy, that for which alone there was expenditure—a return that requires an act of productive consumption, productive because upon the return a space of difference, not one of identity, opens. Bataille is aware of this, and in the preface to the second volume of *The Accursed Share*, he says that he wants to show that "it is *useful* to have useless values" (1993: 16). These useless values, the values that are consumed outside of a relationship of servility, are subjective values. The subjectivity so linked to consumption is what Bataille calls sovereignty.

For Bataille, in the modern world, sovereignty is the return of human dignity, what might counter the process that reduces human beings to things, reification (1991: 131). This is a concrete possibility, for, notwithstanding the reduction to a thing brought about by alienation,

> thought does not at all abandon, in the face of industrial development, man's basic desire to find himself (to have a sovereign existence) beyond a useful action that he cannot avoid. (p. 134)

Here again we see the problem caused by the separation of the unity of life activity into the two different spheres of the useful (that which serves) and of the sovereign (that which does not serve). Unaware of the problem, Bataille believes that sovereignty is the same as the "free disposition of himself" that, for Marx, "man" will acquire in the communal mode of production. Bataille says that in this situation a

> new chapter would begin, when man would finally be free to return to his own intimate truth, to freely dispose of the being that he *will be*, that he is not because he is servile. (pp. 135–136)

However, what here really opens up is the space, not of sovereignty, but of potentialities and the *could*, hence of real freedom. In fact, to see sovereignty as "man's return to himself" (p. 140), or to speak of "the return of being to full and irreducible sovereignty" (p. 189), that is, to say that the return is that whereby a distance and a relation of externality is created, and a measure of power is imposed by man over himself, is, as Maritain notes with respect to the notion of the sovereignty of the people, "nonsensical" (1998: 44). In the notion of human beings making a decision about themselves, yet "separately from themselves and from above themselves" (ibid.; emphasis removed)—as would be the case in a situation of sovereignty, the structure of servility remains, and it is only freedom that is lost.

The concept of the return, which together with that of negation is very important in Bataille's philosophy of the "totality of the possible" presented in the second volume of *The Accursed Share* (1993: 77)—or the "totality of the Real," which is the same as the object of desire (p. 111)—does not show its full capacity if only employed in the movement toward sovereignty. I cannot here deal extensively with Bataille's use of the dialectic to trace the two-fold movement of the return. However, it is important to say that there is, first, a negation of nature, the negation of the given as a revolt and a refusal, and, at a later stage, the negation of that negation, one whereby nature is not found again in its purity, as it were, but rather as "transfigured by the *curse*, to which the spirit then accedes only through a new movement of refusal, of insubordination, of revolt" (p. 78). The negation of the negation, which opens the space of the *sacred* (or divine), of nature transfigured—a movement of transgression—is an apparently solely destructive movement, but it is in reality a movement toward freedom, the movement of the revolution. It is the elimination of any sovereign condition, not its implementation and upholding; it is the elimination of the exception, which is one with the sovereign (as Carl Schmitt notably holds), precisely because everything becomes exceptional, extraordinary. If we need a name, we call it *haecceitas* and say that it is, not a regime of exception (pointing toward a transcendence of sort), but the regime of the *principle of individuation*, an immanent movement, which, insofar as it individuates the specificity of the human being, that is, its singularity, gives rise to the condition of subjectivity. Individuation, not sovereignty, names the condition of the subject and constitutes its ground. This must be so if one is to avoid solipsism and instead be able to see, in the complex reality of subjectivity, the commonality and universality that it always carries with it. In this sense, Paolo Virno speaks of a "*pre-individual reality*, that is to say, something common, universal and undifferentiated" (2004: 76) that lies at the origin of the process of the constitution of subjectivity. This preindividual reality is for Virno biological, linguistic, and historical, that is, having to do with the "prevailing relation of production" (p. 77). With a reference to the French philosopher Gilbert Simondon, Virno explains that "*individuation is never concluded*, that the pre-individual is never fully translated into singularity" (p. 78). Thus, Virno says that

> according to Simondon, the *subject* consists of the permanent inter-weaving of pre-individual elements and individuated characteristics; moreover, the subject *is* this interweaving. (Ibid.)

This is very similar to the philosophy of Jean-Luc Nancy, which was discussed in Chapter 1. We see how distant this thinking is from a theory of sovereignty and of exception, where what is singular and unique would stand by itself, hypostasized in the most traditional sense of metaphysics, necessarily needing what is not sovereign. In fact, singularity itself cannot be thus hypostasized. Virno says:

> It would be a serious mistake, according to Simondon, to identify the subject with one of its components, the one which is singularized. The subject is, rather, a composite: "I," but also "one," unrepeatable uniqueness, but also anonymous universality. (Ibid.)

To say that the subject is "I," but also "one" does not imply, of course, that it is the result of the juxtaposition of two unrelated elements. Rather, the emphasis is on the concept of interweaving. This is what makes the subject. This, not identity or identification, is what individuation brings about. Thus, as the movement toward freedom (and dignity), as the movement of the revolution, the return does not lead toward sovereignty and power, but rather toward its dissolution or anti-power (dignity), as used by John Holloway in *Change the World without Taking Power* (2005).

In Holloway too, the revolutionary subject is something different from a mere "I," or from any other identitarian formula. He calls it an "undefined, indefinable, anti-definitional 'what'" (p. 150), exemplified by the faceless Zapatista rebels. What this *structure*, this *interweaving*, names is the capacity for autonomy (or perhaps we should only say solitude), that is, the ability to follow the law dictated by the return itself—a return to human dignity. It is a law that speaks with one voice, the voice of human dignity, the voice of the many, many voices. In this sense it is universal and common, singular and plural. But this autonomy, which comes to full light in the solitude of the return, and which can be approximated to an idea of self-discipline and self-governance (but even these concepts fall short of saying what it is), has nothing to do with sovereignty, nothing to do with power as domination, nor does it reproduce the structure of which servility is necessarily an element.

Bataille also uses the concept of autonomy, which, he says, is "the same thing as man himself" (1993: 91). But the problem is, precisely, that he equates it with the concept of sovereignty. The same is true of the concept of the totality, in which, outside mere intellectual life, one finds the unity of subject and object. But this is, again, a *sovereign* totality for Bataille. The concept of *surplus*, or excess, is fundamental in the constitution of these realities: autonomy, sovereignty. This concept also is fundamental to Bataille's emphasis on eroticism: it is the consumption of the surplus (of production) that constitutes the concrete totality in which man loses himself (p. 119), precisely by accomplishing the return. However, the return, to what is sacred or simply animal, the return to a transfigured self, eludes the concept of the sovereign because the surplus, the excess, the "more" that opens what-is to its hidden potential, always happens in the modality—to borrow an expression from William Burroughs—of "not really being there." This is not, of course, in line with Bataille's understanding of the erotic experience, where the other too obviously occupies the place of the object. It is rather a situation in which the other displaces one's subjectivity by reconstituting it—really, this is the return, what returns, which is never the same; it cannot be the same. But precisely because of this, all claims to sovereignty are lost. The concrete totality, made of possibilities in addition to what-is, as well as the autonomy of a transfigured subject, a transparent agent, remains. But how could the self-determined movement of what being displaced returns be sovereign? Of course, Bataille's concept of sovereignty is different from the Schmittian concept, and, in Bataille, the sovereign does not decide on the exception. But as we have seen with Maritain, there really is no need of this term once it is voided of its conceptual substance. Instead, what being displaced returns, what strives to end its state of alienation, the subjectivity of labor regaining its hidden power, crosses the totality of a wasteland, where the excess, the surplus, the potential, the "more," seem to have imploded: this is, yes, the sign of sovereignty, as real subsumption to be sure (all is subsumed under what-is; the potential of labor under capital), but the point, precisely, is to go against it and found something new.

Renunciation

Bataille tries to move beyond old conceptions of power and domination without renouncing sovereignty. To the contrary, and precisely by identifying in the renunciation of sovereignty the new form of sovereignty itself, he upholds it as coterminous with subjectivity and communism. Traditionally, sovereignty and domination are different concepts. There can be domination without sovereignty, but there cannot be sovereignty without domination. Sovereignty is the way in which domination is institutionalized.[4] In his unorthodox use of the concept, Bataille opposes sovereignty to labor and servitude in a way that echoes Hegel's dialectic of master and slave, of desire and labor, but is really a Nietzschean torsion of it. In fact, for Hegel, the slave is the ultimate bearer of power—the power of labor whereby the dialectic is overturned. Labor becomes the mediation between dependence and independence. In fact, "work forms and shapes the thing" (Hegel 1977: 118), where the thing is the object of the master's desire. The thing has the character of *independence*, which desire fails to attain in an immediate fashion. By interposing the mediating action of the slave between the desire of the thing and the thing's independence, the master leaves the latter to the slave, "who works on it" and "takes to himself only [its] dependent aspect and has the pure enjoyment of it" (p. 116). However, the slave "*qua* worker, comes to see in the independent being [of the object] [his] *own* independence" (p. 118; last brackets added). Indeed, the slave "realizes that it is precisely in his work wherein he seemed to have only an alienated existence that he acquires a mind of his own" (p. 119). Alexandre Kojève is correct in saying that

> in the long run, all slavish work realizes not the Master's will, but the will—at first unconscious—of the Slave, who—finally—succeeds where the Master—necessarily—fails. (1980: 30)

However, with Bataille's confusion between the useful and the servile, that is, with his inability to distinguish, in what opposes sovereignty, the two—up to a point intertwined—moments of liberating labor and mere servitude, things must stand under a completely different light. By offering this criticism of Bataille, I do not mean to imply that a transitional period of servitude is acceptable in view of a liberated future. Rather, I mean to challenge the view that labor is absolutely the same as servitude, and that liberation means liberation from labor, rather than through labor. In his study of sovereignty, Bataille says:

> What distinguishes sovereignty is the consumption of wealth, as against labor and servitude, which produce wealth without consuming it. (1993: 198)

He is referring here, more specifically, to the consumption of the *surplus* of production, the excess. He continues:

> The sovereign individual consumes and doesn't labor, whereas at the antipodes of sovereignty the slave and the man without means labor and reduce their consumption to the necessities, to the products without which they could neither subsist nor labor. (Ibid.)

If this were simply a description of economic and social life under capital, then it would be accurate. The problem is that for Bataille the exit from this situation does not depend on the potentialities of labor and useful doing, but rather on the unequivocal triumph of the already dominant modality of sovereignty, although conceived in a nontraditional way. Bataille says:

> Let us say that the sovereign (or the sovereign life) begins when, with the necessities ensured, the possibility of life opens up without limit. (Ibid.)

But it is easy to see that this is a description, not of sovereign life, but of the good life for everybody. I must repeat what I have already said: sovereignty only works within a logic of domination, and it is that logic's institutional form. The logic of domination cannot allow the good life for everybody, for that would be a contradiction in terms. However, necessities should generally be ensured, and the limitless potentialities of life should open up for all. Bataille is absolutely correct in pointing out this need, in suggesting this possibility. But he is mistaken in thinking that this should or could happen under the aegis of sovereignty, in the form of sovereignty. The mistake lies in the equation of utility and productivity, for, as he says:

> We may call sovereign the enjoyment of possibilities that utility doesn't justify (*utility being that whose end is productivity itself*). (Ibid.; emphasis added)

But this is incorrect; first, because, if anything, productive activity is that whose end is utility, and second because, particularly under capital, the link between means and end is suspended. Bataille concludes: "Life beyond utility is the domain of sovereignty" (ibid.).

If it is true that the worker "works in order to eat, and he eats in order to work" (p. 199)—a truth which is at the basis of the Marxian notion of alienation—it is not as true that eating without working–as Bataille's concept of sovereignty suggests—would be the solution. Even when one agrees that it is important "to enjoy the present time without having anything else in view but the present time" (ibid.), it is difficult to see why this present time should not also include the moment of labor—of nonalienated, creative labor, of course— and why Bataille would call this enjoyment, again, "sovereign."

Bataille presents a generic conception of alienation, and his critique of production does not have to do with the specificity of capital, but it is a critique of production as such. Thus, when he thematizes the question of time, and particularly the time of labor, he does not see the difference between the reification always taking place under the capitalist mode of production and the "liberating activity," which, according to Marx, labor, as an "overcoming of obstacles," essentially is (1973: 611). Bataille says:

> In efficacious activity man becomes the equivalent of a tool, which produces. The implication of these facts is quite clear: the tool's meaning is given by the future, in what the tool will produce, in the future utilization of the product; like the tool, he who serves—who works—has the value of that which will be later, not of that which is . . . The basic loss of value resides in the fact that man becomes a thing. Not entirely perhaps, but always. (1993: 218)

Linked somewhat incongruously to the theme of death, the anguish of death, this passage shows once again Bataille's confusion between "use" and "servility," production as creation and production as subordination.[5]

The world of subordination is the world of practice, which is opposed to sovereignty (p. 222). Certainly, and notwithstanding my criticism, Bataille says something important and that goes to the innermost depth of social life and existence in general. Thus, it is true that "the laboriously peaceful life" (p. 221) must be refused in order to exit a world of practice as subordination; and so must the fear of death. Obscured by the language of sovereignty, what Bataille says still points to a radical ontology which, notwithstanding his attacks on "humiliating labor" (p. 227), can be called ontology of labor. Indeed, all humiliating labor, all servility, must be eliminated—in this Bataille is absolutely correct. However, what remains after that elimination is not mere passivity, consumption, and thing-like existence. The subjectivity that Bataille ascribes to the concept of sovereignty, the individual form of activity, creative, poetic doing, far from being negations of the concept of labor as such, negate, precisely, the logic of domination, the world of subordination institutionalized in the form of sovereignty. Bare life may very well be what stands opposite sovereign power and thus completes its concept; but this is so precisely from the point of view of one and the same logic—the logic of sovereignty. Outside it, there is the active life, of doing and labor, the life of care, geared toward the joy, the happiness, otherwise denied. This is true not only from the point of view of the ethics of individuality, but also from the world historical perspective, or the general economy with Bataille, of those agglomerates, those "cold monsters" for Nietzsche, that go under the name of states. But here we see how necessary the elimination of sovereignty becomes, for as F. H. Hinsley explains, "the origin and history of the concept of sovereignty are closely linked with the nature, the origin and the history of the state" (1966: 2).

After a critique of traditional sovereignty, in which he also presents the axiom that "Nothing sovereign must ever submit to the useful" (1993: 226), Bataille challenges the fact that sovereignty be reserved for the exception—a "slippage," he calls it (p. 239). Sovereignty should instead be the ordinary and universal condition, but this precisely makes the concept irrelevant and useless. For instance, he defines sovereignty as "being generally the condition of each human" (p. 282). Sovereignty is then the same as subjectivity, individuality, or, more precisely, singularity. It takes on the form of traditional sovereignty when it becomes the prerogative of one subject for whom all others are objects who recognize him (in the Hegelian sense, says Bataille in a footnote) as the sovereign, while recognizing themselves in him. But it can also take on a more diffused, common form when each person is a subject and thus sovereign (pp. 241–246).

Bataille should here distinguish between sovereignty and subjectivity, and his analysis would truly acquire a radical, revolutionary character. He should do so also because he is aware that "the world of sovereignty as a whole" (p. 252) must be opposed. But why oppose sovereignty with sovereignty? The "categorical no" that the rebel says (referring to Albert Camus) may very well be "the full truth of the subject" (ibid.); it is certainly a decision, but it does not follow from this that there is something sovereign in it. True, the decision separates, but the separation points to a condition of individuation and simple difference, not to one qualified as a position of superiority and supremacy, which is what sovereignty always necessarily implies. Of course, sovereignty is here *the sovereign operation*, a concept that constitutes the main subject of Derrida's important analysis of Bataille's work. This sovereign operation, which takes the place of labor, is the result of the inner experience, the extreme of the possible, laughter, and meditation (Bataille 2001: 94). It is, for Bataille, a *moment*, evidently a disposition, which "cannot be acquired," nor can it be *fabricated* (p. 97). It comes to decision as the "sovereign silence that interrupts articulated language" (p. 90), but, as Derrida suggests, it does not really, not fully, come to presence:

> The instant—the temporal mode of the sovereign operation— is not a *point* of full and unpenetrated presence: it slides and *eludes* us between two presences; it is difference as the affirmative elusion of presence. (1978: 263)

Bataille speaks of this movement as *neutral knowledge*, which "overturns the movement of thought" (2001: 93), displaces the dialectics (Derrida 1978: 273–274), insofar as in the sovereign operation sovereignty pertains to both thought and its object (Bataille 2001: 92). The movement is to the extreme of the possible, where subjectivity has the sense, or rather, with Derrida (and Bataille himself) the *nonsense*, of solitude, nudity, and laughter.

Can this laughter, to just recall one of the many important words used here, also ground communism? I think it can, provided that we are aware that it is no longer of sovereignty that we are speaking, or perhaps that we have reached a moment when we become unaware of sovereignty.[6] And I am not able to say whether it is through the dialectics or through transgression that we can reach that moment.[7] Or perhaps the question is not choosing between them. Transgression does not require that one renounce the dialectics *tout court*, but rather, and this is, I think, what Bataille does, that one break it open. A broken, or open, dialectics is itself a language that fails, but precisely in virtue of this, it more closely follows the translucent elements of the real, which include the potential and thus the exit from what was simply there. It is, as Gavin Grindon says in his excellent essay on the breath of the possible, "an impossible third space that attempts to step beyond and outside of the dialectic: an other which refuses recuperation" (2007: 96).

In *The Accursed Share*, the equation of sovereignty and subjectivity, that is, the modality whereby sovereignty becomes ordinary and common, finds its truth in the concept of communism. For Bataille, sovereignty as subjectivity is "no longer alive except in the perspective of communism" (1993: 261). And he defines communism as "that vast world where what is sovereign must come back to life, in new forms perhaps, but perhaps in the most ordinary form" (p. 262). We have already seen the conceptual problems associated with this idea of sovereignty, or with sovereignty in general. The most problematic aspect is his equation of the sovereign with the unproductive. Indeed, Bataille sees in the unproductive the only alternative to the productive. He thus misses the truth that the category of the unproductive forms part and parcel of the same logic of productivity that privileges the productive. He does not even consider the more fundamental, ontological category of the "not productive" (Marx 1973: 308), or what I have called "neither-productive-nor-unproductive," that is, the logic of neither/nor, of neutrality, which constitutes the ontological ground of productivity *and* unproductivity under capital, as well as of forms in which production is immediately a creative act (Gullì 2005). To be sure, a move in that direction takes place in Bataille with the concept of *renunciation*,[8] which really goes past the dichotomy of the productive and unproductive. Here, Bataille comes close to giving up completely the concept of sovereignty. But, rather awkwardly, he gives it up while retaining it as the most fundamental category of his general economy. Thus, after having argued that there is nothing personal in sovereignty, that it is not "the autonomous decision of an individual" (1993: 311), he says that the task of the individual is, precisely, to renounce sovereignty "in a sovereign manner" (p. 325). If traditionally one renounced sovereignty by giving it to another (e.g., the king), the new sovereignty requires renunciation as such, for its own sake: sovereignty is placed in renunciation. But the truth is that, renounced in a sovereign manner, sovereignty is, in the last analysis, not renounced at all.

I have here dealt with Bataille because his work presents a very unusual notion of sovereignty, equated in turn with consumption, subjectivity, communism, and finally the renunciation of sovereignty itself. The merit of Bataille's philosophy is that it moves on the plane of immanence and contingency and it struggles to forge a completely new vision of human existence— one that touches upon the sacred and the animal aspects of it, without privileging either. Yet Bataille's argument for a new notion of sovereignty is not successful. When he speaks of renouncing sovereignty in a sovereign manner, his attempt to move beyond a commonly accepted view, a strong prejudice in philosophy and political thought whereby the lack of sovereignty is a sign of servility, becomes very clear. He certainly means that sovereignty must be renounced without exchanging it with servitude. But there are two problems here: one, which I dealt with extensively above, has to do with the equation of labor with servitude and their opposition to sovereignty; the other, which directly follows from the first, has to do with the idea that there is no exit from the sovereignty/servility dichotomy other than the paradoxical figure of a symbolic renunciation.

Permanent Transgression

The importance of reading Bataille, particularly the Bataille of *The Accursed Share*, is today underlined by a renewed interest in his work. I might simply mention the volume edited by Leslie Anne Boldt-Irons (1995), with contributions, among others, by Bataille's friend Jean Piel, and Denis Hollier, who analyzes Bataille's political thinking as a necessary moment between and past Nietzsche and Marxism. Then, closer to us, is the important volume edited by Shannon Winnubst (2007), who, in her introduction, explicitly calls attention to the importance of *The Accursed Share* and to Bataille's "courageous thinking" (p. 2). I briefly review those contributions that are closer to the discourse I am tracing. In general, I must say, they are all important, although, from my point of view, they all present the problem of lacking an adequate understanding of labor and thus reproducing, one way or the other, Bataille's confusion between the useful and the servile, as well as his exaggerated emphasis on consumption.

Jesse Goldhammer speaks of Bataille's "counter-Enlightenment anarchism" (Goldhammer 2007: 18). He distinguishes between *imperative sovereignty*, which is "servile because it is instrumental and useful," and *subversive or revolutionary sovereignty*, which "derives its power from abjection and uselessness" (p. 21). Obviously, from my point of view this is one instance of the failure to problematize the confusion between the servile and the useful, what I called Bataille's *mistake*. Of course, I did not choose to engage with Bataille's thought in order to show that he made a mistake—nothing could be less interesting than this in writing about such a thinker—or any thinker for that matter. Rather, the idea is to highlight the path to liberation from a logic of servility brilliantly shown by Bataille, and in this I completely agree with Goldhammer. He says:

> In order to liberate themselves, human beings must dare to sacrifice that which enslaves them. (p. 25)

And defining his anarchist approach to Bataille, he says:

> This accursed share, as Bataille calls it, is what violently and sacrificially fragments all instantiations of authority, productivity, and utility. (Ibid.)

But perhaps the most important aspect of his essay is what he himself calls *the most important* of "all the lessons for the left"—and that is "Bataille's view of power" (p. 32). This is very true today when a good portion of the left, dogmatic and resentful, is imbued with the notion that Nietzsche and Nietzscheanism (and this of course includes Bataille before anyone else) are responsible for the left's own failure to imagine an exit from the logic of domination subsuming all aspects of everyday life, including the very form of the political. However, the truth is that *this* left itself has perhaps not been able (or never really tried) to think radically enough about power—despite its assertion to the contrary. It is in this sense that what Goldhammer points out about Bataille's experience with thinking and writing must be borne in mind:

> Against any authority that declares its superiority, Bataille's anarchism holds out the possibility of headless, decentralized, chtonic power. (Ibid.)

Here, we reach the point where, despite the confusion I pointed out above (confusion caused by holding on to the sign of sovereignty), Bataille's thought reaches the plane of real, or total, anti-sovereignty. Of course, *this* is subversive and revolutionary: it does not command. However, we must be clear that this is *not* sovereignty. This is important in order to avoid charging the anarchist discourse, as we saw Schmitt doing (cf. Chapter 2), with the same logic it wants to dismantle—if only at the opposite end of the political spectrum. In truth, the exit from the logic of sovereignty is the access to a non-regime of permanent transgression. This means that there is no subversive or revolutionary sovereignty. And probably this is what Bataille ultimately means when he writes the last words of volume 3 of *The Accursed Share*: "sovereignty is NOTHING" (1993: 430).

Writing on sovereign consumption and energy, Amy Wendling comes close to challenging the use of sovereignty when she says that in Bataille sovereignty is "a conceptual, methodological, and *practical* postulate" (Wendling 2007: 49). However, she opts for a repudiation of the concept of revolution, understood as a bourgeois concept (p. 47). She starts her essay by recalling Bataille's distinction between an economy of scarcity, based on production, or work, and an economy of plenitude, based on consumption (p. 37). There is scarcity because there is bourgeois accumulation, otherwise "Bataille shows that the earth's energy is superabundant" (p. 36). I cannot deal here with Wendling's sophisticated account of the "three genealogies of the concept of energy . . . operative in Bataille" (p. 37). It suffices to say that the sun's energy constitutes the most fundamental aspect of Bataille's immanent and organicist ontology, linking nature and culture, many human cultures among themselves, as well as nonhuman forms of life. What follows from this concept of energy is the notion of sovereign consumption as "noncoercive pleasure or play, consumption that exceeds a productive, work-driven economy" (p. 46). However, as Marx says, production and consumption are part of a cycle, a *totality*, and this is true not only of the capitalist mode of production, but of any mode of production. "Without production, no consumption; but also, without consumption, no production; since production would then be purposeless" (Marx 1973: 91). True, the concept of purposeful activity is what is being called into question in a reading of Bataille's work. But can this be done without undermining even the discourse on consumption itself? Indeed, for Marx the fact that production predominates over the other members of the totality (distribution, exchange, and consumption) cannot be challenged: "That exchange and consumption cannot be predominant is self-evident" (p. 99). The anomaly of capital cannot be solved by giving consumption predominance over production, but by seeing in consumption the immediate end of production. In fact, under capital, the "purpose of commerce is not consumption, directly, but the gaining of money, of exchange values" (p. 149). Production as the general activity of making, labor as the creative power of the social must remain even when the capitalist relations of production are dismantled, when productive labor, as the labor that produces capital, is eliminated. Mere play will not do. What is true instead is that producing, that is, bringing forth the more or less useful (and even the useless), could be a *noncoercive pleasure*. This means that work itself can be a pleasure if within the concept of pleasure one includes that "overcoming of obstacles" that for Marx is "in itself a liberating activity" (p. 611). The point is not distinguishing between work and play, but rather the point is extricating work from the regime of domination typical of capital, as well as of other modes of production built on a logic of domination. The point is breaking the sovereignty of capital, all sovereignty. As I have argued in *Labor of Fire*, it is important to distinguish between productive labor, that is, the labor that produces capital, and living, creative labor, which still produces in the general sense of bringing forth, but it produces use values. Wendling is aware of this when she says:

> In *sovereign consumption*, consumption is not subjected to an end outside of itself. In the terms of classical Marxism, to act sovereignly is to privilege use over exchange value, or individual over productive consumption. In a temporal schema, to act sovereignly is to privilege the present over the past or future. (2007: 46)

But privileging use over exchange value is not the same as privileging consumption over production; it is rather to privilege one *mode* of consumption-and-production over another. Following Bataille, Wendling places all the emphasis on consumption. But, really, the sun's energy is my own, and when I consume it, I bring something into being, I create, I produce, I work.[9] This does not have to take place within, and be subsumed under, a logic of domination. Thus, instead of discarding labor, we should discard sovereignty. Wendling says:

> Bataille situates the real interest of communism in its vision of a human being whose general condition is to play without labor in an economy of plenty. (p. 51)

I can agree with this if by labor in the phrase "without labor" what is understood is productive, alienated, wage labor, not living, creative labor, not labor as such; if by play we understand all aspects and forms of making. In this sense, there is no real difference between liberated/liberating labor and play, for human activity exits, in this vision, the paradigm of servility.

Pierre Lamarche, in his essay, also starts from a similar premise, the "well known" distinction between limited and general economy in Bataille:

> Limited economy is economy predicated on the notion of a primal scarcity and the necessity to produce and accumulate in order to safeguard against this scarcity that perpetually threatens existence. It corresponds to economy viewed from the perspective of fear and anxiety. General economy, within which limited economy is inscribed, is predicated on a primal plenitude; the superabundance of solar energy bathing the entire planet everyday, a source of energy that continuously gives without taking. (Lamarche 2007: 64)

We have here a concise, clear, and elegant exposition of Bataille's thesis, of his vision of excess. For Lamarche, "Volume 3 of *The Accursed Share* elaborates a theory of sovereignty consistent with the primacy of expenditure in a general economy predicated on primal excess" (ibid.).

Here, too, there is no attempt at calling into question the concept of sovereignty in all its forms. Following Bataille, Lamarche fully accepts what he calls "true" sovereignty, although he initially speaks of the sovereign renunciation of sovereignty as of "a Pyrrhic victory" (p. 65). Then he explains that this renunciation, this state of sovereign destitution, is "a state of freedom from things beyond utility, beyond what is simply necessary to continue to survive" (p. 66). Importantly (and in Taoist fashion, I would say), he interprets Bataille's expression "life *beyond utility*" (Bataille 1993: 198) as "*not* to need things beyond what we actually need" (Lamarche 2007: 65). This is important because it does to an extent recuperate the sense of the useful vis-à-vis the servile. I spoke of a Taoist way because this notion of the useful made me think of Zhuangzi's idea that one should use things as things, not be used by things as a thing (see Fung Yu-lan 1983: 245). But the dialectic between using and possessing is also central in Laozi's *Daodejing*. What is here important is to demarcate the limit between use and abuse. Using things, including our own energy, our labor, beyond the need we have for them is abusing things and abusing ourselves, our time. Thus, Lamarche says, "Free yourself from things." And he adds that for the worker this "also means free yourself from looking upon yourself as a commodity, as labor power, as a *worker*, as a *slave*" (2007: 68). However, there are two problems: The first is that this liberation from workerness and labor power should not be seen as liberation from work as such (see p. 69); the second problem is that such liberation should not be conceived as yet another form of sovereignty. For Lamarche these are not problems at all: liberation from work as such is what we need, and this equals the new form of sovereignty. In an endnote, Lamarche actually distinguishes Bataille's thought from that of Italian Autonomism, Zerowork, and other Marxisms precisely on the basis of the meaning of this liberation from work. For him, Bataille "offers an important correction" to these other Marxisms by going beyond the limitations of productive, wage labor. Bataille's path to liberation stresses expenditure and "the enjoyment of nonproductive activity" (p. 71). However, the real problem is that productive and unproductive (or nonproductive) activities belong to the same logic, the logic of capital, and one is not without the other.[10] Lamarche also defines nonproductive activity as "the maximization of life activity that is directed toward no particular end, but rather is the sheer enjoyment of the moment," and he calls this "the only truly progressive revolution" (p. 71). I doubt that this might actually be the case. But I would also ask why having a particular end is in itself a problem. This is a question that (still in the volume edited by Winnubst) I also have for Zeynep Direk and for Allan Stoekl. Direk, in her interesting reading of general economy as the preindividual, impersonal ground of human existence, accepts the formula of sovereignty as "the denial of all *telos* in wasting and squandering the excess of being" (Direk 2007: 100). Stoekl, who approaches Bataille's work from the point of view of ethics and points out the important problem of subjectivity and the necessity of its overcoming,[11] says:

> Contrary to the world of work, the world of expenditure entails spending without regard for the future, affirmation of ecstasy now, and the refusal of things (*choses*) that only serve a purpose and that contribute only to one's own personal security and satisfaction (profit). (Stoekl 2007: 265)

However, it seems to me that the problem has to do with the *type* of end one has, not with the end as such, for the latter is in a sense impersonal, presubjective, and always already pertains to the concept of the activity itself. Thus, to make an example that is particularly relevant because it has to do with both Marx's critique of capital and Aristotle's philosophy of the end, housebuilding is not a problematic activity because it has an end. It becomes problematic when its "natural" end, shelter, is displaced into the logic of profit (and/or status). If use is the end for the sake of which an activity is entered upon, then there is nothing wrong with it. To claim possession and domination opens a completely different level of discourse. To recall Agamben's distinction between life and law, we can say that labor can be a life activity or it can be entangled in the logic of sovereignty determined by the law and, with Benjamin, by the violence that creates the law.

To go back to Bataille and conclude this chapter, let me stress again that the useful and the servile must be held in separation. Only thus will one have a clear sense of the problem associated with all forms of sovereignty. My view is that the dichotomy itself collapses as soon as one renounces one of its terms. The elimination of servility is also the elimination of sovereignty, and sovereignty itself, a rotten concept no matter what form it takes on, becomes absolutely useless when, to refer to Hegel again, the dialectic of master and slave is overturned. In fact, more than an overturning, there is here a dismantling of the whole machinery of domination. The labor that remains, which "forms and shapes the thing," is neither servile nor sovereign. It is the common, ordinary labor that founds new, immanent plenitudes.

Part II

Sovereignty and Labor

Ax and Fire: Knowledge Production and the Superexploitation of Contingent Academic Labor

ૡૢૺૢ

No hay más que un millón de herreros
forjando cadenas para los niños que han de venire

Nothing remains but a million blacksmiths
forging chains for the children yet to be born.

—Federico García Lorca, *Grito Hacia Roma*
(*Cry to Rome*)

With the restructuring of the university, its corporatization, its full acceptance of the logic of capital, the fact of contingent academic labor should not be seen as an aberration, a scandalous (but perhaps temporary) anomaly that could be solved within and by the very system that produces it. Rather, the ever-increasing number of contingent academic workers, and the consequent reduction in the number and power of full-timers, is now the norm. Not only is it the norm, but it is the coherent, logical consequence of the corporatization process. That is, there could be no corporatization without the logic of sovereignty and domination whereby contingent labor in the first place, and all other labor in the second, must be, as it is, superexploited.

As many have noted, the originary idea of the university as a place for learning (perhaps even disinterested learning) is gone.[1] Having faith in that idea at this point in time amounts to having faith in a romantic past; it would be a useless, if not politically dangerous, nostalgia. Yet, if the past is barred, the future is not. Hence, the work for the transformation of the corporate university can be a *concrete* utopia, that is, one already present in the political, radical imagination, as well as in the structure of the real (when this latter is understood as inclusive of the potential). What must be made clear, however, is that the transformation of the university is not possible if society itself is not transformed. If the university has become a capitalist enterprise, if the relationship between the university as such (its administrators) and its workforce (including the often reluctant full-timers) is the relationship between capital and labor, then the antagonism within the university is the antagonism present in capitalist society as a whole. Of course, where this labor is exploited most, which is the case with contingent labor, there the antagonism becomes irreducible. To say that it is irreducible means to say that the only true solution lies in the elimination of such exploitation, which is equal to the elimination of the university as a capitalist enterprise.

Workers' Rights as Human Rights

Following James A. Gross (2006), I take workers' rights as human rights. Once this position is taken, which could be denied only by hypocrisy and double standards (i.e., upholding human rights everywhere and denying them at home, in the workplace), then it will become evident that what goes on in the corporate university, vis-à-vis contingent labor in particular, is a violation of fundamental human rights. For Gross, the recognition of the fundamental truth that workers' rights are in fact human rights requires a reassessment of commonly accepted values; it

> means that property rights-based, "free" market values will have to give way to the values of human rights that have not historically influenced U.S. labor law and policy despite the fact that human rights values are most consistent with the nation's professed democratic ideals. (p. 22)

Gross's essay starts, as does the whole volume edited by Block et al., from a recent Human Rights Watch report (2000), which found that "workers' freedom of association is under sustained attack in the United States" (quoted in Gross: 21). Both Gross and the editors of the volume stress that this freedom of association must also include the right to strike (pp. 1; 25), a notion whose status remains ambiguous within the International Labor Organization (ILO).[2]

In his essay, Gross takes seriously the notion, too often only rhetorically entertained, that

> human rights are a species of moral rights that all persons have simply because they are human, not because those rights are earned or acquired by special enactment or contractual agreements. (p. 23)

This gives the law itself a position subordinate to principles of universal ethics based on dignity—in our discourse, on the dignity of individuation. Gross points out how the law is very often used to legitimize criminal practices, and he gives the historical example of slavery. He says that

> the existence of human rights does not depend upon the approval of legislature, courts, other institutions, or the will of the majority. (p. 24)

One important aspect of his essay is to include economic rights within a general discourse on human rights. This is important because it shifts the discourse from economic security to what in development studies, for instance, is addressed as *human security*. And although this is not Gross's terminology, the substance is the same: the recognition of a universal ethics capable of grounding a life of social justice, the good life. Fundamentally, all human rights, ranging from the personal to the political to the economic, et cetera, underline the essential truth that at stake is "a life of dignity" that must be defended: "Violations of those rights deny a person's humanity" (p. 23). Recognizing workers' rights as human rights challenges the common exceptionalism with which the employer-employee relationship is understood, that is, the primacy of property values shaping labor relations. In reality, "the employer-employee relationship is more than economic in nature" (p. 24). Contrary to the ever-growing awareness of the importance of human rights issues, the employer-employee relationship is still seen as lying outside them, with workers often experiencing conditions of powerlessness and servility. Yet, Gross says, "Servility, or what some call powerlessness, is incompatible with human rights" (p. 25).

A life of dignity means that people must be able to fully and richly develop their potentialities. This is a right that should be independent of the political will of any constituted power, as well as of any legal framework. In the workplace, this right is the freedom of association, "which includes the right to organize, to bargain collectively, *and to strike*" (ibid.; emphasis added). The last mentioned right, the right to strike, is crucial. Without it, there is no exit from the chronic powerlessness in which a given segment of the workforce finds itself. In fact, there is no reason why employers would yield to labor's legitimate demands unless their interests are somehow threatened. Denying the right to strike (as often happens in the public service sector in the United States) means asserting the sovereignty of property and capital over labor with all its force, arrogance, and violence.

Gross challenges the employer speech right, particularly captive audience speech (where employees are compelled to listen to the employers without having the opportunity to reply), aimed at conditioning and threatening the employees' freedom of association. Even when the employer's right is counterbalanced by the employee speech right, the question remains:

> What justification can there be for permitting employers to continue to resist, discourage, and coerce those workers who exercise their human right of freedom of association? (p. 28)

The only justification is a defense of the employer's sovereignty.

Gross also deals with the question of human resource management. After an initial and brief remark on the distinction often made between the old-style personnel administrators and the new human resources management, he points out the fundamental similitude between the two, which comes down to "the ultimate objective of increasing their productivity" (p. 32). However, recently the notion that "human resources professionals become strategic partners in executing business strategy" is openly advocated (ibid.). Rather than advocate for employees, what these managers do is try to make "the employer's goals the personal goals of each employee" (p. 33). The workers are thus treated as things, as means for others' ends, which is an injustice, a violation of basic rights:

> Inducing workers to see the world through their employer's frame of reference to legitimize and maintain employer control of the workplace without changing the power relationship of superior employer and subordinate employee constitutes manipulation that is an affront to human beings and human rights. (pp. 33–34)

In his concluding remarks, Gross also deals with the practical question of unions and organization. He opens this section by summing up the result of his analysis of power relations and power struggle within the U.S. world of labor. Although he does not use these concepts, it is evident that Gross thinks in terms of political antagonism in its most irreducible form: the antagonism between capital and labor, sovereign power and bare life. He says:

> The U.S. labor relations system is dominated by employer power premised on the inequality and helplessness of most workers and rooted in values that justify the possessions and exercise of that power. (p. 35)

This sovereign power is in constant violation of the basic fact of life. Redressing this violation is for Gross not simply a matter of "marginal adjustments or fine-tuning." Rather, it requires "an explicit restatement of property rights as subordinate to human rights, including the human rights of workers" (ibid.). From a materialist point of view, this restatement of property rights can only come through a clear understanding of the meaning of private property and the necessity (if the aim is the creation of a better society) of its structural dismantling. "Property rights" is the political and legal formula encapsulating the power relations of domination on the one hand, servility on the other. In a sense, one could say that one of the reasons, and perhaps the most important reason, why there are no human rights is that there are property rights. Thus, it is not simply a question of subordinating the latter to the former; it is rather a question of understanding that property rights, the cell of productivity and sovereignty, must be exploded so that human ap-propriation (in the sense of coming to what is proper to humans) can be grounded.

It is in this sense, that is, in the sense of coming to the proper, that the question of organization can be posed outside of the logic of bureaucratization and power and in a way that can reconstitute a different sense of social life. For this to happen, the question of labor must be seen in a broader sense than an economist approach may allow, or, which amounts to the same, the economic aspect of life must not be held in separation from the rest—this is indeed what Gross suggests when he looks at workers' rights as human rights.

Workers' organizations, unions, must have, as Andrew Ross (1997) says in his contribution to *Will Teach for Food*, a *utopian* dimension. They will, Gross also says, "need to develop alliances with other social movements" (2006: 36). They certainly "must do more than organize workers" (p. 35).

Although Gross does not deal with the question of contingent labor in particular, his essay remains very important for our discourse, for it allows us to ground the problematics of contingent labor in the broader (universal) context of human rights and international law, hence in a theory of social justice. Moreover, although I am addressing here the question of contingent academic labor, this is to be understood in its relation with other sectors of the workforce within and without the academy.

Flexibility and Contingency

When I earlier spoke in one stroke of full-time (tenure and tenure-track) faculty, contingent academic labor, and other non-academic workers within the university, I did not mean to equate them and their situations. Obviously, there are important differences between those who are protected and guaranteed and those who are not. However, as many commentators have noted, in the long run the present conditions of superexploitation of a growing number of workers will erode the status of relative freedom and power still enjoyed by the more privileged ones. I am not arguing that full-timers should participate in the struggle against the superexploitation of contingent labor in order to safeguard their own interests. I think they should do so in virtue of the requirements of a universalist ethics—at least, that would be the ideal situation.

I am here concerned with contingent labor because in it the antagonism between labor and capital in the age of *real* globalization becomes stronger and more apparent.[3] The choice of contingent labor in the academy, rather than in any other sector, does not intend to give academic labor a special place within the general economy. Most of what is here said of contingent academic labor (and this is limited to the U.S. context) can be extended to other forms of contingent labor globally, and certainly in the latter, workers endure much more difficult and precarious conditions than in the academy. There are also "hybrid" situations, such as the United Parcel Service (UPS) student workers (i.e., students who work) whose precarious conditions of life have recently been brilliantly analyzed by Marc Bousquet (2008). At the same time, the original (but now irremediably lost) spirit of the university, its mission and vocation, give the academy special relevance as one of the last bastions to fall under the progressive regime of real subsumption. Professors become part of the proletariat, as many have argued. The contingent workforce in particular, by being included and excluded at the same time, is, at the same time, the most invisible and the most exposed group.

I would like to start by disambiguating the word "contingent," as used in this context. It means one thing for capital, another for labor. For capital, the university, and its managers, it points to today's widespread notion of *flexibility*. For them, the new workforce, and soon all but a handful of full-timers, is contingent in the sense that it can be gotten rid of at any time if the need arises. Because it makes flexibility possible, contingency has a lot of positive value for the institution. Moreover, it is much cheaper than the regular full-time segment of the workforce. For labor, on the other hand, contingency is not simply an economic category. It has a rather substantial existential and ontological dimension. It is what threatens labor in its essential being—what threatens, disrupts, and often destroys life, the good life, the potential for it. It disables potentialities. For each contingent worker, contingency is a negation of their being. It tends to diminish in importance and annihilate a person's past (for what good work one has done in the past, what strenuous effort one has endured, is deliberately forgotten by the institution and not rewarded in any way; for instance, decades of service as a contingent worker will not yield any security), and it cripples a person's future (for tomorrow one can be dismissed for no reason, with perhaps an academic smile and the advice "take care of yourself"—just like the elderly homeless woman dumped from a shelter on a street corner near a Los Angeles hospital in Michael Moore's *Sicko*). All there is with contingency is the fleeting present: the anxiety of that whirlpool that we call the now, a hectic running from place to place, from campus to campus, and then for many, toward the end of a never-ending semester, the odious (because undignifying) "peer" observation;[4] and at the end of one's career the specter of one's life as a failure. I do not simply say one's *professional* life as a failure, for, as it has been noted by Joe Berry for instance (2005), precariousness on the job has important reverberations at all levels of a person's life, including the way in which others, often starting from one's colleagues and associates, see the person in question. Indeed, as a Calabrian saying goes: "To a fallen tree, ax and fire," which means that there is no return from failure, but more and more negativity and difficulties follow.

I do not need to repeat at this point an account of what it is to do contingent academic labor; it can be found in many books and articles, and I return to it later. Instead, I would now like to ground my discussion in some passages of the *Grundrisse*, for it is very important to get an understanding of contingent labor within the open and fiery dialectic of capital and labor. In doing this I join a tradition in the literature on academic contingency, from Randy Martin (1998a) to Marc Bousquet (2008), just to mention two names. However, this should not be seen as an approach reserved to Marxists. Nor is it something that relates, disciplinarily, only to labor studies. One of the points I am making in this book is that the exploitation and superexploitation of labor (once labor is understood as the constitutive power of the social as a whole; that is, understood as human activity) is the root of all social injustice. The fundamental question of human rights cannot fully and successfully be addressed unless it is seen from this radical perspective.

In the *Grundrisse*, Marx says that the worker, in exchanging her labor capacity, "surrenders *its* creative power" (1973: 307; emphasis added). The phrasing of this is very interesting and important, for it covers the ground from the basic exigencies of economic life to everydayness in its multiform totality, including one's creativity. Although it is not the worker's intention to exchange her creative power, she cannot help doing that: her creative power is part of her labor capacity; in exchanging the latter, she will also exchange the former. Creativity is arguably the most essential element constituting a person's subjectivity. The originary site of one's creativity is the same as the site of one's labor capacity, and it is for this reason that art and labor can be reconciled. When a person's labor capacity is sold, creativity is also gone. Through exchange, this labor capacity is soon transformed into labor power—a commodity. Creativity will be the scoria that must be thrown away. When a contingent academic worker has taught three, four, perhaps five classes in one day, when this is repeated three, four, perhaps five times a week, at the end of the day, at the end of the week, there is no creativity left for what should in principle be a creative life. As much as one likes teaching, one has to recognize that one gives more (much more) than one receives. Teaching is a type of labor of care (see Chapter 5), rewarding on the one hand, yet exhausting and draining on the other (especially when one teaches six or seven classes per semester and at different institutions).

Once one has exchanged one's labor capacity (which includes one's creative power) as labor power, there can be no time and energy for research and writing, for further creative labor. I myself am an example of this. I teach six or seven classes per semester at two different schools in Brooklyn, and I have done this for many years. In order to do my research and write, I need to use most of the time left, including often the nights and the (unpaid) summers. Every semester, I meet at least two hundred new students, with whom I work passionately. At the end of each semester, I feel proud and happy to hear from my students that they have learned a lot; they really enjoyed the class. Yet, as time goes by, I realize that most of my intellectual (and physical) energy (and at some points in the semester, all of it) goes into teaching, and just as Marx explains at the outset of volume 1 of *Capital*, this energy is twofold: use value and exchange value; useful labor and abstract labor. At first sight, and in a more idealistic vein, one could think that the use value is represented by the knowledge that my students and I produce (or reproduce) in the classroom, whereas the exchange value is to be found in the tuition they pay and the wage I get. This would not be so bad, but it is too simple, and ultimately false. Under the university as a capitalist enterprise, the knowledge thus produced or reproduced in the classroom is only coincidentally a use value. In reality, my teaching is for me only an exchange value; and it is a use value, not for the students, but for capital. The students' learning capacity (which is itself work), whereby they participate essentially in the production (or reproduction) of knowledge, is also a use value only for capital, whereas it is for them a mere exchange value. Both my teaching and the students' learning capacity are what capital (in this case, the university) *needs* in order to produce surplus value. It is in this sense that they are both use values for capital.

This is, if I am correct, an application of Marx's analysis from both *Capital* and the *Grundrisse*. Capital would not bother with the process of teaching and learning unless there was in it something *useful for* capital.[5] Capital's only aim is the creation of surplus value. But the latter is already contained in labor (in our case, in teaching and learning), and must be extracted from it. In fact, surplus value is already contained in exchange value, that is, in the twofold character of the commodity form *and* in labor as a commodity.

What appears at the end of the process as a *result* is in truth "already contained in the presupposition" (Marx 1973: 307). The presupposition, as paradoxical as the result, is that, to count as labor power, the use value of one's labor capacity must be seen exclusively as exchange value. If I want to sell my labor capacity, I better not use it myself, as my own use value; if I do, I will be left with nothing to sell. My labor capacity will become a use value for capital, not for me. It is at this point and in this sense that it also becomes productive—in the specific sense of producing capital. But it is here that its creative power is lost.

The above is of course true in general. In the case of contingent academic labor, or of academic labor in general, what must be said is that its use value has now become *productive*. In the past, academic labor was creative when it was good, or simply unproductive otherwise. In the university as a capitalist enterprise, it is productive in the specific sense of producing and increasing capital—and contingent labor (due to its low cost) is more productive than its permanent counterpart. The more productive one can be, the more exploitable and exploited. There is therefore no exit from the present superexploitation of contingent academic labor other than a radical dismantling of it, as well as of its other, its double, the capitalist university, capital as such. As Marx says, "the demand that wage labor be continued but capital suspended is self-contradictory, self-dissolving" (pp. 308–309). This is so because wage labor, if not the ultimate presupposition, is one of the mediations in the process from labor to capital. Marx says:

> It is just as pious as it is stupid to wish that exchange value would not develop into capital, nor labour which produces exchange value into wage labour. (p. 249)

Accordingly, one cannot hope to abolish contingent labor in the academy and keep the corporate university. It would be like having capital without wage labor, without exploitation—but then capital is no longer possible.

In this chapter, I argue that without the superexploitation of contingent labor, the corporate university would collapse. This means that such labor is "contingent" only by equivocation. In reality, it is an essential and structural component of the system itself. Contingent labor is bound, attached to the university, even in the specific sense that after some time it will be impossible for any individual worker to find another job: impossible to be outside, impossible to be inside. Being inside and outside at the same time, this labor is attached to the university as to nothing; it is attached to its own invisible shadow. In a sense, the university itself becomes this contingency. Such is the case, for instance, with the Metropolitan College in the Louisville area discussed by Marc Bousquet:

> The name itself is misleading, since it's not a college at all. An "enterprise" partnership between UPS, the city of Louisville, and [various] campuses . . . , Metropolitan College is, in fact, little more than a labor contractor. (2008: 126–127)

The tendency to transform the university into a full-fledged and successful business is present everywhere. To this aim, contingency itself is not contingent, but absolutely necessary. But if this is the case, if there is such an equivocation about contingency, then something must be done about it. If contingent academic workers (or most contingent workers in general) actually work permanently, experiencing, as Joe Berry says, a "permanent lack of permanence" (2005: 4), then the category of contingency needs careful scrutiny. And because of the inherent powerlessness of contingent workers, due to the limitations in their organizing capacity (limitations that have a legal and material character, from contract insecurity to lack of time due to overwork), I think it is necessary that their issue become an issue in universal justice and international law. Of course, here I am speaking beyond the question of academic contingency, but inclusive of it. The ILO has discussed the question of contingent labor, but there is no clear position about it. I think a passage should be made from a discourse on economic security to one on human security. Then it would be easier to recognize the inherently criminal nature of conditions that bring about a permanent sense of human insecurity.

For instance, at the time of this writing, the contingent workforce at the City University of New York (CUNY) is experiencing difficulties determined by legal and material conditions. With the new contract, soon to pass, contingent workers will see their situation essentially unchanged.[6] Some of the contingents are against the new contract ratification and they even blame the union leadership, which had in the past been rather supportive of contingent workers and at times even explicitly its advocate, for downplaying their plight and demands. While this type of complaint might be an over-reaction to the present situation of deep and legitimate disappointment, the fact remains that it is not through the union's inability to secure a better collective bargaining agreement that the situation of the contingents can change. It might be that, at this point, ratifying the proposed contract is the right thing to do in order to avoid a more unfavorable future settlement. It is therefore a practical question of this kind. Barbara Bowen, president of the Professional Staff Congress (PSC), urges all union members to give their support, while she acknowledges that the "major disappointment of the pro-posed contract is in the area of job security for long-serving adjuncts" (Bowen 2008)—and there are many of them, of us.[7] But waiting a decade or more before possibly gaining access to job security (that is, economic and human security) cannot appeal to anyone. Obviously, this radicalizes many people's positions; it once again highlights the truth that contingent workers are being defrauded of what already and essentially belongs to them. The fact remains, however, that the self-organization of the contingent workforce proves to be an extremely difficult task. Contingent workers have very little time and resources. Moreover, and this is true of all CUNY workers and of the whole public sector in New York, there are legal limitations to what one can do, as one cannot resort to a strike (this is specifically regulated by the Taylor Law); in the case of contingent workers a strike would result in their immediate dismissal.[8] Inevitably, the main question raised by those who dis-sent is: what is to be done? Most suggestions revolve on the task of rethink-ing the concept of the union itself. Apparently, contingent workers now need to fight not only against the administration, but also against the union lead-ership. This is just an illustration of how contingent labor's initial and essen-tial lack of security and power progressively worsens when, attached to noth-ing but its own precariousness, it finds no structural and (traditional) legal weapons to vindicate itself. What is left is, of course, the almost impossible task of building a successful alternative organization. Perhaps the only real exit, to remain within the CUNY illustration (but it could be generalized), is to seek and make a legal case on the basis of an argument capable of dem-onstrating the violation of fundamental human rights being perpetrated in such a situation—this is something that belongs in the territory of the growing relationship of ethics and international law.

If the argument can be made that contingent labor is bound, attached, to the university (or any other enterprise) and that in the long run it ruins and destroys the life of contingent workers, then action should be taken to prohibit it; this means that contingent labor should be recognized for what it really is: noncontingent, permanent labor, which should have all the security and benefits that go with the fact of working, the fact of living. Later I will speak about the importance of union organizing and social movements. Here I want to say that pressure should be put on the ILO to recognize that this form of labor, whereby a human being is reduced to the nothingness she is attached to, must be made illegal. The ILO recognizes four fundamental and universal rights at work: the freedom of association and the freedom to bargain collectively, the elimination of forced labor, the elimination of child labor, and the elimination of discrimination (cf. Block et al. 2006: 1–14). The elimination of contingent labor should be given the same status as the above. It is outside all logic and all ethics to think that people who regularly work for years at the same workplace are contingent workers. These workers fall into a legal and administrative category that is a travesty of the law (at least, of the law aspiring to ethical grounding, such as is the case with international law) and a perversion of what it means to administer, that is, to attend to those conditions that can bring about the common good. But here I need to add something: Even when some type of work is truly contingent, in the sense that it is not performed regularly, such as is the case with seasonal work, its superexploitation cannot be justified, either.

If this is the situation, if the capitalist university lives off the sour blood of contingent labor, then the question arises as to whom the university really belongs (that is, *ought to* belong). The answer is that the university essentially belongs, first of all, to the students. To be sure, they are also part of that contingency that defines adjuncts, part-timers, et cetera. This becomes particularly clear when one reads Bousquet's chapter on UPS student workers (2008: 125–156), but it is true in general, even when students are not formally employed—a situation that, particularly in community college settings, is rare (for most of them work). I have never been happy with the notion that students are customers in the corporate university. In fact, they are more like inmates, or patients in a hospital. They are certainly not simply consumers. They are producers, and they are *consumed*. As Stanley Aronowitz says, they "can still get in, but they can't get out except as intellectual corpses" (1997: 200). Nonetheless, the university belongs to them in the same way in which wealth belongs to labor. Then, in addition to the students, who are also workers, all other workers, the contingents most of all, have a legitimate claim to the university and the knowledge that can be produced in it. Managers, administrators, and trustees of the present kind must be removed from the vision of a future university. From the standpoint of the sovereignty paradigm, this would be the only way in which the equivalent of popular sovereignty in government could also be conceived with respect to the university. However, since in the present study we are seeking to go

beyond the concept of sovereignty in all its forms, we can say that the removal of those in power is the condition for the participation in governance
and management of all those others who in any way contribute, not to the
advance of property, but to the deepening of the measure of humanity, to the
daily, creative, and caring effort of the community to ground the good life.
But those who are utterly indifferent to this daily effort and simply legislate,
those who enjoy sovereignty but live parasitically off the labor of others must
be made to understand that the political goal of dismantling and restructuring the restructured university cannot stop at one or two reforms for the
amelioration of miserable labor conditions; rather, it will go all the way to the
dissolution of the present contingency and from there to a new contingency—
this time one of freedom and creative power, that is, one in which the word
contingency is used philosophically, in the sense of the richness of potentiality, not economically, as referring to a workforce that is present and absent at
the same time.

The word contingency is used in many ways, and this is part of the paradoxical situation defining the lives of many people today. Contingent is also
the fact of human existence itself. However, the way in which *contingent* is
used with respect to contingent labor hides the fact that this labor is most of
the time, if not always, not contingent at all. Economically and legally construed and stigmatized as contingent, it is in reality, that is, structurally and
ontologically, a permanent feature of a given workplace. What is important
here is that the recognition that *we work* rather than not (where "we" includes, in the academy, the whole laboring community starting from the
students) also becomes the recognition of our constituent power, of our dignity, as well as of the fact that the university is not (certainly no longer) a
special institution standing apart from the rest of society. As a capitalist institution, the university belongs to the world of capital as a whole. The struggle
against the university as such an institution is also the struggle against capital, and the latter is essentially a struggle against undignifying exploitation
and for social justice. If capital asserts its sovereignty primarily by means
of the logic and language of productivity, and if productivity is a central
moment of the corporate university, fighting against it—through creative
and caring labor—is ending the sovereign claim, the dominance of capital
and property over labor and life, outlining a model of social justice.

We Work

In this chapter, we see that an important way in which the power of sovereignty over labor is exercised can be easily detected in the production of

knowledge, and particularly in the most precarious of its modalities of actu-
alization, that is, contingency. There are various reasons why this is important. One of them, perhaps the most important, has to do with the seemingly absolutely free character of this type of production—so free that, as
Randy Martin and other contributors to a volume edited by Martin (1998a)
argue, too often—and mistakenly—knowledge production, in the specific
form of academic labor, is not recognized as labor. Of course (and fortu-
nately), the production of knowledge does not take place only in the academy. But it is in the academy, in the sphere of higher education, of what today is called the corporate university that this knowledge is institutionalized
and industrialized. As Martin says:

> It should come as little surprise that what goes on at the university
> is *work*—and a highly organized division of labor at that. (p. 16)

In this chapter, I am focusing on the exploitation of contingent labor within
the corporate university, including the labor of disadvantaged students in
community colleges. Students, in fact, contribute essentially to the production of knowledge. As Stefano Harney and Frederick Moten note, "doing
academic work" (this is the title of their essay in the volume edited by Martin) is not simply a privilege or a task of the academic, the professor. Students
are also always involved as "workers at the point of production" (1998: 167).
    The focus on contingent labor within the academy will let us more read-
ily see the contradiction between sovereignty and free labor. In fact, academic labor, which is usually conceived of as inherently free (also due to the
principle of academic freedom), will appear as a form of bound labor.[9] This
may not still be the case with tenure and tenure-track positions; it certainly
is for the growing number of part-timers and adjuncts, who are desperately
needed by the institution, yet at the same time not given any security. Soon
they find out that they are bound to this lack of security, for fleeing it is very
risky. Paradoxically, it becomes their only security: one made of insecurity
itself, anxiety, and danger. Is not this the typical (psychological and material) situation of anyone who is trapped, imprisoned, bound? I say poetically
that contingent labor is attached to its own contingency as to nothing. However, this statement should be understood literally, as well. Indeed, it names
the nakedness to which the sovereign institution reduces the individual capacity to labor and its creative power. It also represents the powerlessness experienced by the collective contingent workforce, particularly due to its atomi-
zation; it is in fact difficult to come together and organize, difficult even to
know each other (cf. Berry 2005: 114). By appropriating one's vital energy,

the sovereign institution—to paraphrase Marx—confronts one as an alien power. The individual worker, and consequently the collective workforce, becomes a shadow, a trace, a vanishing mediation, approaching nothing, truly falling into it. From this fall, there is often no return. And I say this without exaggeration, without being carried away by language. In fact, there are those who after thirty or forty years of service as contingent workers will retire with no security at all—only perhaps with a sense of failure: Their lives have been thrown into and consumed by the machinery of the institution, its fixed capital. The university (or any other company) calls this flexibility. From the perspective of the contingent workforce, it amounts to an irremediable loss: of time, freedom, and dignity. Also recall that some contingent labor is contingent only in name. Furthermore, most times it is not voluntary, in the sense that workers would gladly have a permanent position, but the latter is denied to them. Consequently, they are *forced* to work *contingently*; that is, although they often work permanently, their jobs are legally construed as contingent jobs. I think that the injustice is here self-evident. Thus, involuntary contingent labor is a type of bound labor. The fact that other times contingent employment (temporary, part-time, etc.) is voluntary and even preferred does not change the injustice committed in the former cases. In the academic context, most of the contingent labor belongs to the nonvoluntary and contingent-only-in-name category. There may be a lawyer who also likes to teach a class, or a full professor at one institution who chooses to work as an adjunct at another; but these are exceptions rather than the rule. It must also be noted that what is called voluntary contingent work is often voluntary only equivocally. For instance, as Jeffrey B. Wenger says, "workers may have to choose some form of contingent work as an earning substitute for UI [unemployment insurance] benefits" (2006: 178). Courtney von Hippel et al. (2006) deal in particular with the question of "volition in the shadow workforce." They start their essay by stressing the fact that "the shadow workforce is not a homogeneous entity." They say:

> Differences between types of contingent workers are so pronounced that, for some workers, the shadow workforce is preferred to the mainstream. For those strongly preferring the mainstream, some parts of the shadow are clearly darker than others. (p. 30)

They present data showing different motivations and preferences in contingent workers. With references to the recent literature on contingent labor and after listing some of the reasons people might have in choosing temporary employment, they conclude that, broadly speaking, some people work as temporary employees because they prefer various aspects of the job such as flexibility, variety, and skill enhancement, whereas others work as temporary employees because they have only limited opportunities to do otherwise. (pp. 49–50)

Although it is very important to recognize these types of differences, one should not be thereby led to justify, totally or partially, the principle of contingency and flexibility. von Hippel et al. say:

Interestingly, although statistics indicate that an overwhelming percentage of the workforce is desirous of permanent employment, anecdotal evidence suggests that an increasing number are viewing contingent work positively. (p. 51)

They give an example from the high-tech area, where some individuals might enjoy the sense of freedom coming with being able to move from one job to another and thus establish a nonstandard type of lifestyle, of "work and nonwork uses of time" (ibid.). What this suggests is that a) there are two completely different categories: voluntary contingency and involuntary contingency; b) it is necessary to better understand what makes some people prefer contingent labor. In order to do that, one should study their situation diachronically, in a lifetime, as well as along the lines of class analysis and power structure. Common sense itself suggests clearly enough that there is an irreducible difference between wanting to work contingently and being forced to do so. Voluntary contingency is contingently contingent; the involuntary type is necessarily so. Blending the two into the same category only creates philosophical and political confusion. This confusion gives the impression that individuals can choose freely—and this is indeed what neoliberal ideology wants: we are all free, in all senses, including that of working contingently or not. In reality, to offer an analogy, the fact that some people may want to sell themselves into slavery does not justify slavery as such, as an institution. Thus, in studying the phenomenon of contingent labor, we should not be deceived by the presence of voluntary or contingent contingency. We should instead focus on involuntary or necessary contingency—also because the former type is often a misguided, ideological travesty of the latter.

Thus, contingent academic labor, like most forms of contingent labor, appears as a form of bound labor. As such, it should be abolished by converting it into full-time, permanent labor; that is, converting the pseudo-jobs of contingency into real, *good* jobs. As Eileen Schell says, it is the responsibility of the institution to "find ways to offer ethical and equitable working conditions" (1998: 14). Although bringing about real changes may be like "moving a mountain" (ibid.), the fact remains that the good life, equal to a situation of social justice, is unattainable without a good job. This can only be a situation in which labor is free. But free labor can only be labor without sovereignty. Then, the time of not-labor will also be free—free, for instance, from the anxiety that comes with constant insecurity; free for the pursuit of all other meaningful activities (themselves part of the full concept of labor) without which the full and rich development of one's potentialities is impossible. The injustice that thwarts one's labor and one's time also disables one's potentialities. In the construction of this form of disability, it is easy to discern the violence of sovereignty, the compliance of the law (which comes from that same violence, as Walter Benjamin says), the obsession with a regime of productivity that grows only insofar as more servility and poverty is created. In the particular context we are dealing with here, it is the sovereignty of capital in its neoliberal specificity (as the power that has also restructured the university), which is of concern. This means that the case of higher education is nothing but an instantiation of a general tendency investing society as a whole—a general tendency, or perhaps an accomplished fact: the subsumption of all human activity *as productive labor* under capital. As Peter McLaren notes, "neoliberal educational policy operates from the premise that education is primarily a subsector of the economy" (2005: 31). This is, of course, part of the *general illumination* that neoliberalism is. As David Harvey says: "Neoliberalization has meant, in short, the financialization of everything" (2005: 33). And it is here good to remark that the critique of the logic of productivity presented in this book is not merely a critique of production. It is a critique of capitalist production, particularly at its present, neoliberal stage, and thus a critique of financialization. Certainly, to go back to the question of education, there are situations in which exchange of ideas and learning outside the logic of sovereignty, productivity, and "the financialization of daily life" (Martin 2002b) take place: to name a few, the Brecht Forum in New York; the Institute for the Critical Study of Society in Oakland (at the Niebyl-Proctor Marxist Library); bookstores like Modern Times in San Francisco and Bluestockings in New York; community centers and study and affinity groups; and the transnational, online edu-factory project. In these situations, through open lectures, reading and study groups, collective exploration of new ideas and dialogue, an anti-hierarchical, horizontal, network of relations can be envisioned and initiated. In this sense, one may also mention the importance, in theory and practice, of revolutionary critical pedagogy described and defended by McLaren (2005). But at the institutional and policed level, what prevails is the system of injustice that the logic of productivity and sovereignty necessarily engenders. The fact that *knowledge* is the produced commodity does not alter the fundamental truth that injustice (exploitation, violence, death) is its substance, just as it is the substance of any commodity.

The question of justice, which I treated in an abstract way in Chapter 1, comes back here (as well as in the next chapter) in a more concrete form. In fact, the aim of a critique of sovereignty and productivity is to highlight the concrete possibility of social justice. At the outset of his essay, the introduction to *Chalk Lines*, Randy Martin explicitly links sovereignty and labor while speaking of Clinton's educational policy in the late 90s: a signal, Martin says, that "educational access and attainment are . . . to link labor and citizenship in a renewed covenant of the sovereign subject" (1998b, p. 4). The truth of this is that "education means business" (p. 5); the end of education is work. Education in general, and higher education in particular, is about increasing productivity (p. 9). Martin says, "Education is merely an extension of labor-market discipline" (p. 12). And the nerve of discipline is sovereign power.

Speaking of the notion of academic labor, Martin refers to the 1996 Yale graduate students' strike, which "forced recognition that a category of human activity was, in fact, labor" (p. 18). As labor, it also must exit the illusion within which it often hides itself, the logic of exceptionalism, and recognize the collective dimension, the "we" Martin says, which characterizes it. Of course, this will be more easily recognized, and with great difficulties hopefully accomplished, by the most exploited segments of the academic workforce. Martin says:

> Insofar as we continue to invest in the mythos of academic hierarchy . . . we will continue to be implicated in the manufacture of our own relative surplus population. (pp. 18–19)

For Martin, this is a matter of choosing between use value and exchange value within the specific field of education, but more generally within the context of work, and life. He continues:

> At stake is not only access to increased disciplinary requirements but also what forms of human association, cooperation, affiliation, and collective fantasy can be accessed through education. (p. 19)

The discourse on the end of domination and hierarchy within the academy signals, beyond the triumphant "universalizing managerialism" (ibid.), or perhaps across it, the possibility of redefining the meaning of academic work (and of work in general) along truly universal lines. In fact, education should not be the privilege of the closed and policed institution, and it should certainly not be geared toward increasing the productivity that hammers and deepens the system of social injustice at the global level and alienates humanity. Recognizing that "what goes on in the university is *work*" (p. 16) is also a step toward changing the idea and the reality of both the university and the work going on within it.

This radical need—changing the university, creatively redrawing the *chalk lines* that define it, in Martin's metaphor—is something that goes well beyond the world of higher education and has to do with fundamental issues of social justice. We will see this again when speaking about the community colleges, with which Martin is also concerned (p. 6).

As Gary Rhoades and Sheila Slaughter say, "Universities are not just servants of or suppliers to the marketplace. They are active players in the marketplace" (1998: 38). They occupy a central position in the reproduction of capitalist relations, and in doing this they forgo their original aspiration of fostering public reason—they become sites for "the pursuit of private profit" (p. 39). Speaking of the "managed professionals," Rhoades and Slaughter say:

> In our view, if faculty are to regain some influence over their work lives and workplace, they must move beyond the ideological and political position of being independent professionals and connect their work and their professional ideology to the interests of the immediate communities and broader publics that they serve. (p. 51)

In fact, as Harney and Moten say, "most professors in the United States are part of the service sector proletariat" (1998: 155)—although, they add, this is not how these professors would see themselves. Recognizing "what it means to do academic labor" (p. 158), rather than cling to a notion of "social positioning" (ibid.) in an empty structure such as the corporate university, which denies all authentic subjectivity and only fosters productivity, competition, and, in the case of those who lack security, failure, is extremely important if the intention is to regain the social and cultural dignity implied in the passage by Rhoades and Slaughter above. The equivocal nature of academic work can also be detected in the language used to describe it. Harney and Moten give a precise sense of this when they render "academic standards" as "levels of production" and "collegiality" as "flexibility and docility on the job" (p. 164).

The principles of flexibility and docility become particularly important in the case of contingent labor (often referred to as adjunct labor). Vincent Tirelli provides a very good description of the typical adjunct situation, especially at the City University of New York (CUNY), where he works. More generally, speaking of "flexible labor and the reserve army of the unemployed," he says:

> Those who make up the contingent faculty workforce are a diverse group, but they share the lower-tier status and all the indignities that accompany it . . . [F]rom whatever place they enter this system, they all share the experience of second-class citizens in the university. (p. 190)

If the notion that one is actually working is in general denied in the university, in the case of the adjuncts what is (this time institutionally) denied is the fact of holding a job. Just like the sovereign, contingent labor is also defined by the modality of being inside and outside at the same time. However, this time the definition is not a sign of power, but of its lack.

The Ambiguous Condition of Contingent Academic Labor

If there is in general no recognition that what goes on in the academy is labor, in the case of contingent labor this becomes not a sign of social positioning, but rather of a marginalization that, in the long run, takes a serious toll on the economic stability of the individual workers, but also on their psychological, existential and *human* well-being. Bill Readings remarked that "few communities are more petty and vicious than university faculties" (1996: 180). Yet the university is still considered "the potential model for free and rational discussion" (ibid.). In fact, what goes on within it is something different, and certainly, from the viewpoint of contingent labor the exact negation of those romantic ideals, one might naively still associate with this *ruined institution* (cf. Readings: 169). Readings' study of the corporate university very much relates to the denial of the actual living labor expended within it. This is evident particularly in his emphasis on the fact that, with its *idea of excellence*,

> the university is not just *like* a corporation; it *is* a corporation. Students in the University of Excellence are not *like* customers; they *are* customers.[10] (p. 22)

But academic labor is still seen as a form of higher vocation, an activity one engages in as one does in, say, writing poetry. And this argument is often used to dismiss the political concern of contingent academic workers: You are not really exploited; what you do is part of a higher mission; it is not a vulgar job. In a similar vein, contingent labor is often seen as the labor of "apprentices," and this is "a means of ignoring and denying their real relationship to the university" (Tirelli 1998: 192). In reality, Tirelli notes, "most part-time faculty . . . have many years of experience, are not in any kind of mentoring relationship," and all they lack is a real job and a career path (ibid.). Under neoliberal policies, that is, under the "corporate domination of society" (McLaren 2005: 30), this lack of permanence is necessary to the university in order to provide that *flexibility* that eventually burns out the adjunct. According to Tirelli, this is also used, at least rhetorically, as a justification for denying them a job: "they eventually get 'burned out' and need to be replaced" (1998: 192).

In his important, militant book on contingent labor, which he describes as "a manual for action," Joe Berry calls this flexibility "the academic equivalent of day labor" (2005: xii). Among many important points made in *Reclaiming the Ivory Tower*, perhaps the most important is Berry's political understanding of contingent academic labor as a labor force and as a movement:

> We are part of a huge campus labor force that has created a vibrant labor movement, including clerical and technical workers, grad employees, food service, maintenance, and housekeeping workers, skilled trades people, and academic professionals of all sorts. (p. xiii)

He continues:

> This movement has spanned the entire spectrum of post-secondary education, from urban adult educators teaching ESL to contingent professors teaching graduate students at the most elite universities. (Ibid.)

From my point of view, this analysis is more important than those dealing with the changes taking place at research universities: it is more immediately political and at the center of the question of social justice. Berry has a clear sense that contingent faculty work, and do *good work*, but that they lack *good jobs* (p. xiv). The importance of this point cannot be overestimated, for too often does one hear, even from well-meaning and informed people, that for a variety of reasons the quality of the work done by contingents is not as good as its counterpart. However, the judgment is made without taking into account the essentially different conditions under which these two groups do their work. Indeed, anyone who has firsthand experience of teaching contingently knows that *the problem is not the quality of work, but the effort required to produce that quality.*[11] Thus, adjuncts and part-timers have to overexert themselves in order to reach the same quality level produced by others. It is because of this overexertion that they often also ruin their health and destroy their lives.

Like many others writing on this issue, Berry also points out the question of the corporatization of the university, of the fact that higher education is in the service of capital. He says that this has happened both internally, as higher education institutions conformed to the rest of the corporate world, and externally, through a restructuring of the university to serve private business. He also makes the point that students are now customers to be trained as workers rather than citizens to be educated (p. 4).

As for the faculty workforce, it

> represents one of the few recent instances in the United States economy (another is taxi driving) where an entire occupation has been converted from permanent career status to temporary, often part-time, status in the space of a single generation of workers. (Ibid.)

He also points out that at this point in time the term "adjuncts" to denote part-time and temporary academic workers, now the majority, is not really accurate; he refers to the entire group as contingents, which emphasizes this faculty workforce's "permanent lack of permanence" (ibid.).[12]

In addition to the injustice permanently experienced by the contingent workforce, another more general social and political problem (but one that makes administrations rejoice) is the erosion of tenure for academics. This entails a loss of "the freedom to search for and speak the truth as one sees it (academic freedom)." Berry concludes:

> Now that most teachers in higher education have neither tenure nor the prospect of even getting it, administrators and trustees have won a great victory. They have much greater flexibility to hire and fire as program and enrollment demands, and the faculty as a whole is less able to set the terms of its own work. (p. 5)

Rather than convert non-tenure contingent positions into tenure ones, which would be one of the solutions to the situation of contingent academic labor, the opposite tendency has asserted itself.

For Berry, contingency is the "most significant of our unprofessional conditions . . . To put it bluntly the employer's flexibility is our uncertainty" (p. 9). He mentions some important aspects of this uncertainty, for instance, impossible schedules, absence or inadequacy of health care, disruption of everyday life. Contingency can destroy social life and limit one's professional horizon (p. 10). In short, it is "dead-end day labor" (ibid.). Once one has entered the cycle and stayed enough time within it, it becomes very difficult (and often impossible) to find an *exit*, for

> the time and energy it takes to maintain a living at contingent academic employment, or at contingent employment outside academia, leaves no time for developing the academic capital that can keep [one] attractive on the job market. (Ibid.)

All this creates a situation in which stress is deeply and daily experienced, although it is "hard to quantify" (p. 11). Instead, the stress accumulated becomes manifest when it suddenly transforms itself into a nervous breakdown or other medical conditions (e.g., stroke, cancer), which are in turn difficult to face given the absence or inadequacy of health care or health insurance: a vicious circle—as vicious as the world of academia itself.

Another important point made by Berry has to do with the exploitation of contingent faculty's commitment to the job. This is, it seems to me, in direct contrast with other less generous views (at times coming from people who are or have been adjuncts themselves) that for various reasons castigate the behavior of most adjuncts, in a way that recalls the widespread mode of "blaming the victim." For instance, in an article that also makes some good points (and that certainly starts with a powerful and lucid denunciation of the situation of contingent academic labor), Walter Jacobsohn criticizes many part-timers and adjuncts for "passing." He says that most of them "do not want to acknowledge that the institution in which they work exploits them shamelessly, that it does not value them as members of its community" (2001: 170). According to Jacobsohn, in this state of denial, they take refuge in teaching and thus disempower themselves, as well as their students. He says:

> Teaching is not an isolated act. It takes place in a community. When part-time faculty do not acknowledge their status, they are enacting

an ideology that degrades them and their students. I call this practice "adjunct passing." (p. 171)

I have some problems with this sweeping statement. The first has to do with the meaning of "community" in this specific context. Certainly, teaching is not an isolated act because, before any other consideration, it involves the teacher and the students. The fact that it takes place in a community is already given in the original relationship of teacher and students, and of students among themselves. But what Jacobsohn probably means by community is the institution, a place which most often precisely lacks the sense of being a community. One could argue that the community needs to be built. However, contingent workers, being included and excluded at the same time, have great difficulties doing that—difficulties that are objective and subjective. The second problem is that it is not clear what acknowledging one's status as a contingent worker, as Jacobsohn requires, would be. If this entails building a position of permanent antagonism within the institution (vis-à-vis the full-timers, administrators, etc.), then the possibility of building a community is forgone and the risk of losing one's job increases. I am not against the formula of antagonism, when it has been made clear that it is a collective, not an individual, effort. In this sense, there is nothing more important than the right to strike. Jacobsohn himself gives an account of his experience with organizing a strike at Long Island University, where he worked. But at the City University of New York, for instance, a strike is made impossible by the Taylor Law. In such a situation, it is more difficult to find a viable formula of antagonism. If, on the other hand, acknowledging one's status means speaking to the students about it, one may risk being misunderstood, seeing one's authority diminished in the classroom, and perhaps being accused of doing politics for personal reasons. I think that it is a very delicate situation. Certainly, one cannot walk around with a special sign that identifies her as an adjunct. Jacobsohn speaks of "adjunct identity" (p. 172) and of how one must appropriate this identity. But I hope he means *consciousness*. The two are not the same. The latter, precisely, is the awareness I have that my work is not valued as it should be—but this perhaps only at the strictly institutional level (that is, not necessarily at the personal level, in my relationship with students and colleagues, including the full-timers). This consciousness is itself a relation, and a reflexive one, which makes room for the determination of a tort and the affirmation of one's right to exit, a *right to flight*.[13] In the sense of Kierkegaard, it is the relation between the reductionism of necessity and finitude and the escape toward possibility and infinitude.[14] Identity, on the other hand, nails one in a position from which there is no escape—unless one looks at it dialectically as the identity of identity and non-identity, similar to Kierkegaard's notion of relation (despite Kierkegaard's opposition to Hegel); but then it is of no simple identity that one is speaking. Yet appropriating the adjunct identity would be a simple and reductionist operation. In reality, one is and is not an adjunct. Of course, the slave, too, was at one and the same time not a slave, and this not abstractly, but concretely; hence, the possibility of rebellion. Indeed, this is true of any identity, incapable of completely encapsulating the being of an individual. The problem here is not "passing" for what one is not, that is, an adjunct or part-timer passing for a "real" professor; rather, the question is that of not being reduced and fixed in a position, a category from which there is no exit and which must in fact be destroyed. The attitude, therefore, must be critical. And if there is appropriation, it also must include nonappropriation. Of course, the adjunct knows he is an adjunct. But why should he assume that as his identity? And where? In which context and circumstances? In the classroom, it would be counterproductive. In the department, it would be simply antagonistic—uselessly so at best, dangerously at worst. The truth is that the invisibility of the adjunct, with which Jacobsohn also deals, the invisibility of the contingent worker in general, is something real, objective, institutional. In this sense, this invisibility itself is visible.[15] At CUNY, for instance, a large public institution, there are about nine thousand adjuncts and part-timers and eight thousand full-timers. The invisibility of the first group cannot go unnoticed. In fact, it is noticed in many ways, and the principle of its presence is justified with subtle arguments—thus, the notion that, if properly used, adjuncts enrich (in the academic, not in the economic sense) the institution. An article from *The Chief: The Civil Employees' Weekly* (November 2, 2007), posted on the PSC website, quotes PSC President Barbara Bowen in this sense:

> Ms. Bowen said the aim [of the union] in New York is to get the ratio to about 70 percent full-time and 30 percent part-time in line with CUNY's goal [that is, the administration's goal]. "Adjuncts have always enriched college curricula when they are actually used as adjuncts," she said. She gave the example of a poet who teaches a course on literature or a lawyer who teaches a course at a law school. "Then the students have the benefit of the experience of a practitioner," she said. "Then the person is truly an adjunct to the academic program of a college." (Kolodner 2007)

In a time of trouble, such as nowadays at CUNY, the problematic aspect of such statements becomes evident. In principle, we can agree that having practitioners working as adjuncts may be a good and resourceful addition to a program; however, this can only be understood as the exception, not the rule. The ratio eyed by both the administration and the union (70 percent full-time and 30 percent part-time) is far from being fair and equitable. Thirty percent would still be a disproportionate number of adjuncts and part-timers. In reality, for a situation of exception, much less than 3 percent would suffice. The union should distance itself from the rhetoric of innocence and piety typical of the administration: adjuncts are an asset; too bad the situation has gotten out of hand. In fact, carried away by one's own rhetoric, one might start seeing more poets and lawyers than there are in actuality. As a matter of fact, this demonstrates the principle of the visibility of the adjuncts' invisibility. After all, it is a general principle of neoliberal policies that it is good to have contingent labor: a sign of the competence of a company's administrators.[16] In reality, the way many CUNY adjuncts and part-timers feel these days, exploited by the administration, unaided by the union, says a lot about their impossible identity. They cannot simply be adjuncts because being that is like being *another* (e.g., the poet, the lawyer); yet they cannot be *that other* because they are reduced to being what they are, with no exit, no escape. Their professional commitment, as well as their identity, is romanticized on the one hand (as that of the poet, the lawyer, etc.); it is dismissed and derided on the other (as that of the apprentice, of the one whose work lacks quality, or of the one who did not quite made it—and will never make it).[17]

To return to Berry, we see that professional commitment is exchanged for "unpaid departmental work, . . . unprofessional wages and little respect, except from our students" (2005: 11). Moreover, this is

> also used to discipline contingent faculty. Employers imply that if one behaves "professionally," one has a greater chance of being re-hired, or even possibly hired into a [full-time] position. (Ibid.)

He adds, "This pressure to act like a full professional naturally exacts a psychological toll as well" (ibid.). And here a new remark must be made as to the question of the *quality* of contingent academic labor. This question often comes up in a very ambiguous way. Although those who raise it may intend to address the poor structural quality within the institution, *of* the institution and *because of* it, it does at the same time seem to imply that the work of adjuncts and part-timers is inherently poor. In fact, contingent workers, as

Berry also notes, do much more than their counterparts; they must, in order to keep up and offer their best. Thus the quality of their work is, generally speaking, excellent. As Bousquet also notes,

> the problem is not with the intellectual quality, talent, or commitment of the individual persons working on a nonprofessional basis; it's the degraded circumstances in which higher education management compels them to work (2008: 4)

In order to keep a high quality despite such degradation, they must ruin themselves: physically, psychologically, and professionally. In truth, what the institution does is injure them, harm their potential. For instance, many promising scholars (after years of abnegation and study) will reach a point when they have to renounce (or realize that they have already renounced) their aspirations—for lack of time, energy, resources. The time comes when it is no longer possible to catch up. What the institution does is consume their lives, destroy their dreams and concrete possibilities. When the failure in their personal lives, of which many commentators speak, looms clear, it also becomes irreversible, and there is no way of undoing the grave injustice done. In this sense, the institution is guilty of moral delinquency and, truly, of a human rights infringement, that is, the right to economic and human security and to the free and full development of one's potentialities (and this fact, which is true of contingent labor in general, should become a matter of concern for international law, specifically the International Labor Organization). For, if we take seriously (as we must) the notion that each individual life has irreplaceable dignity, and if this dignity is thwarted whenever one's potentiality is compromised and disabled, with the dire consequence that one's life is reduced to the finitude of powerlessness and servitude, of unfreedom and nothingness, then speaking in this context of delinquency and crime, of defying morality and disfiguring humanity, is no rhetorical exaggeration.

Interestingly enough, poor quality and failure are not traits of the immediate performance of the contingent worker, for, as we have seen, her performance is generally excellent. They are instead aspects of what Bousquet (2002) calls, in a *Social Text* article, "the waste product of graduate education." Both in said article and in his recent book, he says: "Cheap teaching is a social crime and failure" (2002: 98; 2008: 43). This is extremely important and absolutely true. Cheap teaching ruins society as a whole. Its quality is poor in the sense that it is reversed as such within society, that is, as the sad product of superexploited labor. This teaching is a failure in the subjective sense that it destroys the life of the contingent worker, but also in the objective sense according to which society itself fails. As I have noted above, Berry also argues against the claim of some researchers and administrators that "contingents are actually poorer teachers." He says: "What is clear is that it is a much greater struggle for contingent faculty to do their job well than it is for their [full-time] colleagues" (2005: 15). The question of the quality of education vis-à-vis the use of "cheap" labor has also been a concern of the American Federation of Teachers (AFT) (see Lundy, Roberts, and Becker 2006: 126). However, it is always important to disambiguate the whole relation: cheap labor/poor quality. This labor is cheap only insofar as it is not paid adequately, it has no security, and it is superexploited—certainly not for inherent reasons of its own. Moreover, it is cheap for the employer, but it is not cheap for the worker. In fact, the worker, having to reproduce her labor capacity, must pay a higher price for it than she gets in return. And I say this literally, since often one must resort to borrowing money in order to live. The relation cheap labor/poor quality becomes then the relation superexploitation / debt (with the corollary of stress, illness, disrespect, etc.).

We have already seen the importance of the fact, stressed by many writers, that academics are workers. This is of course particularly true of contingent faculty. We have also seen how workers' rights should be understood as human rights. And in the case of the contingent workforce this recognition is particularly urgent. We do not need to stress again the fact that work, labor, is the power constituting the social. But a labor sickened by a regime of superexploitation cannot produce a healthy society. It will produce a sick society, like the one we have now. Only free labor will be able to bring about a free society. As we have seen in the previous chapters, all forms of sovereignty over labor must end for this to become a concrete possibility. What is at stake here is not simply the question of higher education, nor of the contingent workforce. This is of course an extremely important and urgent question; yet, it is one case of a much more widespread situation, that is, the exploitation and superexploitation of labor in general. What is at stake, really, is human dignity, the destiny of humanity, social justice. Whenever labor, understood as all life activity, is subjugated, the dignity of individuation is lost. The relation of subjugation and servility, which we have seen in particular in Chapter 3, must be highlighted in those areas where, because of the rhetoric of innocence I mentioned above, it seems to be completely absent, such as in academia.

Among others, Berry makes the point that contingent faculty "are now just workers" (2005: 12). He also distinguishes, more sharply than others, between contingent and noncontingent workers: "Many of those considered by higher administration as 'faculty' are, to us, 'bosses'" (p. 13).[18] This is true even when individual full-timers are, as is often the case, sympathetic to the situation of contingents. Of course, the power relation is structurally built in the institution. For instance, whereas contingents are regularly *observed* by full-timers, a situation in which contingents *also observe* other contingents *and* full-timers would count as outrageous. Contingents are observed by noncontingents, that is, by their bosses.[19]

Berry's task is to build a movement able to "change the conditions of contingency and thereby change all of higher education—and perhaps the labor movement itself in the process" (p. 17). This movement needs to challenge both the proletarianization of the new faculty, due to the current corporatization in the academy (similar, Berry says, to the introduction of Taylor's "scientific management" in industry), and the "mixed conscious-ness" built up by contingents, which leads them "to pursue, sometimes for years and even decades, the search for individual solutions" (p. 18). Instead, it is important to "transform a primitive and individual rebel-liousness into something collective" (ibid.). This requires that one focus, not on the notion of merit, but on the notion of labor. In fact, "the objec-tive fact that we are now workers allows us to join the world of the broader labor movement, and most of our students who are working-class people themselves" (ibid.).

For Berry the question of organizing is taking a new shape in the corpo-rate university. He says that

> while in some ways the difference between FTTT [full-time tenured and tenure-track] faculty and contingent faculty is greater than ever, in other ways the forces acting upon both groups have created the basis for a firm alliance. (p. 22)

Obviously, the conditions for the alliance do not imply its actual existence. And there are many reasons why this alliance needs careful and detailed organizing—one of these reasons being the reticence of many full-timers to share their goals with the part-timers. However, for Berry, such an alliance would add a lot to the struggle and benefit both groups, full-timers and part-timers (p. 23).

But the most important question is that of respect and dignity. Among the signs of disrespect Berry also sees the "lack of names in class schedules and catalogs" (p. 28). Contingents, moreover, have no office of their own—a situation that is not satisfactorily explained by the fact that they are contingents. Berry also says:

> One seldom recognized aspect of the exploitation of contingent faculty is that in addition to doing the same work in the classroom as the FTTT faculty, we must also maintain "professional behavior" despite our invisible status within the institution. This emotional work imposed upon us is draining because not only is it required but it is also completely unsupported and unacknowledged. And this is just another way in which we are placed in a position of superexploiting ourselves in order to do the job. (Ibid.)

There is here the making of a *double consciousness*, "similar to what W.E.B. Du Bois described for African Americans, who have to maintain a dual social face" (ibid.). He continues by addressing a theme similar to the one addressed by Jacobsohn, as well as others. That is the theme of the "adjunct identity." However, more careful than Jacobsohn, Berry understands the difficulties of contingent faculty, for instance, the fear some (or many) might experience to reveal "their true status to students for fear of losing respect and the ability to teach effectively" (ibid.). And the same can be said, Berry notes, of the relationship contingent workers have to the rest of academia.[20] In this sense, Berry looks at the problem from a human/existential point of view (in the sense one might say of Kierkegaard, who always underlines the fear, the anxiety, the distress). This is very important, for it would be wrong to ask this shadow workforce to unduly expose itself as a ghost, a deviation from the norm, only to find out that its powerlessness and servility increase thereby. It is important to remember that the policed university, just as any other institution, has no compassion, and that it will do anything in its power to crush any movement that challenges its sovereignty. By this I do not mean to imply that it is useless to organize. In fact, it is a necessity and a priority. We must organize first of all for the right to strike when it is prohibited, for this prohibition denies labor its dignity and freedom. Secondly, we must draw the attention of international law to the grave injustices done to labor, that is, to the constituting power of the social, the source of common wealth. In fact, one cannot expect much from the pettiness of any institution and its regulations, nor can one expect anything but fierce resistance and irrational regulations from city laws, state laws, and national laws. Regulation is very important, but for it to be fair it must proceed from the most disinterested level, and that is, at the present time, the level of international law. This would actually be an interesting application of the principle of subsidiarity I treated at the end of Chapter 1. Without a recognition of the human rights dimension of the issue of contingency, all one can get is the right to a less crowded office, to an increase in wages, et cetera. One would certainly not be able to formulate thereby the most fundamental question, usually passed under silence: what precisely justifies the almost universally accepted notion that contingent labor, because of its contingency, can be exploited? It is as if, inherent in contingent labor, there were not simply the formula of its exploitability and exploitation but also the legal and moral justification for this fact. What I am saying is that even in those cases of voluntary contingency (which are often equivocal, as I have noted above) economic and human security should be guaranteed; this is evidently truer in the many more numerous instances of involuntary contingency. The notion that any form of labor might be exploited must be removed from a thinking that thinks a better world, a world that makes room for a better thinking. That is, without this removal and elimination, without the fall of sovereignty, no discourse on social justice and human rights can really make sense, really be sincere.

No change is possible without organization, but this runs into problems of individuality and everydayness that cannot be overlooked. Berry says, "The main obstacles to self-organization among contingent faculty are fear, fatalism, and ignorance" (p. 105). However, Berry also challenges the notion of the leader. For him, the right position in order to have a good political organization is: "We are all leaders" (p. 108). This is indeed important because very often what happens is that the political organization takes on the same logic of sovereignty it ought to combat. And there are those who, while professing a progressive and even revolutionary ideology, are only too eager to posit themselves as the leaders and managers at the expense of the real movement, of the improvements that could be made in the political struggle for the common good. Berry's book is also important in that it provides practical suggestions on how to organize—suggestions that take into account both the objective limitations of contingent faculty, that is, isolation, fear of retaliation from the administration, et cetera, but also a critical stance vis-à-vis power. The latter, it seems to me, is a position whose importance can be appreciated along the lines (within the Zapatista tradition) of Holloway's discourse on anti-power (see Chapter 3).

Perhaps more important is the way in which the actual struggle against constituted power within the institution can take place. This is due to the fact that often the option of a strike is unavailable and at times even collective bargaining is against the law (p. 116). These are both examples of a political and social crudity that needs to be challenged and altered, and I have called attention to the human rights dimension involved in this. Berry also makes the point of the legal constraints on the ability to organize and of the imperative to go beyond them. This is in fact the struggle inherent in, produced by, the logic of sovereignty itself.

The fundamental point with respect to the question of organization has been made by many, including Berry; that point is that organization needs to work at the level of the constitution of a movement capable of overcoming the present situation of superexploitation. In an interesting essay in which they interview participants in the 1996 Yale strike, Corey Robin and Michelle Stephens clearly phrase the either/or faced today:

> Either we hope for the best and depend on the good intention of those who are driving these trends [to corporatization], or we organize ourselves into a concerted, national movement that will force administrators across the country to make the necessary reforms. (1997: 78)

The organization of this movement must actualize itself and act at the local as well as national *and international* level. I repeat that the international or transnational moment should also be understood in the sense of starting to think in terms of global social justice and universal ethics, that is, beyond national sovereignties, which are too often themselves the participants in the system of superexploitation.

The Work of Students

No aspect of the question of social justice and for the good life (including the problem of inadequate or no education) can be left to the whimsical and anarchic movements of capitalist growth and the national laws implicated in it. Evidently, economic growth does not guarantee social well-being. The point is also made by John Levin in a recent, important book on community college students in the United States. At the outset of his study, Levin says that while being acknowledged as the world leader in many fields and endeavors, the United States "lags behind other countries in the more humanitarian domains" (2007: 1). He focuses on the question of justice—"the conflict of justice and neoliberalism," as his title says—in order to give the universal measure of a reality constructed and justified according to "the needs of the nation-state or the state or the community" (p. 5). The basic point, similar to Paul Willis's in *Learning to Labor* (1977), is that students in underprivileged institutions "are denied justice" (Levin 2007: 3).

Levin's book is relevant to our discourse because it shows the link between learning and working from the point of view of students. The claim is that community college students are denied justice "both within their institution and as an outcome of their education" (p. 4). This is another way of saying that within the world of higher education in the United States, large groups of people have their potentialities disabled, that learning is understood only in terms of training for the specific aims and interests of capital and its institutions. In contrast to the common reductionist view of students as simply customers, in a more complex manner Levin says that students "become both commodities and consumers—sources of revenues and products to be sold" (p. 5). Obviously, this reality, which is a general tendency of society, becomes more evident in the world of the community college, which "is *de facto* an institution for nontraditional students because it serves the most disadvantaged populations in higher education" (p. 11). Levin also notes the importance of the presence of people with disabilities within these populations. In this sense, going to the bottom of the issue of injustice within higher education, he identifies the main problem in the fact that these students find themselves in conditions of *segregation* and *beyond the margins*. He says:

> While mainstream community college students might conform to the human capital model of the community college, suggesting that students are potential workers and thus economic investments, those students who are outside the mainstream, outside the margins, are almost invisible not only to scholars, policymakers, and government officials, but also to administrators and faculty in their institution. (p. 32)

He challenges the claim that the community college provides *open access* both because the notion of open access is not absolute (due to selection admission rules such as test score results) and because the institution is often unable and/or unwilling to *accommodate* nontraditional, disadvantaged students (p. 12). The importance of this lies in the fact that if traditional students "continue to be viewed as the norm" (p. 22), in reality nontraditional students "are now the rule, not the exception" (p. 23). It is in this context that Levin emphasizes again the issue of people with both physical and mental disabilities, whose general destination in terms of higher education is precisely the community college (p. 29). Other groups constituting the category of nontraditional students include the working poor, welfare recipients, undocumented immigrants, and ESL students (p. 30). He says:

> These students are beyond the bureaucracy: They are rarely captured in national or even state data-collection machinery; often classified as "noncredit," they also can be students who are physically separate from the mainstream in off-campus programs—at work sites, in church basements, or in prisons. Yet, they are a component of the institution that claims to be an "open access" college. (p. 32)

Applying Rawls's principle of justice as fairness, the "difference principle," and social contract theory, Levin concludes that "we can judge a nation's or a state's educational apparatus by how well it facilitates actual, not merely formal, equal opportunity for the worst-off citizen" (p. 47). However, his explicit attack on neoliberalism, that is, capitalism (p. 50), places him beyond Rawls's theoretical view of justice, on a terrain which is more immediately political—for Rawls's conception of justice does not necessarily challenge the logic of capital, but it can do so only implicitly. The need to go beyond the formal aspects of a theory of justice lies in the fact that higher education "has become a global business" (p. 52). The logic of productivity and sovereignty typical of neoliberalism is necessarily "in conflict with the needs of disadvantaged students in higher education—those who require basic skills, social education, and personal attention" (ibid.). But the new managerialism in colleges and universities, one founded upon principles of profitability and superexploitation, cannot address, let alone solve, the system of injustice it has created in the first place and upon which it rests. As Levin notes, its slogan is "better products; better profits" (p. 55). Individual labor, including the students' learning process, originally and ontologically grounded in difference, undergoes the "art of homogeneization and standardization" (ibid.); that is, in Marx's terms, it becomes abstract. With difference, identity is also lost. The dignity of individuation disappears. And this is particularly serious when at stake is an identity and an individuality that starts off with greater precariousness and fragility, such as is the case with disabilities.

Levin's critique of productivity is in line with what we have seen so far in the literature against corporatization in the university. He says:

> Learning is thus structured for economic purposes: for workforce development and for individual skills required for initial employment, retraining, or career advancement. (p. 167)

This is particularly important in the community college where "contract training has become a mainstream activity to serve business and industry" (ibid.). Consequently, the community college becomes "a vehicle of neoliberalism, appropriating the concept of lifelong learning and shaping the concept with a decidedly economic purpose" (p. 169). The euphemism "lifelong learning" serves the purpose of covering up the logic of real subsumption in the realm of knowledge production. Individuals will produce and reproduce knowledge throughout their life, but their learning is, to use Willis's expression again, only a "learning to labor," a training for the aims and interests of capitalist expansion and growth. Levin says:

> We have arrived at a society of lifelong learning, not because we have evolved to accept that learning *per se* is a defining or developmental characteristic of being human or because we have much to learn to be human and realize our capacities, but because the new economy requires us to serve its masters and to adjust to changing technical requirements. (p. 178)

It is, he continues, "an adaptation to the corporation, to the company, to the institution, to the state" (ibid.). The real aims of this process are high productivity and global competitiveness, certainly not individual formation and growth (p. 179). Because of this, instead of an "open door" or "open access," the community college becomes *exclusionary* (ibid.). Large segments of the disadvantaged populations, those who would slow down rather than hasten the pace of productivity, are excluded from the potential gains of the learning process. In the last analysis, it seems that the community college has become the central cell within higher education for the reproduction of a workforce still conditioned by the dichotomy of productivity and unproductivity: productive labor, which alone produces and increases capital, and unproductive labor, which does not. This overlooks the fact that what is often viewed as unproductive, typically the various labors of care, is very useful to society and unproductive only from the point of view of capital. Not only is it very useful to society, but also—although often undervalued—it requires exceptional skills. Such is the case with childcare, which, in the words of Eva Feder Kittay, requires "a talent as precious as an artist's" (1999: 156). She says:

> Childcare work has been viewed as one of the least skillful occupations, second only to janitorial work. To see an exceptional childcare worker engage a child dispels, in an instant, such devaluation of this oldest and most universal of women's work.[21] (Ibid.)

The main point made by Levin, the conflict of justice and neoliberalism, shows very well how the reproduction of the productive/unproductive distinction in the economic realm, of which the educational system is a vehicle, is an impediment to the flourishing of social justice. Toward the end of his study, Levin repeats: "Neoliberal ideology and its related practices are antithetical to justice for the disadvantaged populations" (2007: 193). The question of human rights, the right to human security, with which I have opened this chapter, is here central again. As I have noted, this question cannot be left to the state and its institutions, which serve and guarantee the interests of capital, but it must be viewed as a question of universal social justice, regulated by universal principles. With the notion of the public community college as "an extension of the state" (p. 185), Levin also says: "Whereas, historically, the community college has opened its doors to the underserved of society, the state was, true to neoliberal ideology, closing its doors" (p. 194).

The aim of this chapter was to look at contingent labor in the academy and the production of knowledge from the point of view of a critique of productivity and sovereignty. This critique shows the way in which labor, which, I repeat, should be understood as human activity (i.e., not simply as productive labor, wage labor, etc.), is dominated by the forces and movements of capital, superexploited, and construed as either productive or unproductive following the needs of capital itself. This mode of domination and superexploitation amounts to a violation of basic human rights, and this violation cannot be remedied by the same system that produces it. In the specific realm of knowledge production and learning, this critique also shows how basic human potentialities, the source of wealth and happiness, are deactivated, disabled, in order to enable and enhance the gears of productivity, profit, and competitiveness. Disabling potentialities has devastating consequences in the life of individuals and in society as a whole, producing pathologies that could instead be avoided from the start.[22] In fact, learning is nothing but the activation of potentialities. But learning to labor in a regime of domination and superexploitation is a path to injustice, poverty, unhappiness, unfreedom, and illness. Learning, as it is in itself, is already labor, but a form of labor that is free from sovereignty, and whose value is determined by the lack of violation toward that which is to be learned.

When the opposite is the case, the labor of teaching and learning appears as unfree, bound, and any appeal to categories such as contingency and flexibility is only a way of masking a more violent and crude reality: that there is no exit and all forms of production (in our instance, of knowledge production) are subsumed under the logic of productivity of capital. The only exit is therefore the total dismantling of this logic itself. The reference I have often made to the principles of human rights and international law should not be understood as a hope that a radical and real change might come from above. Rather, it is a way of problematizing the antinomies constituting those very spaces of institutional thinking and practice; a way of calling attention to the fact that a discourse of human dignity (of absolute urgency today) cannot prevail as long as forms of life-activity, forms of labor, continue to be exploited and oppressed. Thus it is not a mere upholding of human rights doctrine that can change things, but rather a critique of productivity and sovereignty, as well as the political actions that it engenders and from which it is sustained.

CHAPTER FIVE

Sovereign, Productive, and Efficient: The Place of Disability in the Ableist Society

❧

Look: this is my reward / For taking care of you
—Sophocles, *Antigone*

"What is that word 'menial'? I never heard it," said Edith.
"It is obsolete now," remarked her father. "If I understand it rightly,
it applied to persons who performed particularly disagreeable and
unpleasant tasks for others, and carried with it an implication of
contempt. Was it not so, Mr. West?"
—Edward Bellamy, *Looking Backward. 2000–1887*

The rule of capital through the wage compels every ablebodied person
to function, under the law of division of labor, and to function in ways
that are if not immediately, then ultimately profitable to the expansion
and extension of the rule of capital.
—Mariarosa Dalla Costa and Selma James,
The Power of Women and the Subversion of the Community

The critique of productivity and sovereignty yields a radically different concept of labor. This is the concept of labor as care, which has been recently worked out in gender and feminist philosophy. Eva Feder Kittay (1999), in particular, speaks of it as the work of dependency—a concept which, not confined to the economic sphere, has the power to redraw the map of political philosophy as a whole, as well as of the study of culture.[1] It does so by showing the falseness of the notion of the independent, fully autonomous, individual, and by replacing it with the infinitely more sensible notions that dependency is an inescapable condition of human experience and care is the only truly adequate way to relate to the fact of dependency. Typically, the independent and fully autonomous individual is male;[2] the work of dependency and care is, as typically, seen as what "naturally" belongs to women; it is, as Diemut Elizabeth Bubeck says, "women's work" (1995: 24).[3] Needless to say, this is only due to the fact that historically the work of care has been done (and it is still mostly done) by women (pp. 40–41). As Kittay also says, the fact that this type of work is "largely gendered" does not entail that it needs to be (1999: xiv).

The aim of this chapter is to show that the centrality of the concept of care requires that the logic of productivity and sovereignty be dismantled; in other words, care cannot become the new *essential difference*, the new modality of organizing political communities and society as a whole, of managing individual lives and communal situations, unless the realities of exploitation and domination are eliminated. Under such realities, care can be a bureaucratic and mechanical application of police measures, a paternalistic attitude and practice, but it could not become the adequate response to the condition of dependency—a response that includes adequate agency. Indeed, adequate agency constitutes the univocal and common ground of the carer and the cared for; in true care, they can both display and experience adequate agency—adequate not to some institutional measures of society, but to the actual conditions of their existence.[4] At the same time, the critique of productivity and sovereignty would reach a blind spot without a concept such as care, capable of offering a viable and powerful alternative to the condition of the present, and, indeed, to the history of the human adventure. It is in this sense that I review here some of the literature on the labor of care and on the question of disability (where the inescapability of dependence and the necessity of care become most evident). That is, I try to think care, dependency, and disability in the light of the critique of productivity and sovereignty and, at the same time, confirm the importance of such a critique from the point of view of the centrality of care and the inescapability of the condition of dependency, which includes what is problematically called disability.[5]

In *Labor of Fire*, I indicated—along the lines of a concretely utopian thinking—that after productive labor (as the labor that produces and increases capital), the time/space of creative labor would open up. Yet, the category of creative labor did not acquire there a specific connotation. It was only put in relation to its most obvious occurrence, artistic labor; yet it was not given the amplitude required by an activity responsible for the constitution of the social as a whole. In reality, creative labor, and this includes the specificity of art, is nothing but labor as care; or, put it another way, care is the result of the merging of labor and art. This approach effectively challenges the view that both art and care are forms of unproductive labor, or rather it problematizes the productive/unproductive labor dichotomy. With respect to artistic labor, a similar analysis can be found in the recent work of José Maria Durán (2008).

In volume 3 of *Capital*, Marx distinguishes between freedom within the realm of necessity and the (true) realm of freedom.

> The realm of freedom really begins only where labour determined by necessity and external expediency ends; it lies by its very nature beyond the sphere of material production proper. (1981: 958–959)

However, he soon makes clear that these two spheres or realms are not, as they would be in a metaphysical scheme, completely separate and independent from one another; rather, in a way that recalls the base/superstructure model, freedom (even "true" freedom) always remains grounded in necessity. In the following passage, Marx says what freedom is when it remains within the realm of necessity and what true freedom is *beyond* necessity. Interestingly, even the second moment, of true freedom, is not completely detached from necessity and material production but it *flourishes* on the basis of it:

> Freedom, in this sphere [i.e., the sphere of necessity and material production], can consist only in this, that socialized man, the associated producers, govern the human metabolism with nature in a rational way, bringing it under their collective control instead of being dominated by it as a blind power; accomplishing it with the least expenditure of energy and in conditions most worthy and appropriate for their human nature. *But this always remains a realm of necessity. The true realm of freedom*, the development of human powers as an end in itself, *begins beyond it, though it can only flourish with this realm of necessity as its basis.* The reduction of the working day is the basic prerequisite. (p. 959; emphasis added)

We are reading about the inescapability of necessity and dependency. The two spheres, of necessity and freedom, are not stages that are at one and the same time separated yet connected by a transition; rather, they belong together insofar as necessity itself is socially reappropriated, that is, insofar as it returns from the realm of alienation and death and becomes proper to the human condition, structural to the good life for everybody. There cannot be true freedom unless freedom itself is first found in necessity and necessity redefined in freedom. The communal positing of needs for the sake of liberating time and grounding human dignity is the overcoming of the necessity posited by capital. Only on the basis of this, can true freedom flourish. This flourishing, "the development of human powers as an end in itself," is nothing but the flourishing of *time* and *care*. Indeed, time and care are the most important concepts in the above quoted passage. When necessity is *collectively controlled* instead of being a *blind dominating power*, time is liberated and true care becomes possible. Thus, Marx ends the passage with the notion of the reduction of the working day as a prerequisite. And indeed, as Dalla Costa and James say, "[t]o 'have time' means to work less" (1972: 40).

It is evident that all labor does not end with the liberation of time. In the *Grundrisse*, speaking of automated labor, Marx says that, at one point, the contradiction created by machinery (i.e., the simultaneous creation of *disposable time* and its conversion into surplus value) can no longer be contained. Then, "the mass of workers must themselves appropriate their own surplus labour" (1973: 708). He continues with one of the few descriptions in his work of the labor of the future:

> Once they have done so—and *disposable time* thereby ceases to have an *antithetical* existence—then, on one side, necessary labour time will be measured by the needs of the social individual, and, on the other, the development of the power of social production will grow so rapidly that, even though production is now calculated for the wealth of all, *disposable time* will grow for all. For real wealth is the developed productive power of all individuals. (Ibid.)

Although Marx is here using the expression "productive power," it might be important to note that "productive" has nothing to do with the logic of productivism, but is instead related to the creative dimension of labor. This labor is called *productive* either by equivocation or because the word *productive* itself has returned to its originary meaning of *bringing forth*—thus, inclusive of the labor which, under capitalism, is known as *unproductive* (typically, "women's work").[6] Even more important is the fact that the *growth* of disposable (free) time will make it possible for individuals to *care* for those activities and situations that remain beyond the range and power of automated labor. In fact, disposable time cannot be a time in which one does nothing at all. Rather, it is the time in which time itself grows, the time of fertility (to recall Neruda),[7] poetic time, when the doing is done in accord with the spirit of the end, which is the doing's own essence.

It is the time of care, when the subject and object *merge*, not into the one, but into the other—other from subject and object alike. This is not the other of alienation and antithesis, but that of the return to the proper. Yet, upon the return, there is no rest. Most of the work is yet to be done. The freedom with which the return was accomplished finds a new necessity in the object of care, as impenetrable now to the logic of automation as it was earlier ignored and disdained by the traditional logic of productivity and sovereignty.

Obviously, Marx's analysis of automated labor points in the direction of the labor of care only implicitly—whereas liberated time is explicitly thematized by him. As Bubeck notes, there is "a part of necessary labour that Marx obviously overlooked completely because it certainly does not lend itself to being mechanized or automated." She continues: "I mean (a part of) that part of necessary labour that is overwhelmingly performed by women—women's work" (1995: 24). Bubeck divides this work into three categories: housework, child care, and caring work. Focusing on care, she says, "Completely automated 'care' for the needy is an abandonment of people to machines. It ceases to be care" (p. 29).

The work of care has the liberation of time as a precondition. It is the labor that must be done even when most of the remaining necessary labor is accomplished *with the least expenditure of energy* by means of machinery. In this sense, it is the time and labor that flourishes in the true realm of freedom—a labor that has human welfare as its main aim, that is, the *development of human powers as an end in itself.* For the end of care is the activation and development of human potentialities, not for the sake of profit, but rather for the sake of letting the dignity of individuation emerge in full visibility, outside of the dichotomy of norm and exception, productivity and unproductivity, paid and unpaid labor. As Bubeck says, it "involves human beings, carers and those cared for as human beings, communicating and interacting with each other" (p. 29). This labor must be highly creative, and indeed constitute an art, for it

> requires the exercise of our most distinctive capacities: language and thought and a complex emotional life which allows us to empathize with and understand others and meet their very individual needs. (Ibid.)

The fact that care has been historically seen as the work of women does not imply that this should continue to be the case in the future society of liberated time and labor. For Bubeck, the "theory of women's work as *care*" only shows the historically unjust treatment and exploitation of women (p. 11). Obviously, "women's work" can also be (and to an extent is) performed by men. This has been the case historically and even more so presently, particularly in the regime of flexibility and contingency characteristic of globalization, where the problem is recognized as the feminization of labor.[8] Whether it is performed by women (which is overwhelmingly the case) or by men, women's work, the labor of care, always remains in a state of super-exploitation. Although its social importance is seldom recognized, for it is taken for granted that someone (usually women) will do it, the labor of care, Bubeck says,

> could be seen as a paradigm or model of social interaction, and *persona carans* could replace *homo economicus* as the individual theorized in social and political theory. (p. 12)

This is a very important point, which stresses the possibility of rethinking the fundamental fact of the economy as a total social fact. The *nomos* of the *oikos*, that is, the way in which the space and time of life must be run, the management of a dwelling (which has both a spatial and temporal connotation), is contained in the concept of the *caring person*. This would not simply be a description of the *household economy* in Aristotle's sense, for instance, for which women and children and slaves were totally or partially excluded from citizenship, and the household itself, just like the city-state, was a place of inclusion and exclusion, ruled by the master, husband, and father, yet truly managed and cared for by those who did not rule it. Typically, in Aristotle too, one of the central concepts is time, more precisely, the distinction between the time of necessary labor and the time liberated from that necessity. Someone will have to perform the necessary tasks: slaves in the household, common laborers in the community (1998: 1278a5–10). However, the caring person, *persona carans*, does more than perform the necessary tasks, for she is the force reinventing the community, the being-with, the merging of object and subject in the mode of care.

Bubeck's analysis shows the complexity of care: " 'Caring' can refer to an emotional state or to an activity or to a combination of the two" (1995: 127). After reviewing some traditional, broad definitions of care and caring, she offers her own, restricted definition:

> Caring for is the meeting of the needs of one person by another person where face-to-face interaction between carer and cared for is a crucial element of the overall activity and where the need is of such a nature that it cannot possibly be met by the person herself. (p. 129)

For instance, she distinguishes between care and service: "the housewife cooking a meal for her husband is providing a service, whilst her cooking the same meal for an infant would be care" (p. 132). Although Bubeck's restricted definition is very precise and useful, for the purpose of this chapter I employ a broader concept of care in order to indicate that virtually any type of work and activity might and perhaps should relate to the mode of care. Kittay stresses that care is work (1999: 30). Of course, Bubeck is right in saying that "presumably nobody would think it adequate to describe the production of a car as 'caring'" (1995: 130). Yet it is not inadequate to think of caring as a fundamental disposition of human praxis. Thus, for instance, caring for the environment is not a form of care essentially different from that which relates to a person in need (and in this sense even the production of a car falls into the problematics of care). Certainly, it is not different in terms of the disposition required of the carer, although it may entail a completely different set of activities. And although there are different types of needs, some of them met by service, others by care in a more precise and restricted sense of the word, it might be argued that a general mode of care is essential to both; that is, service itself—redefined outside the paradigm of hierarchical relations and sovereignty—requires care as its essential moment.

For Bubeck, care and activities that are an expression of love *may* coincide, although they do not need to. Restricted to activities that "meet a need which the person in care could not meet herself" (p. 134), care does not always have to have an emotional dimension. For instance, "in the public sphere, care does not require the existence of an emotional bond between carer and cared for" (ibid.). Nor are, Bubeck says, "activities and acts of an emotional bond . . . necessarily care according to my definition" (ibid.). Ofelia Schutte notes that "dependency work is work," regardless of its motivation (2002: 138).

Indeed, a *general economy of care* (I here use "general economy" in Bataille's sense),[9] cannot be exclusively concerned with one's emotions, nor with one's fundamental ethical disposition and sense of justice; it is instead a *total fact*, linking an individual to a world. However, it is precisely because of this that a broader concept of care might be more useful than a restricted one. The fact that the work of care has historically been *assigned to* women on the basis of the still now commonly accepted notion of a "natural" distinction between the genders in terms of emotionality and rationality (women being considered more emotional, men more rational) only shows that generalizing the concept of care so as to make it a prerequisite of human praxis signals the exit from a regime of productivity and sovereignty alike. As Bubeck notes, "What has characterized women's work in history so far is precisely that it has been done by women" (1995: 40). Typically, men stay aloof from the mode of care, as if by caring they might lose the essence of their masculinity. Bubeck also says:

> Women are supposedly "naturally" caring and nurturing and therefore naturally suited to do women's work. Women's work, therefore, seems to be irredeemably women's work. (pp. 40–41)

But it is evident that domination and slavish labor (that is, sovereignty and productivity) cannot end until men start doing women's work on a regular basis and women's work itself consequently ceases being women's work. This is not entirely different from the Marxian idea that revolutionizing society entails the dissolution of the proletariat as a class. Indeed, the logic is the same. The end of dominated labor equals a new distribution of labor. The reduction of the working day cannot be limited to wage labor, but it has to take into consideration the time of reproduction of that labor, the work of care, unpaid labor, "women's" work. Necessary labor (not of the necessity posited by capital, or by any other sovereign regime) must be done by all, but it can be done slowly, carefully, and creatively. The division of labor along the lines of gender is one of the most persistent and stubborn modalities of social domination. Too often, even in situations that should be characterized by progressive and open thinking and praxis, for instance among left intellectuals and activists, women's work continues to be women's work—even when occasionally performed by men. However, if the mode of care becomes the univocal and common concept of human praxis, if it is care that labor finds upon its return from alienation, that is, if labor *is* care, then caring is no longer an ancillary (although in truth structural) moment aiding the more serious occupation of production; rather, production itself becomes bringing forth in the mode of care: a creative activity, an art. It is in reality the coming together of poiesis and praxis: a poetic praxis, a practical poiesis.

As I noted in Chapter 4, Eva Feder Kittay says that some forms of caring, such as childcare, require "a talent as precious as an artist's" (1999: 156). Indeed, this might be true of most or all forms of caring. In the introduction to *The Subject of Care*, Kittay and Ellen K. Feder, who co-edited the volume, speak of caregiving in general as "a thoughtful, intentional work" (2002: 2). What has been historically considered as women's work, and devalued on that account in societies in which sovereignty pertains to men, contains within itself the seed of a future society, the future of labor. For Kittay this is the labor of dependency and care, which becomes most visible in one of the most invisible existential realities, the reality of disability, particularly of severe mental disability.

Kittay sees dependency as the inescapable condition of human life. Care is socially necessary because of the inescapability of dependency. Disability is one of the names given to the fact of dependency. Although degrees of dependency are always present in everybody's life, dependency is most conspicuous at the beginning of life, in illness, and in frail old age, for those who reach that stage in life. No one would say that a newborn is disabled, provided that he or she is "normal," but the category of disability can be attached to people who become seriously ill (for instance stroke victims) and to the very elderly. In addition to these cases, and in a more specific manner, the category of disability is reserved for those who have permanent physical and/or mental impairments. Although the attention to disability, from the academic and institutional worlds, is growing, our societies are far from placing this question at the center of political, social, philosophical, and quotidian discourse. To be sure, what is essential to radical change in our societies is not simply that disability issues be discussed, academically or otherwise. Rather, the essential thing is that structures are put in place so that people who are regularly marginalized under the stigma of disability can develop their potentialities, secure the good life, and flourish rather than wither in oblivion and lack of developmental activities. The essential thing, in other words, is the constitution of a society in which ability is not the measure of all things. To this end the critique of productivity and sovereignty is a prerequisite.

In *Love's Labor*, Kittay formulates the concept of *dependency work* as "the work of caring for those who are inevitably dependent" (1999: ix). She offers a "dependency critique of equality" (p. 4), since the latter concept "masks inequitable dependencies, those of infancy and childhood, old age, illness and disability" (p. xi) and it remains "elusive for women" (ibid.; also pp. 4–5). The critique of the myth of independence and of society as an association of equals shows dependency as an inescapable condition of human life and care as the adequate response to the fact of dependency. While recognizing the general category of interdependence (yielded by the critique of the myth of independence), Kittay focuses on the more fundamental fact of dependence, from which interdependence itself may arise.

She reviews various critiques of equality before speaking of the dependency critique. They are the difference critique, the dominance critique, and the diversity critique. Generally speaking, however, the traditional concept of equality proves incapable of becoming common, for it entails the idea of "man as the measure of humanity" (p. 5). It is then *equalities*, if anything, that might reach into the common with a view to the fundamental aspect of *difference*: "We are different *from* another and we are equal *to* another" (p. 11). Indeed, difference is a relative category, whether understood together with identity or with equality. In the former case, every being is different from any other in virtue of being identical with itself; but precisely in this there is commonality. In the latter, a being is different from those to which it is not equal in virtue of being equal to those that are not different from it. Obviously, the former situation is, ontologically speaking, more fundamental and common than the latter, of which it must constitute the inner structure.[10] Of the latter, Kittay gives an example that might be useful to quote:

> For instance, to insist that difference is the property of a deaf child in a class of hearing children—and so the deaf child must accommodate herself to her hearing peers—is to ignore the fact that the hearing child is also different from the deaf child. *Neither hearing nor deafness is inherently a difference. Instead the difference is in the relation these children bear to one another.* (Ibid.; emphasis added)

The last two sentences show that the most fundamental and common reality is given by a being's self-identity, or rather by it singularity, its *thisness*, which points to the commonality of difference as a relational concept, as well as to the problematic nature of a hastily posited equality.

For Kittay, it is only the dependency critique that moves toward "an appreciation of the inevitable variety of human interaction and a more adequate understanding of what is morally acceptable in asymmetric relations" (p. 15). This critique addresses the question of a gendered labor and the necessity of its redistribution; it also challenges the traditional logic of inclusion and exclusion, typical of the distribution of labor and justice. In particular, Kittay argues, it highlights the *contingent* nature of the difference that has historically assigned women the role of dependency workers and caregivers (p. 16). However, she also notes that even among women the work of dependency has not been evenly distributed (p. 28), for class and race are equally fundamental moments in the division of labor. Obviously, dependency work "must be done by someone" (ibid.). The question for Kittay is how to end the stigmatization of this type of work and of those who do it. One of the main reasons for this stigma, particularly in modern, capitalist societies, is that the work of care is not productive. In this sense, the critique of productivity and sovereignty becomes fundamental. Kittay says:

> Rather than ask if women's care of dependents results in them being marked as different, we need to ask whether doing dependency work

excludes those who do it from the class of equals, and if so, what we must understand and do to end this exclusion. (Ibid.)

It is here that the concepts and realities of productivity and sovereignty show their persistence, here that their critique must be incensed and their danger exposed. Thus, for Kittay, the "dependency critique considers . . . the inescapable fact of human dependency and the ways in which such labor makes one vulnerable to domination" (ibid.). In this sense, a formal discourse on justice remains far from creating the structures of true equality, which only an emphasis on non-productive, non-sovereign, care can bring about. In other words, the truth of a fundamental inequality cannot be altered by a formal positing of the principle of equality (who is equal to whom?) that operates through a logic of inclusion and exclusion. True equality cannot be established empirically; that is, the standard of the equal must be a transcendental and univocal concept, such as the dignity of individuation—certainly not *man as the measure*.[11] Otherwise, as in Aristotle, justice would remain equality for equals and inequality for unequals (*Politics* 1280a10–15). When the latter are excluded from the society of equals, the semblance of equality obtains; so does the shadow of inequality. Merely demanding equality does not solve the problem of who will do the work that generates inequality in the first place: the labor of support and care, the labor without which there could not be a human community. As Kittay says, what is important is a new and fairer distribution of this labor "across the population" (1999: 19). Care and equality are to be brought into "a dialectical relation" (ibid.). In this sense, equality is not a reduction of difference to the same, with the consequent exclusion of the irreducible one(s). Rather, it is the neutrality of subject and object, of carer and cared for—the substance and product of care. It is "being with," in Nancy's sense (see Chapter 1). It is also *care* in Heidegger's sense, as "being-ahead-of-oneself-already-in (the world) as being-together-with (innerworldly beings encountered)" (1996a: 180).

Kittay speaks of connection-based, rather than individual-based, equality. This is a concept that is very close to the Heideggerian notion of being-together-with other beings encountered. Beyond Kittay, it is also a concept that points to the construction of genuine communism, that is, the meeting of need and (labor as) care. But it is Kittay herself who describes this as a community that transcends equality as the right of an individual, or as a right in general, and emphasizes the mutual and social responsibility inscribed in the concept and reality of care, on the basis of need (1999: 28). She is here speaking of the *system of exploitation* in and by which dependency work, the labor of care, is undervalued, with a consequent decrease of "the moral worth of the caregiver as well as the person cared for" (ibid.). She continues:

> A society in which such a system of exploitation is the norm cannot be said to be a society in which equality, as both a moral and social value, thrives. (Ibid.)

Later on in her book, criticizing Rawls's views, she says:

> Principles of right and traditional notions of justice depend upon a prior and more fundamental principle and practice of care. (p. 108)

The social responsibility of care requires a new distribution of dependency work (p. 32), which in turn entails the elimination of the division of labor. The latter, in fact, is always based on an idea of domination, on fixed categories hierarchically arranged. However, the new distribution of dependency work, and of work in general, should happen on a horizontal plane, certainly across the genders.

The new distribution of work, and of dependency work in particular, certainly requires a critique of productivity. Indeed, as Ofelia Schutte notes,

> it is necessary to identify unpaid care work as productive work and to determine what proportions of time women and men spend, respectively, in unpaid work in the home. (2002: 140)

This work is considered unproductive because it is invisible and consequently cannot be measured (p. 143). Moreover, frustratingly for the political economist, it does not result in a physical object, a commodity—it does not appear to have an end other than the activity itself (at least from the point of view of the logic of production). In reality, this labor is *not* productive *only from the standpoint of capital*. When Schutte says that it should be considered as productive, the implicit assumption is that the word "productive" is no longer inscribed within the logic of capital, the logic of domination and exploitation, but it is instead understood as a social category. Thus, this labor is productive in a wider, or rather essentially different, sense. It is certainly important to grasp the distinction between productive and unproductive labor as a major source of social inequalities. It is as important to realize that the solution cannot lie in making all unproductive labor productive, but rather in eliminating the distinction as such. True equality cannot be brought about by reducing all human doing to the category of productivity (under the aegis of capital or other sovereign regimes), but rather by liberating its power for the necessity of care, the necessities of life, and of the good life for all. True equality then is the projecting and the being-with of care. This equality is not the result of the movement whereby an "inferior" is forced to measure up to a "superior," nor is it the mere equation of two terms. Rather, it is their displacement into the neutral (the neither/nor) and the common. It is the pronounced parallax whereby the universal comes into sight.[12] True equality can only be commonality and universality.

Disabling Potentialities

In her dependency critique of Rawls's theory of equality and social justice, Kittay points out the reiteration in the latter of a problem common to the Western tradition of political thought, that is, the exclusion of many from equality and citizenship. She calls attention to the fact that if we "begin our inquiry concerning the principles of justice with the idealization of a fully functioning person" (1999: 88), which is what Rawls requires, we will end up with a society in which equality, social justice, and full citizenship cannot belong to all. Given the fact that dependency is unavoidable, the concept of *person* cannot be adequately formulated by bracketing dependency out.

Forms of dependency include very young and very old age, illness, and disability. In the case of disability, particularly in severe mental disability, where dependency often constitutes a permanent feature of a person's life, the difficulty and danger of a formal discourse on equality become apparent. Here, too, the logic of productivity and sovereignty shows its problematic nature. In fact, a society that values productivity (for productivity's sake)— and on the basis of productivity raises a hierarchical order of values for inclusion and exclusion—will invariably and necessarily marginalize and exclude those who cannot be productive in the same way and who, because of the high degree of their dependency, are not *sovereign*. A discourse on equality and social justice will have to make this a high priority: dismantle the logic of productivity and sovereignty, *slow down* the gears, in the sense stressed by Kittay in her chapter on Sesha, her daughter, who has a severe mental disability,[13] and raise the mode of care to the univocal and unsurpassable condition of the good life for everyone, that is, to the dignity of individuation.

The common objection of the need for efficiency cannot stand. A society is not efficient that speeds toward useless production and consumption while overlooking the needs of the neediest. The *caring mode of production*, distribution, and consumption, seems to be the only exit from the obsessive logic of productivity that, as noted by William DiFazio (2006), *purposefully forgets*.[14]

This new mode is what in substance Bubeck (1995) also suggests when she replaces the figure of *homo economicus* with that of *persona carans* (see above). What is produced through and by this obsessive logic is actual or potential disability: potentialities are systematically disabled whether there is a real (physical or mental) impairment or not; the full growth of individuals, regardless of the ways in which and the degree to which this growth might happen, is hampered; disabilities are made. By contrast, in the caring mode of production, which has the dignity of individuation as a precondition, what counts is the singularity of being-in-the-world and being-with-one-another. Moreover, the mode of care is a vindication of unproductive labor over speed, profit, and exploitation, the becoming common of *women's work* over productive labor (as the labor that produces and increases capital), a coming into full view (and recognition) of the highly creative yet often invisible skills required by the art of making the good life possible and, eventually, common.

As one of the clearest examples of almost total social exclusion, the reality of disability, particularly severe mental disability, shows the importance of the mode of care as the negation of the logic of productivity and sovereignty. To give full and fully radical meaning to the notion that another world is possible (a better world, of the good life for all), disability must become the measure of humanity.[15] Concrete examples of how true, loving, and *enabling* care can alter the lot of individuals condemned otherwise to oblivion and waste, to a life of disability and poverty in a rich and able-bodied world, are found in the literature on disability. I have already mentioned Kittay's chapter on Sesha, her daughter. Among other things, Kittay there shows how, in a situation of severe disability, only adequate and true care can on the one hand alter the pattern and neutralize the specter of institutionalization while, on the other hand, providing the conditions for the full development of one's potentiality. It is important to understand (and Kittay's chapter is fundamental in providing this understanding) that the measure of a person's flourishing, thus the value of a person's life, cannot be determined by quantity and pre-established external standards. Full development is not fuller if it develops more (a logical and ontological impossibility), nor is adequate agency more or less adequate according to whether it meets or does not meet these same standards of externality. The dignity of individuation places value on the inherent potentialities of an individual being (regardless of the kind of potency they sustain; and, indeed, even delicate potency, the potency of a little flower, is potency all the same). It places value on the *thisness* of this being, its identity and difference. The completeness and actuality of such thisness, a *such this* (Aristotle *Metaphysics* 1030b24), is the measure of its universality. It is, as McRuer puts it, *a contingent universalization* (2006: 157).

Equally critical of Rawls's contractarian theory, but also critical of Kittay's emphasis on dependency as the most fundamental moment of the human condition, Martha Nussbaum proposes her capabilities approach, which focuses on the individual and is therefore to be understood in the tradition of liberalism. However, Nussbaum's would be "a new form of liberalism" (2006: 221). In her critique of Kittay's "anti-liberal direction" (p. 218)—for, as we have seen, Kittay denies the importance of the notion of the independent individual—Nussbaum says:

> By contrast, although my view insists that human beings are inevitably dependent and interdependent, and holds that dignity may be found in relations of dependency, citizens enjoy full equality only when they are capable of exercising the whole range of capabilities. (Ibid.)

For her, liberalism runs into problems in relation to notions such as a contract for mutual advantage, but it is not altogether *disabled* (p. 221) insofar as its defense of individuality, that is, "the equal worth of persons and their liberty" (ibid.), still stands. However, the question is whether the individual and its individuality can adequately be understood in the atomistic way proposed by the liberal tradition. The individual is, of course, always social and that means, never truly independent from other individuals. Individuality, as we have seen in Chapter 1 (dealing with Nancy), is the result of a being-with, a plurality of more original singularities.

For Nussbaum, "the person, not the group, is the primary subject of political justice, and policies that improve the lot of a group are to be rejected unless they deliver the central capabilities to *each and every person*" (p. 216). I do not see how this is necessarily *liberal*, provided that the concept of individual is properly defined and understood. Indeed, nothing can be more closely associated with the full growth of the individual than Marx's statement: "From each according to his ability, to each according to his needs." However, to become an axiom of political justice, this truth cannot be left to the mere individual (in his independence and isolation), but it has to become common—that is, common to all individuals, to society, to the individual as an inherently social being. Yet, while renouncing the contractarian view of an "idealized rationality" (p. 216), Nussbaum suggests a vision of the individual as the irreducible and independent subject of political justice—something which, it seems to me, would amount to the end of politics (a premature end). In this sense, Kittay's suggestion of *departing* from the liberal tradition (p. 217) in order to grasp dependency as the inescapable fact of the human condition seems not only more innovative and progressive, but also more attuned to the reality of everybody's and everyday life.

Nussbaum says:

> All citizens should have the chance to develop the full range of human powers, at whatever level their condition allows, and to enjoy the sort of liberty and independence their condition allows. (p. 218)

This is a function of the capabilities approach. However, this approach cannot deny the facts of dependence and interdependence, which turn sheer independence into a *fiction*, as Kittay says. Nussbaum herself has to agree with this: "To be sure, nobody is ever self-sufficient; the independence we enjoy is always both temporary and partial" (pp. 218–219). But Nussbaum thinks "we need a lot more" (p. 219). Yet, this "more" (notably, *liberty*) cannot be the total negation of the fundamental condition of dependence. It is rather *being-with*, which must be at hand even in solitude and without which solitude itself would be unbearable. I think that what is most important in Nussbaum's position is not her insistence on liberalism, but rather her attention to the ways in which society must organize its public policy to "fully include" people with disabilities and their caregivers (p. 222). It is also very important that, in her critique of the social contract (and implicitly of productivity), she recognizes that the kind of social change able to end the stigma of disability cannot happen "because we think we will gain thereby, in a narrow economic or self-interested sense of 'gain'" (ibid.). As a matter of fact, here the fact of independence is weakened by the recognition of the unsurpassable condition of being-with, which forms the substance of Kittay's notion of the inescapability of dependence. Nussbaum says that this change can only happen "out of our attachment to justice and our love of others, *our sense that our lives are intertwined with theirs and that we share ends with them*" (ibid.; emphasis added). However, this seems precisely to disqualify liberalism (even a new form of it) from being the theory of justice society needs.

In addition to Kittay's chapter in *Love's Labor*, there are other works that, often through personal accounts, show the importance of the mode of care in order to neutralize the stigma of disability and emphasize the dignity of individuation, which is proper to life, and, certainly, to human life. Among these works I can mention Michael Bérubé's book on his son, Jamie, who has Down syndrome (Bérubé 1996), some essays in Pothier and Devlin's *Critical Disability Theory* (2006), and Sophia Wong's essay on her brother,

Leo, who also has Down syndrome (Wong 2002). In the already cited *Frontiers of Justice*, Martha Nussbaum (2006) also constantly refers to her nephew, Arthur, and his disability, as well as to Sesha Kittay and Jamie Bérubé. Regardless of the difference in philosophical approach, these works share the notion that the end of the mode of care must be empowerment and the constitution of those conditions able to bring about *adequate agency*; adequate not to some external standards but to the *thisness* of any given existence. Certainly, from the point of view of the present study, they share a common understanding, whether implicit or explicit, of the problematic nature of a society built on categories of productivity and sovereignty; a society in which the end is often not that of enhancing people's capacities, but rather of disabling and deactivating their potentialities. In particular, they all show how problematic the notion of disability is and that, certainly, *"people with impairments and related disabilities are not unproductive"* (p. 105; emphasis added)—if it were not for the stigmatization of individual existential conditions *as disabilities*, the confinement of forms of human activities to the realm of the unproductive, and the inability or unwillingness of society to foster the necessary structural conditions for the full and adequate development of potentialities, or as Nussbaum (2006) and Sen (1999) say, capabilities.

In her version of the *capabilities approach*, a theory also developed by Amartya Sen in economics (Nussbaum 2006: 70), Martha Nussbaum says that "we begin with a conception of the dignity of the human being, and of a life that is worthy of that dignity" (p. 74). The concept of dignity she uses is *political* in the tradition of Aristotle and Marx, linking rationality and animality, rather than limited to the concept of the person, as in Kant and contractarianism, particularly Rawls (p. 159). In this sense, and once the question of liberalism is bracketed, I would say that the concept of dignity of individuation I am trying to formulate here is in some important ways similar to Nussbaum's conception of dignity. She calls the capabilities approach "fully universal" and "similar to the international human rights approach" (p. 78). From the point of view of the capabilities approach, Nussbaum also points out the problem of productivity, although she is not interested in a critique of productivity as such. Indeed, she sees productivity as "necessary, and even good," although not as "the main end of social life" (p. 160). Of course, this is correct when one uses, as Nussbaum seems to do, a broad and transhistorical concept of productivity. It might then be good to observe here that when I speak of the necessity of undertaking a critique of productivity, I mean productivity under the regime of capital. However, this is an important observation in order to highlight the fact that without an adequate concept of what it is to produce, to create, to make, any discourse on dignity and human rights risks losing sight of the material conditions of life, and of their production and reproduction. For instance, under the capitalist mode of production, in which productivity as the making of surplus value and profit *is* "the main end of social life," all values, including dignity, are subsumed under exchange value and price. It is consequently not possible to overcome the distinction between productive and unproductive labor under the sovereignty of capital, for the elimination of that distinction is the elimination of capital itself. As I have already noted, Nussbaum stresses that

> people with impairments and related disabilities are not unproductive. They contribute to society in many ways, when society creates conditions in which they may do so. (2006: 105)

And again: "Their relative lack of productivity *under current conditions* is not 'natural'; it is the product of discriminatory social arrangements" (p. 113; emphasis added). Productive here means useful. However, under capital (i.e., under "current conditions"), some forms of human activity are called unproductive not because they are not useful in a general sense, but because they are not useful in the sense specified by capital itself, that is, the creation of surplus value. Thus being unproductive is not the result of unqualified *social arrangements*, but it has to do, and fundamentally so, with the mode of production of capitalist society and with the notion of productivity arising from it. What I am saying is that the important move is not creating the conditions whereby people with impairments and related disabilities might more fully join the mechanism and machinery of capital. This might prove an unsurpassable obstacle, given capital's ends, as well as the objective reality of some forms of physical and, especially, mental impairment. Rather, it is important to understand that a new mode of production (geared toward the constitution of real wealth, proper to genuine human needs, and available to all) is necessary. This is the mode of *enabling* and *empowering* care, where the caring person and the person cared for reach an agency adequate to the *this-ness* of the situation at hand, not determined by the demands of productivity and profit. Under this mode, enabling and empowering do not go in the direction of normalization; rather, they subvert the norm, as they dwell (and build new being) in the marginal spaces and interstices negated by the norm.

What I am saying is that the activities of people labeled as mentally disabled cannot be truly appreciated unless the *substance* and *spirit* of these activities is understood. This is an effort that it is the task of "normal" individuals to make. As long as these people's activities are seen as useless because of their obvious unproductive character from the standpoint of capital and, more generally, of efficiency, no real change can take place. But when they are placed at the center of the attention, interests, and well-being of society, of a community (the family, for instance), they acquire a different meaning, that is, they are valorized, for they are eventually grasped not only as useful, but also as creative (and, at times, highly creative) acts. Such valorization is possible when there is not compassion, but admiration—as is the case, for instance, in the Bérubé family with Jamie (Bérubé 1996) and in my experience, in my own family, with my younger brother, Pino, to whom this book is dedicated. This is certainly the lesson anyone who has not had direct experience with the condition of mental impairment can draw from Bérubé's book, from Wong's account of her family life with her brother in her essay on gender and disability, or from Kittay's chapter on Sesha. Both Bérubé's son, Jamie, and Wong's brother, Leo, have Down syndrome, thus a condition that does not impair what society might consider the accomplishment of "normal" and even great achievements, such as holding a job or even writing a book, as Bérubé hopes his son might one day be able to do, and as some with the same condition have already done. However, the same holds true even when more severe conditions are present, such as is the case with Kittay's daughter, Sesha: her ability to communicate her joy is a creative act.

Without a critique of productivity, that is, the displacement of priorities and ends from the strictly economic realm onto the social and ontological realms, there may be no sufficient reason for radically changing the existential conditions of people stigmatized as people with disabilities other than a recourse to moral principles (largely left to the disposition of individuals) or charity. As Nussbaum argues, contractarianism cannot adequately address the question. Indeed, the notion of a social contract always seems to involve and be based upon a logic of inclusion and exclusion, which makes the social contract *invisible* to many, and that is, to those who in the contract figure as the excluded and invisible ones.[16] Even when cooperation is eyed, full inclusion remains a problem insofar as the ability to co-operate varies largely among people; moreover, if the end of cooperation is the making of profit, speed, high efficiency, and productivity, it is evident that those who cannot keep up the required rhythm and pace must be necessarily excluded. In this sense, Nussbaum criticizes Rawls's idea of mutual advantage based on "*normal" social cooperation* (2006: 118).

In her response to Nussbaum, Wong defends "a Rawlsian conception of moral personhood that explicitly includes all human beings, including those labeled 'mentally retarded'" (2007: 583). She argues that "an idealizing approach to personhood accords people labeled 'mentally retarded' the respect

and dignity that they deserve on a par with all other human beings"
(pp. 583–584). Going much beyond the limits of Rawls's theory (which excludes non-autonomous individuals from moral personhood and social contract capacity), yet claiming close affinity with it, Wong shows how it is
possible to virtually (i.e., in an idealized manner) confer autonomy to the
nonautonomous. She starts from noticing that Rawls's two moral powers
(the capacity for a sense of justice and the capacity for a conception of the
good) are "*potential,* rather than always actualized" (p. 586).[17] Because they
are potential properties, they can develop and become actual depending on
the presence of what Wong calls "Enabling Conditions" (p. 589). In Wong's
view, while "every human being has the capacity to develop the two moral
powers" (p. 592), the Enabling Conditions depend on the social circumstances of life. As a matter of fact, she notes: "This is the difficulty faced by
people labeled 'mentally retarded' who grow up in institutions and have
minimal or no contact with their families" (p. 589). However,

> being included as members in families and other social associations
> along with peers of their own age and with competent adults en-
> ables them to develop the moral capacities of community members.
> (p. 590)

Here the theme of true care comes back as the determinant feature of the
production of social life. In her defense of contractarianism and against
Nussbaum, Wong opposes mere care and favors a fully inclusive social contract (although the inclusion may for some be only idealized). She says:

> I argue that treating people as potential participants in negotiating
> principles of justice (even if they never actually participate in such
> negotiations) is better than treating them as recipients of care en-
> gaged in loving relationships designed to maximize their capabilities
> (p. 593).

For Wong this is a way of granting (idealized) autonomy to a person who,
instead of being the mere recipient of someone's care, becomes "a potential
interlocutor" (ibid.).

Leaving aside the philosophical problems inherent in the notion of a social contract, always hypothetical in nature and thus perhaps necessarily incapable of full inclusion, I do not think that a choice must be made between
the care that maximizes potentialities (or capabilities) and the establishing of
an idealized relationship whereby the needs, desires, and interests of the less

advantaged person may find adequate expression. Indeed, the difference between these two attitudes may be one of presentation more than of substance. What I mean to say is that the latter can be understood from a perspective of true care, while the former accomplishes its goal (the maximization of a person's capabilities) only insofar as the person in question is provided with those conditions whereby her agency can flourish in a manner that is adequate to her actual situation. In my view, what is fundamental in either case is understanding that no real change can take place as long as our society remains entrenched in the sovereign logic of capital. True, an individual's sense of justice will always make a difference in any given situation. However, a universal ethics of the good life for everybody requires a passage to a transformed social order. This is an order in which, I repeat Bubeck's formulation, *homo economicus* is replaced by *persona carans*, that is, one in which the essence and spirit of economic discourse and activities are not economic in nature (certainly not in the capitalist sense of the word) but ontological. This means that they have to be brought into a relation to the making and doing constituting a being other than that originally found in the immediacy of nature. On the one hand, the labor of care constituting this new being has the highest regard for the least advantaged; on the other, the labor of the least advantaged themselves (certainly useless from the standpoint of capital or other sovereign modes geared toward accumulation and, in an exclusive way, toward efficiency) is of the highest kind, for it is the closest to art and poetry. It is closest to the heart of art and poetry, the essence of the earth, in the sense that, in this labor, any achievement uses the full potency of being, always fully contracted in any *this*. To the contrary, any efficient expenditure of energy, which leaves an excess, or surplus, is merely instrumental.

Sovereign, Productive, and Efficient

In his book on queerness and disability, McRuer offers a critique of productivity as compulsory able-bodiedness, "which in a sense produces disability" (McRuer 2006: 2). The alternative to able-bodied dogmas is that "a disabled world is possible and desirable" (p. 71). The idea that a better world *is* a disabled world is very provocative, but it is the necessary outcome of a critique of productivity. Of course, what this means is that disability must stop being "the raw material against which the imagined future world is formed" (p. 72)—an idea, McRuer says, typical of liberationist models. Whenever able-bodiedness is the goal, perhaps unwanted, the specters of normalization, independence, productivity, and sovereignty also linger. For McRuer, the construction of able-bodiedness is linked to the construction of heterosexuality: "The institutions in our culture that produce and secure a hetero-sexual identity also work to secure an able-bodied identity" (p. 151). These normalizing identities, essential to the logic of the same, are not differences among differences, nor do they open up the realm of the universal. They are not differences because they have closed the gap between the norm they have established and the moments of anxiety that brought them to establish the norm. Indeed, they are not different from that anxiety, as in having moved away from it. Rather, that anxiety no longer exists, and it has never existed. They are what they have always been; what they will always be. Dif-ference to them is a matter of indifference. Yet, they are not universals be-cause they are incapable of the leap into what they are not, incapable of reaching into the univocal and neutral structure that connects the one to the other, the structure of otherness as such. They have lost their contingency, no longer able not to be. McRuer speaks of *"those [desirable] disabled/queer moments"* as of *"temporary or contingent universalization"* (p. 157; emphasis added), that is, moments in which, as I understand it, we are what we have not been and would not be, able not to be what we are, and thus, able to reach into the other. However, it is not the idealized other that we encounter, nor ourselves *as* and *in* the other; rather, we encounter our own otherness, which is the same with what is different from us, for it is difference itself—not merely what-is, but what-could-be. The universalizing potentiality pres-ent in this, that is, in the "dis-" of disability, just as in the "ab-" of the abnor-mal (the *abyss* surrounding the norm), subverts the logic of the contract and of a multitude united under the sovereign sign. The *disunited multitude* feared by Hobbes (1994: XVIII) the multitude that commits injustice, reaches, through the "dis-" of its disunity, and bears witness to, the most extreme forms of exclusion whereby citizenship is nothing but dis-citizenship.

In their introduction to *Critical Disability Theory*, Dianne Pothier and Richard Devlin speak of "a system of deep structural economic, social, po-litical, legal, and culture inequality in which persons with disabilities experi-ence unequal citizenship, *a regime of dis-citizenship*" (2006: 1; emphasis added). Their critique of contractarianism, of Rawls in particular and of liberalism in general, is very strong:

> Rawls is quite blatant in expressly excluding the disabled from his social contract model, on the premise that their "fate arouses pity and anxiety" [Rawls 1999: 84].[18] (p. 11)

What for Rawls is "beyond the theory of justice" and relating to "persons dis-tant from us" (1999: 84) becomes the basis of Kittay's dependency critique, as we have seen above, as well as of the *politics of transformation* sought by critical disability theory (Pothier and Devlin 2006: 12). This politics of transformation starts by acknowledging the fundamental truth that disability is "a social construct" (p. 13), "a systematically enforced pattern of exclusion" (p. 14). One of the fundamental moments of this politics of transformation has to do with the critique of productivity. Obviously, Pothier and Devlin do not deny the reality of physical and mental impairments, the "functional limitations" (p. 13) not equally experienced by all individuals in a society. However, these functional limitations and impairments are of such a broad variety (some visible, others invisible; some mild, others severe) that to simply label them as disabilities neutralizes their existential importance and specificity (for the individual and for society as a whole). They become nothing but "categories of inclusion and exclusion" (p. 14).

From the point of view of the present study, Pothier and Devlin's introduction, as well as the other essays in *Critical Disability Theory*, is very important. Pothier and Devlin explicitly address not only the question of productivity, but also that of sovereignty, confirming the basic insight of *Earthly Plenitudes* as to the importance of the critique of these concepts and realities in the effort to theorize the possibility of genuine social change: a world of all-inclusive citizenship, based on an appreciation of labor as adequate agency—adequate to the specificity and singularity (that is, the *thisness*) of every and each individual. This singularity is what I refer to as dignity of individuation. This is not the concept of the individual, certainly not one in the liberal tradition; it is rather what sustains an individual in its singularity.

Pothier and Devlin's challenge to liberalism and its concept of the individual is very explicit:

> Liberalism tends to put great emphasis on the individual, assuming that the self is both *sovereign* and a foundational unit for analysis. However, critical disability theory forces us to reflect on a number of profound ontological questions. *Who is a self?* Is there such a thing as an authentic self? What is the significance of disability to the conception of the self?. (p. 16; emphasis added)

I have already dealt with this question, especially in Chapter 1 of this book. The ontological critique of the self was part of the critique of sovereignty and of the formulation of the concept of the dignity of individuation. The importance of the critique is intensified when one deals with disability. Here, a defense of the independent individual cannot be justified on the ground that those whose individuality has historically been denied deserve access to it (see Nussbaum 2006: 221–222), for these are the very people whose existential conditions eminently show the fictitious character of the independent individual, as Kittay has convincingly argued. As Pothier and Devlin say, liberalism "has put great store in the principles of liberty, autonomy, and choice" (2006: 16); however, these are principles that need to be challenged for reasons that are not dissimilar from those we saw in Kittay's dependency critique. In Pothier and Devlin we also find a question that is seldom explicitly asked: the question of productivity. They ask: "What is meant by productivity?" (p. 18). This question is central to the present work, as I have often repeated. Pothier and Devlin also ask: "And, most importantly, why should productivity . . . be a legitimate criterion?" (ibid.). Indeed, if productivity itself is not called into question, all discourse about ending a regime whereby large multitudes are excluded from citizenship and the good life ends in contradictions and aporias. In criticizing productivity *and* efficiency (most eminent functions of sovereignty), Pothier and Devlin say:

> Efficiency and productivity are irretrievably ableist discourses that can only condemn (some) persons with disabilities to a presumptive inferior status. An enabling citizenship needs to be unshackled from the ideology of productivity and efficiency. (p. 18)

Conclusion:
Labor without Sovereignty

A t the end of the last chapter of this book, Pothier and Devlin's critique of the ideology of productivity and efficiency points to the possibility of unshackling labor from the yoke of sovereignty. This labor, or rather the many labors expressing human creativity and praxis, human activities, can enter a completely new dimension, take on a new form, and be, not sovereign in turn, but free of the schema of sovereignty. To put it in a succinct and paradoxical form, the sovereignty of labor is labor without sovereignty.

We have seen how the concept of sovereignty is a problem at various levels of human political life. Interestingly, it might still serve some purpose when, in a world of sovereign states, a people is denied sovereignty. However, this should not lead one to justify sovereignty as such, but rather to see that there are other possible configurations for the world than that dictated by the paradigm of sovereignty. If another world is indeed possible, it must be one in which the notion of a relation of a superior to an inferior, that is, the notion of sovereignty, is eliminated. Difference and diversity do not necessarily entail sovereignty.

When sovereignty is associated with productivity, as is particularly the case under the regime of capital, it takes on a more dangerous character than it might have in the sphere of state politics. Indeed, such association determines people's everydayness more than state politics does—and the latter, as Peter Bratsis (2006) shows, is really a result, rather than a presupposition, of the former. It does so by serving as the structural moment of relations such as the productive/unproductive labor distinction, or the division of labor itself. Typically, the fact that some forms of human activity are seen as unproductive, and undervalued on that account, speaks clearly enough of the injustice inherent in the hierarchical constitution of these relations. By being unproductive, they are considered lower than the productive ones. Obviously, everybody knows that they are not. Everybody knows that without those forms of labor dubbed unproductive, human life would be impossible, certainly it would not even approach the possibility of aiming at the good life, but stay *solitary, poor, nasty, brutish, and short.*

However, even for Hobbes, whose work I have not treated in this book, it is not the sovereign who alone ensures the possibility of a better life. The sovereign only inspires the fear necessary for the observance of the covenant. For Hobbes, the covenant is not between the united people and the sovereign, but rather among the united people under the sovereign, who choose the sovereign as a guarantor. Yet, it is still the same idea of sovereignty that keeps people from wrongdoing, the fear that that power inspires—as if caring would necessitate fear as a precondition.

True care, the labor of care is that which is performed not because of the fear that in not performing it one could be found guilty of wrongdoing. Rather, true care is motivated by one's attitude in relation to the dignity of individuation, by one's experience of the plenitude of each singularity, and of oneself as plenitude.

In this book I have proposed the labor of care as an alternative to productive labor and as an adequate expression of the notion of labor without sovereignty. A caring mode of production is not one in which nothing but affection is produced. Rather, it is the mode that allows labor to return to its original disposition of producing the necessary and useful for the good life, not of this or that group of people, but of the plenitude full of plenitudes.

Notes

NOTES TO INTRODUCTION

1. This is the word used in Saro-Wiwa's *rotten* English, which is the language employed throughout the novel. The word "uselessed," in particular, is very interesting from the point of view of the present study. It indicates both the idea of unproductive labor and the notion of the construction of disabilities.

2. I say "*real* suspension" in the sense of Walter Benjamin's "*real* state of emergency" (see Chapter 2).

NOTES TO CHAPTER 1

1. See Kojin Karatani's treatment of the problem (2003: 100–112).

2. See Loiret 2003: 123. Loiret quotes the following passage by Thomas Aquinas: "In a more special and perfect way, the particular and the individual are found in rational substances which have dominion over their own actions, and which are not only made to act, like others, but which can act of themselves; for actions belong to singulars" (*Summa Theologica* I, q.29, a.1).

3. There is some similarity between the concept of the dignity of individuation I am presenting here and that of subsidiarity, another contender of sovereignty, especially when applied to international human rights law, as Paolo Carrozza (2003) does in his excellent article on this subject. However, they are ultimately two different concepts. I briefly discuss subsidiarity and point out its difference from the dignity of individuation in the remark at the end of this chapter.

4. For a discussion of individuation in the Middle Ages, including the legacy of the Early Middle Ages and the Scholastic background of modern philosophy with a particular reference to Leibniz, see the volume edited by Jorge J. E. Gracia (1994).

5. On the problematic aspect of the concept of autonomy and independence, see also Kittay 1999. I deal with Kittay's work in Chapter 5.

6. Some of these questions are concretely treated in Chapters 4 and 5.

7. I deal more extensively with Pothier and Devlin's position in Chapter 5.

8. "The passage from potentiality to act, from language to the word, from the common to the proper, comes about every time as a shuttling in both directions along a line of sparkling alternation on which common nature and singularity, potentiality and act change roles and interpenetrate" (Agamben 1993: 20).

9. I refer to Marx's slogan again in Chapter 5.

10. As David Held says, "The doctrine of sovereignty has . . . two distinct dimensions: the first concerned with the 'internal' aspect of sovereignty; the second concerned with the external. . . . The former involves the belief that a political body established as sovereign rightly exercises the 'supreme command' over a particular society. . . . The latter, external, dimension involves the claim that there is no final and absolute authority above and beyond the sovereign state" (1995: 100).

11. On subsidiarity, see the remark at the end of this chapter.

12. The distinction between right and law is, of course, present in Hobbes as well. But whereas in Hobbes it is used to defend the doctrine of sovereignty, in Leibniz the opposite is the case.

13. Being a Christian philosopher, Leibniz cannot completely dismiss the notion of miracle, but he has to justify it somehow, saying that even "miracles conform to the general order." To do this, he distinguishes between God's most general laws, which are *without exceptions,* and what he calls "certain subordinate maxims," which are the same as what "we call the nature of things." These latter are simply "God's custom, with which he can dispense for any stronger reason than the one which moved him to make use of these maxims." Thus, God "has particular volitions which are *exceptions* to [the] subordinate maxims" (1989a: 40; emphasis added). This is perhaps one of Leibniz's weakest moments. He recuperates the notion of exception, typical of sovereignty, which he attributes to God only. However, the truth he has established remains valid, and that is that God does not use his volition in ways other than those determined by his understanding.

14. See Karatani's treatment of this question, although in the context of Kant's philosophy, where the other is the transcendental (2003: e.g., 53, 70).

15. The relationship between singularity/universality and particularity/generality is rather difficult. Going back to Deleuze, Karatani says that "while the connection between particularity and generality requires a mediation or a movement, that between singularity and universality is direct and unmediated" (2003: 102). But what of plurality? And in what sense can one speak of a singular universal and a singular plural? As Duns Scotus says, "It is one thing to conceive singularity as an object or part of an object. It is quite another thing to have singularity as a mode of conception or as the aspect under which the object is conceived." It seems that in the first case the singular would really be the particular: "an object or part of an object"; in the second case, it would be singularity proper, that is, a mode of the particular and what characterizes it. Duns Scotus continues: "For example, when I say 'a universal', the object conceived is plurality, but singularity is the mode of conception, that is, it is conceived as a singular thing. . . . When I say 'singular', it is singularity that is conceived, but the mode of conception is that of a universal, for what I conceive is indifferent to being more than one" (1987: 91–92).

In other words, the universal entails the multitude (plurality) of possible beings or aspects of beings under the mode of conception of the singular; the singular names, not the plurality or multitude of beings or aspects of beings but only *this one*, which, understood this time under the mode of conception of the universal, is *whatever this*.

16. "Pronounced parallax" is Kant's expression in *Dreams of a Visionary* that names the gap between the subjective and the objective viewpoint, the empirical and the rational (see Karatani 2003: 1–2, 47–48). On this, see also Slavoj Žižek, who says, "The standard definition of parallax is: the apparent displacement of an object (the shift of its position against a background), caused by a change in observational position that provides a new line of sight. The philosophical twist to be added, of course, is that the observed difference is not simply 'subjective,' due to the fact that the same object which exists 'out there' is seen from two different points of view. It is rather that, as Hegel would have put it, subject and object are inherently 'mediated,' so that an epistemological shift in the subject's point of view always reflects an 'ontological' shift in the object itself" (2006: 17).

17. Here Žižek does not elaborate on the difficult question of the relationship between substance and subject, which can also be taken, notably in Aristotle, as interchangeable. But in *The Ticklish Subject* (1999) there is a section on "The *Speculative* Identity of Substance and Subject," where, speaking of Hegel, Žižek says that "the split which separates Subject from Substance . . . is inherent in the Substance itself" (p. 88). This split is the subject itself, perhaps its emergence, which is inherent to the substance insofar as "caught in self-division" (p. 89). Similarly, however, in *The Parallax View*, he speaks of the subject as "ecstatic." With a reference to Lacan, he says that "the subject is the void [S-barred] which emerges when a substance is 'dispossessed' through ecstasy" (2006:45).

18. Jean Bodin says, "La souveraineté est la puissance absolue et perpétuelle d'une République" (1993: 111).

19. This view is really the opposite of that of Hobbes, for whom if there is no law there is no (in)justice.

20. Patrick Riley notes, "Bits of Leibniz can be pulled rightward, or pushed leftward—even if Leibniz took himself to be a tolerant moderate traveling on a broad *via media*" (1996: 273).

21. On the distinction between appetite and love in relation to the will, see Loiret 2003: 41.

22. See the outset of *Grounding for the Metaphysics of Morals*.

NOTES TO CHAPTER 2

1. See note 10, Chapter 1.

2. See Schwab's introduction to *Political Theology*.

3. The notion of the utter destruction of the enemy is of course not completely novel in history. Schmitt himself mentions, in this context, the extermination of the Native Americans of North America (1996: 54).

4. The initial name of "Operation Infinite Justice" for the war on terror started in 2001, soon changed to "Operation Enduring Freedom," evidently belongs to the same logic of the utter destruction of the enemy.

5. I have dealt more fully with Agamben's study of the state of exception in another work (Gullì 2007).

6. See Machiavelli's *Discourses* (I, V) and *The Prince* (IX).

7. See *Discourses* (I, III).

8. This is Bodin's expression, from *Les six livres de la République*, Book I, chapter 8.

9. On the prehistory of the concept of sovereignty, see also Hinsley's lucid chapters in *Sovereignty* (1966).

10. "We may dislike the State machinery; I do not like it. Yet many things we do not like are necessary, not only in fact, but by right. On the one hand, the primary reason for which men, united in political society, need the State, is the order of justice. On the other hand, social justice is the crucial need of modern societies. As a result, the primary duty of the modern State is the enforcement of social justice" (Maritain 1998: 20).

11. See Chapter 5.

12. For the philosophy of the common, and its advantage over a theory of democracy, see Negri 2003.

13. For a recent treatment of Vico's poetic metaphysics or ontology, see Sandra Luft's *Vico's Uncanny Humanism* (2003); for Marx and living labor, see for instance Antonio Negri's *Time for Revolution* (2003), Jean-Marie Vincent's *Critique du travail* (1987), and my own *Labor of Fire* (2005). Vincent, in particular, conjugates Marx's and Heidegger's philosophies, with respect to labor, in an original way.

14. For an extreme, nay aberrant, formulation of this argument, see Geoff Waite's book on Nietzsche (Waite 1996), really an insult to the tragic thinker, whom Henri Lefebvre, already in 1939, courageously called "a great philosopher and a great poet" (2003: 100).

15. I am here simply giving an account of Heidegger's interpretation of Nietzsche in this respect. I engaged with it critically when I wrote my master's thesis, "The Problem of Metaphysics in Heidegger's Confrontation with Nietzsche" (Gullì 1992).

16. I have discussed the *as-structure* more fully in *Labor of Fire* (Gullì 2005).

17. See my discussion of this in *Labor of Fire* (2005: 71–74).

NOTES TO CHAPTER 3

1. The importance of distinguishing between the servile and the useful will become particularly evident in Chapter 5, in which I deal with the work of care.

2. In this respect, see my book on the ontology of labor (Gullì 2005).

3. See also Foucault 1984: 63.

4. In this sense, see Hinsley 1966.

5. The theme of death, the fear of death, is also central in Hegel's dialectic of master and slave. It is only after that experience that the slave's process of self-recognition begins. For Bataille it is only what impedes sovereignty.

6. Derrida says: "At stake in the operation, therefore, is not a self-consciousness, an ability to be near oneself, to maintain and to watch oneself. We are not in the element of phenomenology. And this can be recognized in the primary characteristic—illegible within philosophical logic—that sovereignty *does not govern itself*. And does

not govern in general: it governs neither others, nor things, nor discourses in order to produce meaning" (1978: 283). This means that sovereignty *is not* sovereignty. He also characterizes the sovereign operation as *nonmeaning* (p. 271) and, quoting from *The Inner Experience*, as the "relation to the loss of meaning" (p. 270).

7. In "Preface to Transgression," his essay on Bataille, Michel Foucault says: "Would it be of help, in any case, to argue by analogy that we must find a language for the transgressive which would be what the dialectics was, in an earlier time, for contradiction? Our efforts are undoubtedly better spent in trying to speak of this experience and in making it speak from the depths where its language fails, from precisely the place where words escape it, where the subject who speaks has just vanished, where the spectacle topples over before an upturned eye" (1977: 40).

8. The logic of neither/nor is also present, as we have seen, in Bataille's concept of *neutral knowledge*.

9. In her very engaging review of *Labor of Fire*, Wendling asks whether a category other than labor, for instance "creation," would not better serve the purpose of describing the ontological power that, following Marx, I attribute to living labor. She says, "Marx undoubtedly does . . . deploy labor as an ontological category in some of his texts. But is this a merit of Marx's philosophy, as Gullì also claims? Could it not also be a symptom of Marx's inability to escape the Hegelian conceptuality [and] the concomitant bourgeoisification of his thought?" (Wendling 2006: 627). This question is also very much present in her Bataille essay. My answer is that the concept of labor, work, or production (not as capitalist production, but as the capacity and actual practice of making) is a necessary moment of the human experience. Fundamentally, creation and production are the same, although we need to disambiguate the latter term because it has been usurped by the logic of capital and become its distinctive sign, and the former because it has been relegated to the compensatory and supplemental sphere of art. One of the most urgent revolutionary acts is to destroy this false distinction.

10. The fact that productive and unproductive labor belong to the same logic, and that they are both different from the labor which is *not productive* (or neither-productive-nor-unproductive) but creative, constitutes one of the main points in my discussion in *Labor of Fire* (2005). There the distinction is made between political economy and ontology, but it could be said that the distinction between limited and general economy is very similar to the former. For what is limited economy if not that dictated by capitalist relations of production and their science, and what is general economy if not the new science of the totality of the *oikos*, our habitat, the world? As for Lamarche's essay, it really depends on what he means by "nonproductive." If he means "unproductive," then he does not really abandon limited (or political) economy; if on the other hand he means "not productive" (but I do not think this to be the case), then his antiteleological description of it requires further discussion. In fact, labor that is "not productive" is not labor that does not have an end, but rather that which does not produce and valorize capital without falling, on account of this fact, into the category of unproductivity—a category still devised by capital itself. Under capital, labor that is "not productive" has only the status of a conceptual reality.

11. Stoekl correctly says that "Bataille's theory is not only an economic one but an ethical one that criticizes the affirmation of the *self*" (Stoekl 2007: 265).

NOTES TO CHAPTER 4

1. See, for instance, Readings 1996 and Slaughter and Leslie 1997. I often use the phrase "the university" to mean higher education as a whole. Obviously, there are important distinctions within it. Stanley Aronowitz says: "At the top are two tiers of research universities, which are dedicated to the production of knowledge for the socioeconomic system. Their products are destined for use in economic and social domains, chiefly corporations and the state—especially, but not exclusively, the military. The third tier consists of nearly all liberal arts and technical colleges. Whether intended to train elite or plebeian students, these colleges *transmit* the knowledge produced in research universities and, conventionally, have a major responsibility in the elite schools to impart the Western intellectual and moral traditions to students" (1997: 188). He continues: "The fourth tier includes the community colleges and two-year technical schools; their main job is to provide technicians to business and industry. A declining group of students use these schools as a stepping-stone to four-year programs, and in recent years the two-year degree has increasingly become terminal for the majority of community college students. And, given the shrinking demand for technical workers of all kinds, the community college is increasingly important as an *ideological* institution insofar as it fulfills, but only in a bureaucratic sense, the promise of higher education for all" (p. 189).

It must be noted that the *transmission* of knowledge always also includes new *production* of it, whether this is institutionally acknowledged or not.

2. Gernigon, Odero, and Guido say that although the right to strike has *surprisingly* not been set out explicitly by ILO Conventions and Recommendations (besides, they add in a footnote, being incidentally mentioned in one Convention and Recommendation), it has often been discussed within the ILO, and two of its resolutions "in one way or another emphasized recognition of the right to strike in member States" (2000: 7).

3. I say "real" globalization to stress the fact that in our days the globalizing process, which for some is as old as the human adventure, has reached its full-fledged status. The choice of the adjective "real" is also intended as a reference to Marx's concept of real subsumption.

4. The problem of the observation is not very often spoken about, but it is very important to challenge this practice of control and this (really unjustified) burden placed on contingent workers. In some institutions, such as CUNY, adjuncts and part-timers are observed for ten consecutive semesters, that is, five years. And if by chance or necessity one goes from one college to another after some years, the process starts anew. Some people argue that the good thing about the observation is that if an adjunct is not reappointed, she has a case. But there is really no logic in this. First, because adjuncts and part-timers can be dismissed for no reason, and second because an observation can go badly for a variety of reasons, including the subjective disposition of the observer. Moreover, once hired, contingents should be reappointed automatically, perhaps observed once or twice, but years of this practice cannot find a meaningful justification. In truth, this practice becomes a despicable institution, which does not even try to disguise its true nature but openly manifests it, that is, of being what it is: the *observation* by a superior of the activity of an inferior. The use of the word "peer"

to qualify this practice is actually offensive. Do part-timers observe full-timers? And if not, why? A good account of the possibility of injustice inscribed in the practice and institution of the observation can be found in Thelin and Bertoncini 2004.

5. Here, I think again of Bousquet's analysis of the UPS "earn and learn" program (2008: 125–155).

6. Some time after I wrote this, the proposed contract at CUNY was ratified by an overwhelming majority of voters. Of a total of 7,245 votes, there were 6,764 "yes," one was void, and 480 (including mine) were "no."

7. After the contract ratification, in President Bowen's message of gratitude toward the PSC team that worked on the contract, and of congratulations to CUNY Chancellor Matthew Goldstein (whose position on contingent labor had been unassailable), the disappointment note on adjuncts' job security completely disappeared. It stands to reason that if the union leadership had taken, in relation to contingents' job security, a position as intransigent as the chancellor's, it would have been in the interest of the university to rethink the terms of the contract in this respect.

8. In the words of Frederick P. Schaffer, CUNY's General Counsel and Vice Chancellor for Legal Affairs, in the event of a strike, "no notice or hearing is required prior to termination" of adjunct faculty's employment (see "CUNY Matters Online," http://www1.cuny.edu/portal_ur/cmo/i/5/19/).

9. For a theoretical and historical understanding of how "free" labor might ultimately always be bound, see Moulier-Boutang 1998.

10. However, as I have noted, I find the notion that students are customers problematic.

11. See, for instance, the interesting autobiographical opening in Schell 1998, where the question of the quality of teaching versus job security is illustrated. Schell also pays special attention to the fundamental question of gender.

12. For the choice of the word "contingent" rather than "adjunct" or similar words, also see Schell 1998.

13. On the principle of the right to flight, see Mezzadra 2001 and Moulier Boutang 1998.

14. See Kierkegaard 1980.

15. For what I may here call *the invisibility paradox*, also see Schell 1998. Schell says: "Because they hold lesser rank and status, contingent faculty, although a statistically visible presence in higher education, are often 'invisible' in the decision-making processes of departmental and professional life" (p. 63). Needless to say, they are invisible precisely because they are too visible, but this visibility is, to say the least, embarrassing. Bluntly put, the paradox itself can only be explained in terms of a logic of apartheid.

16. See, for instance, Nelson 1997: 4.

17. "The final blow is that after a few years of working under these conditions, you'll find yourself stigmatized on the job market as a 'part-timer' by those who know perfectly well what the market is like but wonder what was wrong with you that you didn't get a job" (Ray Pratt 1997: 269).

18. In this sense, see also the volume edited by Bousquet, Scott, and Parascondola (2004).

19. On the question of the observation, see note 3.

20. In this sense, see also Nelson 1997. He says: "Improbably enough, the academy has become a place to build workplace solidarity that crosses class lines" (p. 6). He also addresses the question of the ambiguity and danger of contingent faculty's identity (p. 9).

21. I deal with Kittay's work and with the general idea of the labor(s) of care in Chapter 5.

22. In this sense, see also Amartya Sen's concept of poverty as capability deprivation (Sen 1999).

NOTES ON CHAPTER 5

1. Kittay says she prefers the expression *dependency work* to *dependency care* "to emphasize that care of dependents *is work*" (1999: 30).

2. As Kittay says, ". . . the independent individual is always a fictive creation of those men sufficiently privileged to shift the concern for dependence onto others" (1999: 17).

3. See also Dalla Costa and James 1972: 33.

4. Adequate agency can be the result of the correct application of the principle of subsidiarity, which I have treated in Chapter 1 of this book. The *help that does not destroy* affirmed by this principle requires that the agency of both the carer and the cared for be displayed and respected.

5. Kittay speaks of dependency as the inescapable condition of human life. That disability is also an inescapable condition may be important to say as a provocative statement. For instance, Robert McRuer says: "Everyone is virtually disabled . . . , disability being the one identity category that all people will embody if they live long enough" (2006: 30). However, the emphasis on disability in this respect is less certain and convincing than the emphasis on the broader, and more immediately evident, category of dependency.

6. Important in this sense is the work by Dalla Costa and James, *The Power of Women and the Subversion of the Community.* They say: "*Where women are concerned, their labor appears to be a personal service outside of capital*" (1972: 28; Dalla Costa and James's emphasis).

7. In *Canto General*, Neruda says: "In fertility time grew." I used this line as the epigraph to *Labor of Fire.*

8. The feminization of labor, a feature of contingent labor in general and of the contingent academic labor I treated in Chapter 4, in developed countries often affects "men of color, low-income, immigrants, and men who do not speak the local language" (I owe this remark to Sophia Wong, email exchange).

9. For a discussion of Bataille's thought, see Chapter 3.

10. In this sense, Leibniz's insight into the reality of individual substances is fundamental. I deal with this topic in Chapter 1.

11. This is what I show in the discussion of Leibniz's notion of the common concept of justice in Chapter 1.

12. For a discussion of the notion of pronounced parallax, see Chapter 1.

13. The title of Kittay's chapter is " 'Not my way, Sesha. Your way. Slowly.' A Personal Narrative" (1999: 147–161).

14. DiFazio (2006) writes about purposeful forgetting in relation to poverty and the making of poverty. That poverty is a function of the logic of productivity should not be difficult to grasp. Poverty should then be understood as a form of constructed disability, that is, an instance of disabled potentialities. In this sense, see also Amartya Sen's notion of "capabilities deprivation" (Sen 1999).

15. I am here thinking of Kittay's challenge of the notion of man as the measure of humanity (see discussion above).

16. I owe this connotation of the social contract to Michelle Sadkovets, a student of mine at Long Island University.

17. This is part of the passage from Rawls's *A Theory of Justice* quoted by Wong: "[E]qual justice is owed to those who have the capacity to take part in, and to act in accordance with the public understanding of the initial situation. One should observe that *moral personality is here defined as a potentiality* that is ordinarily realized in due course. It is this *potentiality* which brings the claim of justice into play [Rawls 1999: 442]" (quoted in Wong 2007: 586; Wong's emphasis).

18. This point is of course also emphasized by Kittay (1999) in her dependency critique of equality.

References

Agamben, Giorgio. 1993. *The coming community*. Trans. Michael Hardt. Minneapolis: Univ. of Minnesota Press.

———. 2005. *State of exception*. Trans. Kevin Attel. Chicago: Univ. of Chicago Press.

Aristotle. 1979. *Metaphysics*. Trans. Hippocrates G. Apostle. Grinnell, IA: Peripatetic Press.

———. 1998. *Politics*. Trans. C.D.C. Reeve. Indianapolis, IN: Hackett.

———. 1999. *Nicomachean ethics*. Trans. Terence Irwin. Indianapolis: Hackett.

Aronowitz, Stanley. 1997. Academic unionism and the future of higher education. In Nelson 1997b, 181–214.

Babich, Babette. 2007. Heidegger's will to power. *Journal of the British Society for Phenomenology* 38(1), 37–60.

Bataille, Georges. 1991. *The accursed share*. Vol. 1: *Consumption*. Trans. Robert Hurley. New York: Zone Books.

———. 1993. *The accursed share*. Vol. 2: *The history of eroticism* and Vol. 3: *Sovereignty*. Trans. Robert Hurley. New York: Zone Books.

———. 2001. *The unfinished system of nonknowledge*. Trans. Michelle Kendall and Stuart Kendall. Minneapolis: Univ. of Minnesota Press.

Bellamy, Edward. 2007. *Looking backward, 2000–1887*. New York: Oxford Univ. Press.

Benjamin, Walter. 1968. Theses on the philosophy of history. In *Illuminations*, trans. Harry Zohn. New York: Schocken Books.

———. 1978. Critique of violence. In *Reflections*, trans. Edmund Jephcott. New York: Schocken Books.

Berry, Joe. 2005. *Reclaiming the ivory tower: Organizing adjuncts to change higher education*. New York: Monthly Review Press.

Bérubé, Michael. 1996. *Life as we know it: A father, a family, and an exceptional child.* New York: Random House.

Bloch, Ernst. 1987. *Natural law and human dignity.* Trans. Dennis J. Schmidt. Cambridge, MA: MIT Press.

Block, Richard N., Sheldon Friedman, Michelle Kaminski, and Andy Levin, eds. 2006. *Justice on the job: Perspectives on the erosion of collective bargaining in the United States.* Kalamazoo, MI: W. E. Upjohn Institute for Employment Research.

Bodin, Jean. 1993. *Les six livres de la République. Un abrégé du texte de l'édition de Paris de 1583.* Paris: Librairie Générale Française.

Boldt-Irons, Leslie Anne, ed. 1995. *On Bataille: Critical essays.* Albany: State Univ. of New York Press.

Bousquet, Marc. 2002. The waste product of graduate education: Toward a dictatorship of the flexible. *Social Text* 20 (Spring): 81–104.

———. 2008. *How the university works: Higher education and the low-wage nation.* New York: New York Univ. Press.

Bousquet, Marc, Tony Scott, and Leo Parascondola. 2004. *Tenured bosses and disposable teachers: Writing instruction in the managed university.* Carbondale: Southern Illinois Univ. Press.

Bowen, Barbara. 2008. What we have achieved in this contract. *Clarion: Newspaper of the Professional Staff Congress / City University of New York.* Contract Special / Summer: 12.

Bratsis, Peter. 2006. *Everyday life and the state.* Boulder, CO: Paradigm.

Bubeck, Diemut Elizabeth. 1995. *Care, gender, and justice.* Oxford: Clarendon Press.

Calarco, Matthew, and Steven DeCaroli, eds. 2007. *Giorgio Agamben: Sovereignty and life.* Stanford: Stanford Univ. Press.

Carrozza, Paolo. 2003. Subsidiarity as a structural principle of international human rights law. *American Journal of International Law* 97(1): 38–79.

Dalla Costa, Mariarosa, and Selma James. 1972. *The power of women and the subversion of the community.* Bristol, UK: Falling Wall Press.

Deleuze, Gilles. 1994. *Difference and repetition.* Trans. Paul Patton. New York: Columbia Univ. Press.

Derrida, Jacques. 1978. *Writing and difference.* Trans. Alan Bass. Chicago: Univ. of Chicago Press.

DiFazio, William. 2006. *Ordinary poverty: A little food and cold storage.* Philadelphia: Temple Univ. Press.

Direk, Zeynep. 2007. Erotic experience and sexual difference in Bataille. In Winnubst 2007, 94–115.

Du Bois, W. E. Burghardt. 1987. *John Brown.* New York: International Publishers.

Duns Scotus, John. 1987. *Philosophical writings.* Trans. Allan Wolter. Indianapolis: Hackett.

Durán, José Maria. 2008. *Hacia una crítica de la economía política del arte.* Madrid: Plaza y Valdés Editores.

Elden, Stuart. 2004. Between Marx and Heidegger: Politics, philosophy and Lefebvre's *The Production of Space. Antipode* 36:86–105.

Eluard, Paul. 1988. *Selected poems*. Trans. Gilbert Bowen. London: Calder Publications.

Faye, Emmanuel. 2006. Nazi foundations in Heidegger's work. *South Central Review* 23(1): 55–66.

Foucault, Michel. 1977. *Language, counter-memory, practice: Selected essays and interviews*. Trans. Donald F. Bouchard and Sherry Simon. Ithaca, NY: Cornell Univ. Press.

———. 1984. *The Foucault reader*, ed. Paul Rabinow. New York: Pantheon Books.

———. 1990. *The history of sexuality*. Vol. 1: *An introduction*. Trans. Robert Hurley. New York: Vintage Books.

Fung Yu-lan. 1983. *A history of Chinese philosophy*. Vol. 1: *The period of the philosophers: From the beginning to circa 100 B.C.* Trans. Derk Bodde. Princeton: Princeton Univ. Press.

Gernigon, Bernard, Alberto Odero, and Horacio Guido. 2000. *ILO principles concerning the right to strike*. Geneva: International Labor Organization. First published in the *International Labor Review* 137 (1998): 4.

Gleason, Sandra E., ed. 2006. *The shadow workforce: Perspectives on contingent work in the United States, Japan, and Europe*. Kalamazoo, MI: W. E. Upjohn Institute for Employment Research.

Goldhammer, Jesse. 2007. Dare to know, dare to sacrifice: Georges Bataille and the crisis of the Left. In Winnubst 2007, 15–34.

Gracia, Jorge J. E. 1994. *Individuation in scholasticism: The later Middle Ages and the Reformation, 1150–1650*. Albany: State Univ. of New York Press.

Gramsci, Antonio. 1971. *Selections from the prison notebooks*. Trans. Quintin Hoare and Geoffrey Nowell Smith. New York: International Publishers.

Grindon, Gavin. 2007. The breath of the possible. In *Constituent imagination: Militant investigations, collective theorization*, ed. Stevphen Shukaitis and David Graeber. Oakland, CA: AK Press, 94–107.

Gross, James A. 2006. A logical extreme: Proposing human rights as the foundation for workers' rights in the United States. In Block et al. 2006, 21–39.

Guibernau, Montserrat. 1999. *Nations without states: Political communities in a global age*. Cambridge, UK: Polity Press.

Gullì, Bruno. 1992. The problem of metaphysics in Heidegger's confrontation with Nietzsche. Master's thesis, San Francisco State Univ.

———. 2005. *Labor of fire: The ontology of labor between economy and culture*. Philadelphia: Temple Univ. Press.

———. 2007. The ontology and politics of exception: Reflections on the work of Giorgio Agamben. In Matthew Calarco and Steven DeCaroli 2007, 219–242.

Hardt, Michael, and Antonio Negri. 2000. *Empire*. Cambridge, MA: Harvard Univ. Press.

Harnecker, Marta. 2005. *Understanding the Venezuelan revolution: Hugo Chávez talks to Marta Harnecker*. Trans. Chesa Boudin. New York: Monthly Review Press.

Harney, Stefano. 2002. *State work: Public administration and mass intellectuality*. Durham, NC: Duke Univ. Press.

Harney, Stefano, and Frederick Moten. 1998. Doing academic work. In Martin 1998a, 154–180.

Harvey, David. 2005. *A brief history of neoliberalism*. New York: Oxford Univ Press.

Hegel, G.W.F. 1977. *Phenomenology of spirit.* Trans. A. V. Miller. Oxford: Oxford Univ. Press.

Heidegger, Martin. 1966. Only a god can save us: The *Spiegel* interview. In *Heidegger: The man and the thinker,* ed. Thomas Sheehan. Chicago: Precedent, 1981.

———. 1977. *The question concerning technology and other essays.* Trans. William Lovitt. New York: Harper and Row.

———. 1979. *The will to power as art. Nietzsche.* Vol. 1. Trans. David Farrel Krell. New York: Harper and Row.

———. 1996a. *Being and time.* Trans. Joan Stambaugh. New York: State Univ. of New York Press.

———. 1996b. *Hölderlin's hymn "The Ister."* Trans. William McNeill and Julia Davis. Bloomington: Indiana Univ. Press.

———. 1998. Letter on humanism. In *Pathmarks,* ed. William McNeill. Cambridge: Cambridge Univ. Press.

———. 2000. *Introduction to metaphysics.* Trans. Gregory Fried and Richard Polt. New Haven, CT: Yale Univ. Press.

Held, David. 1995. *Democracy and the global order: From the modern state to cosmopolitan governance.* Stanford: Stanford Univ. Press.

Heller, Agnes. 1987. *Beyond justice.* Oxford: Basil Blackwell.

Hinsley, F. H. 1966. *Sovereignty.* London: C. A. Watts.

Hobbes, Thomas. 1994. *Leviathan,* ed. Edwin Curley. Indianapolis, IN: Hackett.

Holloway, John. 2000. *Change the world without taking power: The meaning of revolution today.* London: Pluto Press.

———. 2005. *Change the world without taking power: The meaning of revolution today.* London: Pluto Press.

Holloway, John, and Eloína Peláez, eds. 1998. *Zapatista! Reinventing revolution in Mexico.* London: Pluto Press.

IJsseling, Samuel. 1992. Heidegger and politics. In *Ethics and danger: Essays on Heidegger and continental thought,* ed. Arleen B. Dallery and Charles E. Scott with P. Holley Roberts. New York: SUNY Press, 3–10.

Jackson, Robert H. 1990. *Quasi-states: Sovereignty, international relations and the Third World.* New York: Cambridge Univ. Press.

Jacobsohn, Walter. 2001. The real scandal in higher education. In Schell and Stock 2001, 159–184.

James, Alan. 1986. *Sovereign statehood: The basis of international society.* London: Allen and Unwin.

Kant, Immanuel. 1981. *Grounding for the metaphysics of morals.* Trans. James W. Ellington. Indianapolis: Hackett.

Karatani, Kojin. 2003. *Transcritique: On Kant and Marx.* Trans. Sabu Kohso. Cambridge, MA: MIT Press.

Kierkegaard, Søren. 1980. *The sickness unto death.* Trans. Howard V. Hong and Edna H. Hong. Princeton, NJ: Princeton Univ. Press.

Kittay, Eva Feder. 1999. *Love's labor: Essays on women, equality, and dependency.* New York: Routledge.

Kittay, Eva Feder, and Ellen K. Feder, eds. 2002. *The subject of care: Feminist perspectives on dependency.* Lanham, MD: Rowman and Littlefield.

Kojève, Alexandre. 1980. *Introduction to the reading of Hegel: Lectures on the "Phenomenology of Spirit" assembled by Raymond Queneau*. Trans. James H. Nichols, Jr. Ithaca, NY: Cornell Univ. Press.

Kolodner, Meredith. 2007. Adjuncts: CUNY's migrant workers. *The Chief: The Civil Employees Weekly*. November 2, 2007. www.thechief-leader.com/news/2007/1102/news/016.html.

Lamarche, Pierre. 2007. The use value of G. A. M. V. Bataille. In Winnubst 2007, 54–72.

Lebowitz, Michael A. 2006. *Build it now: Socialism for the twenty-first century*. New York: Monthly Review Press.

Lefebvre, Henri. 2003. *Nietzsche*. Paris: Éditions Syllepse.

Leibniz, G. W. 1972. *Political writings*, ed. Patrick Riley. Cambridge: Cambridge Univ. Press.

———. 1989a. Discourse on metaphysics. In *Philosophical essays*, trans. Roger Ariew and Daniel Garber. Indianapolis: Hackett.

———. 1989b. The monadology. In *Philosophical essays*, trans. Roger Ariew and Daniel Garber. Indianapolis: Hackett.

Leopardi, Giacomo. 1997. *Selected poems*. Trans. Eamon Grennan. Princeton: Princeton Univ. Press.

Levin, John S. 2007. *Nontraditional students and community colleges: The conflict of justice and neoliberalism*. New York: Palgrave Macmillan.

Loiret, François. 2003. *Volonté et infini chez Duns Scot*. Paris: Editions Kimé.

Lorca, Federico García. 1996. *Poeta en Nueva York*. Madrid: Ediciones Cátedra.

Luft, Sandra Rudnick. 2003. *Vico's uncanny humanism: Reading the "new science" between modern and postmodern*. Ithaca, NY: Cornell Univ. Press.

Lundy, Catherine M., Karen Roberts, and Douglas Becker. 2006. Union responses to the challenges of contingent work arrangements. In Gleason 2006, 99–132.

Maritain, Jacques. 1998. *Man and the state*. Washington, DC: Catholic Univ. of America.

Martin, Randy, ed. 1998a. *Chalk lines: The politics of work in the managed university*. Durham, NC: Duke Univ. Press.

Martin, Randy. 1998b. Introduction: Education as national pedagogy. In Martin 1998a, 1–29.

———. 2002a. *On your Marx: Rethinking socialism and the left*. Minneapolis: Univ. of Minnesota Press.

———. 2002b. *The financialization of daily life*. Philadelphia: Temple Univ Press.

Marx, Karl. 1973. *Grundrisse. Foundations of the critique of political economy*. Trans. Martin Nicolaus. New York: Vintage Books.

———. 1981. *Capital*. Vol. 3. Trans. David Fernbach. New York: Vintage Books.

———. 1994. *Selected writings*, ed. Lawrence H. Simon. Indianapolis, IN: Hackett.

Mauss, Marcel. 1990. *The gift. The form and reason for exchange in archaic societies*. Trans. W. D. Halls. New York: W. W. Norton.

McLaren, Peter. 2005. *Capitalists and conquerors: A critical pedagogy against empire*. Lanham, MD: Rowman & Littlefield.

McRuer, Robert. 2006. *Crip theory: Cultural signs of queerness and disability*. New York: New York Univ. Press.

Mezzadra, Sandro. 2001. *Diritto di fuga: Migrazioni, cittadinanza, globalizzazione*. Verona: Ombre Corte.

Moulier-Boutang, Yann. 1998. *De l'esclavage au salariat: Économie historique du salariat bridé*. Paris: Presses Universitaires de France.

Nancy, Jean-Luc. 2000. *Being singular plural*. Trans. Robert D. Richardson and Anne E. O'Byrne. Stanford: Stanford Univ. Press.

Negri, Antonio. 2003. *Time for revolution*. Trans. Matteo Mandarini. London: Continuum.

Nelson, Cary, ed. 1997. *Will teach for food: Academic labor in crisis*. Minneapolis: Univ. of Minnesota Press.

Nussbaum, Martha C. 2006. *Frontiers of justice: Disability, nationality, species membership*. Cambridge, MA: Harvard Univ. Press.

Owens, Joseph. 1951. *The doctrine of being in the Aristotelian "Metaphysics."* Toronto: Pontifical Institute of Mediaeval Studies.

Plato. 2002. Euthyphro. In *Five dialogues*, trans. G.M.A. Grube. Indianapolis, IN: Hackett.

Pothier, Dianne, and Richard Devlin. 2006. *Critical disability theory: Essays in philosophy, politics, policy and law*. Vancouver: Univ. of British Columbia Press.

Ramonet, Ignacio. 2002. Servile state. *Le monde diplomatique*. October 2002.

Rasch, William. 2007. From sovereign ban to banning sovereignty. In Matthew Calarco and Steven DeCaroli 2007, 92–108.

Rawls, John. 1999. *A theory of justice*. Cambridge, MA: Harvard Univ. Press.

Ray Pratt, Linda. 1997. Disposable faculty: Part-time exploitation as management strategy. In Nelson 1997, 264–277.

Readings, Bill. 1996. *The university in ruins*. Cambridge, MA: Harvard Univ. Press.

Rhoades, Gary, and Sheila Slaughter. 1998. Academic capitalism, managed professionals, and supply-side higher education. In Martin 1998a, 33–68.

Riley, Patrick. 1972. Introduction. In Leibniz 1972, 1–44.

———. 1996. *Leibniz' universal jurisprudence: Justice as the charity of the wise*. Cambridge, MA: Harvard Univ. Press.

Rilke, Rainer Maria. 1939. *Duino elegies*. Trans. J. B. Leishman and Stephen Spender. New York: W. W. Norton.

Robin, Corey, and Michelle Stephens. 1997. Against the grain: Organizing TAs at Yale. In Nelson 1997, 44–79.

Ross, Andrew. 1997. The labor behind the cult of work. In Nelson 1997, 137–143.

Sahlins, Marshall. 1972. *Stone Age economics*. New York: Aldine.

Sands, Philippe. 2005. *Lawless world: The whistle-blowing account of how Bush and Blair are taking the law into their own hands*. New York: Penguin.

Saro-Wiwa, Ken. 1994. *Sozaboy: A novel in rotten English*. New York: Longman African Writers.

Sartre, Jean-Paul. 1981. *The family idiot: Gustave Flaubert, 1821–1857*. Vol. 1. Trans. Carol Cosman. Chicago: Univ. of Chicago Press.

———. 1985. *Existentialism and human emotions*. Trans. Bernard Frechtman. New York: Citadel Press.

Schell, Eileen E. 1998. *Gypsy academics and mother-teachers: Gender, contingent labor, and writing instruction*. Portsmouth, NH: Boynton/Cook.

Schell, Eileen E., and Patricia Lambert Stock, eds. 2001. *Moving a mountain: Transforming the role of contingent faculty in composition studies and higher education.* Urbana, IL: National Council of Teachers of English.

Schmitt, Carl. 1996. *The concept of the political.* Trans. George Schwab. Chicago: Univ. of Chicago Press.

———. 2005. *Political theology: Four chapters on the concept of sovereignty.* Trans. George Scwab. Chicago: Univ. of Chicago Press.

Schutte, Ofelia. 2002. Dependency work, women, and the global economy. In Kittay and Feder 2002, 138–158.

Sen, Amartya. 1999. *Development as freedom.* New York: Anchor Books.

Slaughter, Sheila, and Larry L. Leslie. 1997. *Academic capitalism: Politics, policies, and the entrepreneurial university.* Baltimore, MD: Johns Hopkins Univ. Press.

Sophocles. 2001. *Antigone.* Trans. Paul Woodruff. Indianapolis, IN: Hackett.

Stankiewics, W. J., ed. 1969. *In defense of sovereignty.* New York: Oxford Univ. Press.

Stoekl, Allan. 2007. Excess and depletion: Bataille's surprisingly ethical model of expenditure. In Winnubst 2007.

Strong, Tracy B. 2005. The sovereign and the exception: Carl Schmitt, politics, theology, and leadership. Foreword to Schmitt 2005, vii–xxxv.

Thelin, William H., and Leann Bertoncini. 2004. When critical pedagogy becomes bad teaching: Blunders in adjunct review. In Bousquet and Parascondola 2004, 132–142, 252–282.

Tirelli, Vincent. 1998. Adjuncts and more adjuncts: Labor segmentation and the transformation of higher education. In Martin 1998a, 181–201.

Vico, Giambattista. 1948. *The new science.* Trans. Thomas Goddard Bergin and Max Harold Fisch. Ithaca, NY: Cornell Univ. Press.

Vincent, Jean Marie. 1987. *Critique du travail: Le faire et l'agir.* Paris: Presses Universitaires de France.

Virno, Paolo. 2004. *A grammar of the multitude: For an analysis of contemporary forms of life.* Trans. Isabella Bertoletti, James Cascaito, and Andrea Casson. New York: Semiotext(e).

von Hippel, Courtney, Venkat Bendapudi, Judith Tansky, David B. Greenberger, Stephen L. Mangum, and Robert L. Heneman. 2006. Operationalizing the shadow workforce: Toward an understanding of the participants in nonstandard employment relationships. In Gleason 2006, 29–61.

Waite, Geoff. 1996. *Nietzsche's corps/e: Aesthetics, politics, prophecy, or, the spectacular technoculture of everyday life.* Durham, NC: Duke Univ. Press.

Wendling, Amy. 2006. Review of *Labor of Fire. Contemporary Sociology* 35(6): 626–627.

———. 2007. Sovereign consumption as a species of communist theory: Reconceptualizing energy. In Winnubst 2007, 35–53.

Wenger, Jeffrey B. 2006. Public policy and contingent workers. In Gleason 2006, 169–200.

Willis, Paul. 1977. *Learning to labor: How working class kids get working class jobs.* New York: Columbia Univ. Press.

Winnubst, Shannon, ed. 2007. *Reading Bataille now.* Bloomington: Indiana Univ. Press.

Wong, Sophia Isako. 2002. At home with Down syndrome and gender. *Hypatia* 17(3): 89–117.

———. 2007. The moral personhood of individuals labeled 'mentally retarded': A Rawlsian response to Nussbaum. *Social Theory and Practice* 33(4): 579–594.

Žižek, Slavoj. 1999. *The ticklish subject: The absent centre of political ontology.* London: Verso.

———. 2006. *The parallax view.* Cambridge, MA: MIT Press.

Index